CHASING JESSOP

CHASING JESSOP

The Mystery of England Cricket's Oldest Record

SIMON WILDE

BLOOMSBURY PUBLISHING
LONDON · OXFORD · NEW YORK · NEW DELHI · SYDNEY

BLOOMSBURY PUBLISHING
Bloomsbury Publishing Plc
50 Bedford Square, London, WC1B 3DP, UK
Bloomsbury Publishing Ireland Limited,
29 Earlsfort Terrace, Dublin 2, D02 AY28, Ireland

BLOOMSBURY, BLOOMSBURY PUBLISHING and the Diana logo are
trademarks of Bloomsbury Publishing Plc

First published in Great Britain in 2025

A catalogue record for this book is available from the British Library

ISBN: HB: 978-1-5266-9253-5; EBOOK: 978-1-5266-9426-3

2 4 6 8 10 9 7 5 3 1

Typeset by Newgen KnowledgeWorks Pvt. Ltd., Chennai, India
Printed and bound in Great Britain by CPI Group (UK) Ltd, Croydon CR0 4YY

To find out more about our authors and books visit www.bloomsbury.com
and sign up for our newsletters

For product-safety-related questions contact productsafety@bloomsbury.com

For Gayle

Contents

Introduction

This is a story about speed. A story of a cricketer who batted at a rate that was not seen again for several generations. A cricketer who set a record for the fastest century scored in a Test match for England that survived for more than 1,000 games. He altered previous notions of what was possible in terms of batsmanship, and challenged the very way the speed of scoring was measured.

For England against Australia at The Oval on 13 August 1902, Gilbert Jessop played one of the most celebrated innings in cricket history – arguably the greatest in the history of the game. It was a lightning counter-attack, the like of which is rarely seen. Walking to the wicket with his side floundering at 48 for five in pursuit of 263 on the final afternoon, with skies overcast and rain threatening to spoil whatever slim hope England clung to, Jessop launched a breathless assault on the dominant Australian bowling, reaching his hundred off what was later calculated as only 76 balls. He was out just after reaching his century but had lifted his team within sight of the winning line and, amid scenes of high drama, they crept home with their last two batsmen at the crease. It ranks as one of the most thrilling victories in England's Test history.

English cricket was at a low ebb at the time. Australia were a superb team, strong in all departments, brilliant in the field and well led by Joe Darling, and England had not beaten them on home soil in nine matches – a barren run of the sort they had not known before. If they had lost again they would have gone down 3-0 in the series, a margin of defeat that they in fact suffered only once at home against any team in their first 70 years of Test cricket. Jessop not only helped snatch victory from the clutches of defeat, but restored some much-needed pride. In a leading article entitled 'Life in the Old Dog', the *St James's Gazette* the next morning proclaimed that the result should end 'gloomy prognostications on the decay of cricket in the Old Country'.

Until Ben Stokes scored a similarly unlikely century to engineer a miraculous win at Headingley in 2019, which is the only other time England have won a home Test against Australia by one wicket, Jessop's was widely regarded as the most brilliant Test innings played by an England batsman. But by some metrics Jessop's performance remains the more remarkable. His starting point was certainly more dire: 215 runs still to win, only five wickets left, whereas Stokes began with 218 needed and seven wickets left. Their approaches could not have been more different: Stokes stayed at the crease 330 minutes to score 149 not out, while Jessop in a whirlwind of destruction blazed his way to 104 in a quarter of that time. There is no question that his runs were scored in trickier batting conditions.

Jessop's incredible century cemented his popularity. It was his first three-figure score in a Test match, but he had made 21 hundreds in first-class cricket in the previous five years and many had come at astonishing speed. Indeed, eight of them took less time than he was estimated to have batted against Australia. For Gloucestershire against Yorkshire at Harrogate in 1897 he reached his hundred in just 40 minutes, which stood as the fastest century in any first-class match until 1920. Feats like this, and his singularly attacking style, meant that Jessop was an established favourite with the public at a time when county cricket attracted big crowds, especially on Saturdays and during holidays. A year after the Oval Test, he reached 200 against Sussex at Hove in just 120 minutes; this remained the swiftest first-class double-century for more than 80 years. 'No man has ever driven a ball so hard, so high and so often in so many different directions,' wrote C. B. Fry, one of England's leading batsmen of the time, and also a busy journalist. 'No man has ever made cricket so dramatic an entertainment.'

Jessop only ever played one way and it was a method of all-out attack that was not replicated in consistent fashion until the global expansion of one-day cricket in the 1980s led to a gradual synthesis of batting styles, with scoring strokes developed for the shorter formats finding their way into the longer game of Test cricket.

To what extent Jessop was a really serious batsman is a moot point. He started out in 1894 as a fast bowler, and when he first played for England in 1899 was selected to open the bowling and bat at No 8. Even when he was recalled to the team for the Oval Test of 1902, he was still theoretically cast as an all-rounder, with the selectors checking on his availability to bowl (in the event he sent down six overs) and slating him to go in at No 7. In his early days, his bowling was genuinely fast and he took more than 500 first-class wickets in six years before a back problem reduced his effectiveness; his workloads with the ball would certainly have influenced how long he was willing and able to bat. He was more than a slogger, though – he typically batted No 5 for Gloucestershire and scored more than 50 first-class centuries across his entire career, placing him fourteenth on the all-time list when he stopped playing. By general standards, though, he took scant care of his wicket. In only 35 of his 855 innings did he stay at the crease for an hour and a half, and only ten times did he bat as long as two hours. He never batted as long as Stokes did at Headingley in 2019. Many purists tut-tutted at his outrageous unorthodoxies.

Jessop's relentless big hitting and fast scoring may have been revolutionary, but they chimed with an accelerated rate of change across a whole range of physical and creative activities around the dawn of the twentieth century. The start of the modern Olympic Games in 1896 generated a wide push for sportsmen to propel themselves faster, higher, further. Walter Baker, an American, became the first person to drive a car at 100mph in May 1902 and was matched by Frenchman Louis Rigolly two years later.

In July 1902, only three weeks before 'Jessop's match', English newspapers reported excitedly about Britain's first 'Mile-a-Minute' trains. In 1903, the Wright brothers undertook the world's first manned flight. The Eiffel Tower in Paris, constructed in 1889, set a new mark for the world's tallest structure and was visited by 2 million people at the Paris Exposition in 1900. Jessop himself was an accomplished sprinter capable of running 100 yards in 10.2 seconds when the record at the turn of the century was 9.8 seconds.

Even if the public at this time didn't quite grasp how the new cars, trains and planes worked, they were astonished and delighted by all manner of scientific advances, including electric lighting, gramophone records and transatlantic radio messages. By the end of the 1890s, most English cities had cinema halls, transforming the way people viewed themselves. As the French writer Charles Péguy famously remarked in 1909: 'The world has changed more in the last 30 years than in all the time since Jesus Christ.'

How Jessop did what he did was no less exciting and wondrous. In a profile of him in the *St Andrews Citizen* in 1913, J. T. Bolton mused:

> When one sits down to describe the man, his method, his power and his wonderful personality, a pause soon comes. Describe Jessop! It cannot be done with mere pen and ink. The only way to do justice to him is to set a cinematograph machine at work while he is at the wickets. Even then you would want more than one machine, for there are the spectators to be taken into consideration, too; the look of anticipation on every face, the pure joy with which every characteristic hit is greeted ... How Jessop does it is a mystery of which I have not yet heard a satisfactory explanation.

That Jessop rose to the occasion in quite the way he did in August 1902 perhaps owed something to the particular circumstances in which the match was played. The Oval Test was no ordinary game. The series may have been won, with

Australia already two up going into this final contest, but London, a city of more than 6.5 million, was in celebratory mood and looking for further cause to rejoice. Two days before the Test began, the Coronation of Edward VII, the eldest son of Queen Victoria, who had died the previous year after more than 60 years on the throne, took place at Westminster Abbey, just across the river from Kennington's Oval. An estimated one million people lined the streets for the procession and among 8,000 guests at the Abbey were the prime ministers of the British Dominions, including Sir Edmund Barton, the premier of Australia, who subsequently attended the final day of the Test. No wonder Jessop's great innings was described in some quarters as 'Coronation cricket'.

That Jessop's heroics occurred in such close proximity to the Coronation had about it shades of the news coming through of Edmund Hillary and Tenzing Norgay scaling Mount Everest as Elizabeth II ascended the throne in 1953, and of Ian Botham single-handedly beating Australia in the days around the wedding of Prince Charles and Lady Diana Spencer in 1981.

There was more, though. It was less than three months since the Treaty of Vereeniging had finally brought an end to the Boer War, a conflict that lasted three years and cost Britain 22,000 lives and the equivalent of £25 billion in today's money. The Relief of Mafeking in May 1900 had led to unprecedented scenes of delight on the capital's streets and the arrival of peace two years later was every bit as welcome. But the war continued to cast its shadow. It had had a particular impact on Jessop as well as a number of leading English cricketers who had gone to fight in Southern

Africa. Jessop had recently become engaged to an Australian, Millicent Annie Osborne, whose previous partner, to whom she was engaged, had been killed in the war. Stanley Jackson, who shared a century partnership with Jessop during the run-chase at The Oval, and Frank Mitchell, Jessop's captain at Cambridge University, both served extensively in the war. Frank Milligan, a Yorkshire fast bowler who was in the attack when Jessop struck his 40-minute hundred at Harrogate, died in the Transvaal in 1900, and Frank Townsend, elder brother of Jessop's best man, Charles Townsend, was killed in action at Kimberley in 1901. Dozens of Australian troops who served in the war and were in London for the Coronation parade, came en masse to The Oval – probably the largest number of 'opposition' fans to watch a Test match to that point. Their noisy presence added to the festive atmosphere.

It seems that Millie Osborne may well have been there, too, the *Daily Express* commenting at the time of her wedding in London a few weeks later that 'the bride has been much admired by every cricketer when seen at several matches during the past season'.

This is a story not only about speed, but also a chase – in fact, two chases. Fast scoring was Jessop's hallmark, but the question which came to consume me, and spurred me to write this book, was: exactly how quickly had he scored his runs at The Oval; was it actually the case that his hundred came off 76 deliveries, as generally supposed? When Jessop's mark started to come under threat from an England batting line-up charged by Stokes, after he took over the Test captaincy in 2022, with being ultra-aggressive, this became a matter of topical interest. Could we be sure that the record for England's fastest century was genuine?

My curiosity was piqued. I wrote an article reviewing the evidence as to how many balls Jessop faced which appeared in the *Cricketer* magazine in March 2023, but that proved to be only the start of my journey of discovery.

It is only in relatively modern times – pre-digitisation and electronic scoring, and post the emergence of one-day cricket – that systems were developed to routinely calculate the number of balls faced by each batsman. Previously, generally only a batsman's scoring shots were listed alongside his name in scorebooks, with the 'dot balls' (balls off which no run was scored from the bat) logged only against the bowler. Moreover, many of the early books in which the official scorers recorded the progress of matches have been lost, and there is no evidence of them surviving from the Oval Test of 1902. That said, in some instances scorers and journalists were in the habit of keeping separate notes about the balls faced by a particular batsman, and especially in the case of someone such as Jessop who scored so fast.

The 76-ball claim for Jessop's century surfaced in 1974 with the publication of *The Croucher*, a biography of Jessop by Gerald Brodribb. That work referred to an unsourced cutting contained in a scrapbook owned by the Jessop family which provided a list of the balls Jessop received and how many he scored from each of them. As a result of my article in the *Cricketer*, Dr Lucy Jessop, Gilbert's granddaughter, who still possesses the scrapbooks, contacted me and with her help it was possible to establish that the cutting came from the *Athletic News*, a sports weekly, published five days after the match.

But what was the evidence beyond this one claim? Could the *Athletic News* ball-by-ball list be verified by other means? I found myself hunting through dozens of publications contained in the British newspaper archive and similar databases in an effort to solve this mystery. My interest became an obsession with the discovery of a report in a little-remembered London morning paper which carried, remarkably, not only a list of every ball Jessop faced but also who bowled each ball, and in the case of the deliveries off which he did not score whether he played a shot or left the ball alone. Such analysis is commonplace now, but I know of no other case of it being done so long ago. Exactly how many balls this second list suggested Jessop faced I will leave the reader to find out.

Drawing on this and other long-forgotten contemporary accounts, this book is a recreation of Jessop's match, and Jessop's innings, in an attempt to establish what really happened.

Such a forensic reconstruction was only possible because of a rich array of newspaper reports, both daily and evening, national and regional. It is hard to comprehend nowadays, in an age of live television and radio, and social media clips, quite how much society once depended on newspapers for their information, and how comprehensive they were in their accounts of major events. Built on a revolution in telegraphic and telephonic communication, the dawn of the twentieth century was a boom time for newspapers, with an explosion of new titles entering the market, including the *Daily Mail* in 1896, the *Daily Express* in 1900 and the *Daily Mirror* in 1903, all of them playing their part in a shift towards more popular, human-interest stories. In sport, former or active players were recruited to write columns, and Jessop himself would become part of this process. But the competition for stories was fierce. 'The communications revolution ... enabled news to be gathered, processed and distributed at a pace and on a scale which became almost an obsession of the Victorians,' Alan J. Lee wrote in *The Origins of the Popular Press in England 1855–1914*. 'The question of speed was crucial, for it was the speed of communication, together with the speed of production, which made a mass press possible.'

This is where the second chase comes in. The story of Jessop's hundred and England's nail-biting run-chase took place as numerous London and regional evening newspapers approached their deadlines. It created a race to be first with one of the biggest stories English sport had seen. I counted more than 30 eyewitness accounts, the number probably swollen by reporters who had initially assembled in London for the Coronation and stayed for the Test. They raced to tell a dramatic tale as it unfolded, hour by hour, minute by minute. It was as near to rolling news as the public could then experience.

This is the story of the longest standing major record in England cricket, a story that has never been fully told – until now.

PART ONE

THE BUILD-UP

WHAT MADE JESSOP THE CRICKETER HE WAS

UNORTHODOX UPBRINGING, UNORTHODOX STYLE

GILBERT JESSOP had an unusual upbringing. He left formal education at the age of fifteen following the death of his father, a surgeon, and then led an itinerant life before entering university six years later. By that point he had played an inordinate amount of club cricket without receiving any of the formal coaching he would have had at the type of private school from which many of the other leading English amateur batsmen of the day emerged. Jessop was almost entirely self-taught and said that had he undergone the usual cricket instruction he would not have played as he did.

Exactly how different things would have been but for his father's death is, of course, impossible to know, but had he stayed at Cheltenham Grammar School for another three years before going on to Cambridge directly afterwards, as might have been expected in the normal course of events, his early cricket would certainly have followed a more conventional path. As it was, he pursued the game during his formative years in an uncomplicated, free-spirited fashion. When he was bowling, he went all out for speed, and when he was batting he went all out for attack. As a fielder, he specialised in diving interceptions and bullet-like throws from short range. By the time he accepted that his batting needed refinement, he was already playing county cricket for Gloucestershire and not minded to change his aggressive approach, simply the means by which he went about it. He continued to play with unbridled energy.

Born on 19 May 1874, Jessop was the eleventh of 12 surviving children, one of five boys and six girls, to Henry and Susannah Jessop. Henry was a physician and surgeon, and the large family lived at 30 Cambray Place, Cheltenham. Gilbert's eldest sibling Ada was 14 years older and Osman, his youngest brother, three years junior. Jessop had a ball in his hand from as early as he could remember, but he said that his parents did not particularly encourage him to pursue cricket. It was said that he was named after William Gilbert Grace, himself a doctor from Bristol, who by the time Gilbert was born was already known as the greatest cricketer the world had seen. There was little scope for outdoor games at a house with a garden measuring about 8 x 8 yards around a central rockery. That did not stop the five Jessop boys from staging their own cricket matches, though, and Gilbert reckoned that the distinctive parameters of their outdoor space shaped his game: 'On the leg aside of the wicket lay safety; on the off the surgery windows ... small wonder, therefore, if a pronounced penchant for the pull should have affected my batting.' There was also a passageway in which matches could be staged after dark by candlelight. Gilbert would also become a good footballer.

Henry was a popular and respected figure in the community. He was a big man, not a characteristic he passed on to his famous son, and a natty dresser with distinctive ties and check trousers. When he died of heart disease in March 1890, aged fifty-three, the *Cheltenham Chronicle* noted that his cheery bonhomie 'was known to all'. His passing had a profound practical impact on the family, not least Gilbert, who had to forfeit a place at the grammar school that was dependent on his father's long-standing position on the board of governors. The composer Gustav Holst, four months Jessop's junior, was a contemporary at the school.

A year after Henry's death, the 1891 census showed Susannah residing elsewhere in Cheltenham along with three of her grown-up daughters and young Osman – a widow 'living on her own means'. By this point Gilbert, not yet seventeen, was working as an assistant master at a grammar school in Alvechurch, 40 miles to the north, in return for which he received free board. It must have been a difficult time for him, wrenched out of a school at which he was seemingly content, and deprived of paternal guidance.

For the next few years he remained in teaching, moving from Alvechurch to South Woodford in Essex, then to Burford in Oxfordshire and Beccles College in Suffolk, until such time as it was possible for him to sit entrance exams for Cambridge. Such a life afforded him many opportunities to play cricket, both for the schools themselves – masters being expected to join pupils – and for local clubs. Jessop had first appeared for Cheltenham Grammar's first XI aged thirteen and was regularly involved with several clubs in and around the town, so that when he returned to Cheltenham in the summer holidays he would pick up his old connections.

'Village cricket flourished around Gloucester[shire] in those days, and matches could be obtained for the asking,' he once wrote. 'Two and often three games in a week were of regular occurrence ... To us, cricket had no season. Any old time and any old place was good enough.' He would often make six-mile round trips on foot three times a week to play local matches. He produced many exceptional performances, including his first century at eighteen, and was often clearly in a different class from those around him. He viewed his time at Burford as particularly helpful as he began playing matches of a higher standard. While at school, he was also involved in arranging the first recorded Boys v Girls cricket match in the UK.

His breakthrough came in August 1893, when by chance he took part in a trial match for aspiring county players at Gloucestershire's ground in Bristol between a Public Schools XI and the Rest of the County. An invitation had been sent to his cousin Hylton Jessop, himself a good club player, but he was unable to accept so Gilbert took his place. Jessop scored 53, took four wickets and athletically ran out W. G. Grace's son Bertie off his own bowling. W. G. himself was watching and was immediately convinced that Jessop should be tried in the county first team the next summer. Discussing Gloucestershire's prospects the following spring, the *Bristol Mercury* stated that Jessop was 'reputed to be a fine field, a free bat, and a fair right-hand bowler'.

Jessop made his first appearance against Lancashire at Old Trafford in July 1894, during the school holidays. Gloucestershire lost by an innings and 98 runs, but Jessop's spirit and determination were widely admired. Most notably, he hit the first ball he faced for four off Arthur

Mold, one of the most feared fast bowlers in the country. Admittedly, it was a half-volley, but Jessop nonetheless drove it to the boundary and repeated the stroke later in the same over. Afterwards, his delighted captain declared prophetically: 'Well, we've found something this time!' Jessop played in all but one of Gloucestershire's remaining matches that season.

Jessop never lost his unquenchable enthusiasm for the game and played an enormous number of matches during his career. In 1895, he was granted leave from school duties to appear for Gloucestershire in term time – W. G. Grace himself wrote to Beccles College for permission – and as a result featured in all but four of the county's 18 championship games. By the following year, when Jessop entered Christ's College, Cambridge, he was appearing regularly for university and county. In a career that lasted until he turned forty, Jessop took part in 493 first-class matches, more than any of the other five amateurs who represented England in the 1902 Tests.

Jessop's stated aim in going to Cambridge was to become ordained for the Church, for which he required a degree, but his ambitions were remote from the outset given his disrupted schooling. His prospects were further harmed when on a return voyage from a short cricket tour of the United States in October 1897 he caught a severe chill and also developed renal colic, missing an entire term in convalescence. It took him a year to fully recover. He considered going to Southern Africa to work as a tutor in what would have been a better climate for his health, but was eventually persuaded to stay on by an offer of the Cambridge captaincy in what proved to be his final summer. He went down in 1899 without a degree, having attended only seven terms, aged twenty-five.

To an extent, cricket became a career instead. He played as an amateur – as was expected of someone of his social background – so he was not paid directly to play, but amateurs received expenses which covered daily living costs and, as Gloucestershire captain from 1900, Jessop would have also been paid an additional allowance. Also, through various contrivances, the more valued amateurs were often given even greater financial support to encourage them to turn out regularly.

Typically, a star amateur might be found a position with their county club as secretary, assistant secretary or treasurer, and paid accordingly, without them being required to do much, if any, work in return. Through abstruse convention, these roles were deemed not to breach amateur status. Archie MacLaren, England captain in 1902, had been made assistant secretary at Lancashire on just such an arrangement, and it was widely understood that few counties were without one or two amateurs who were paid in this way. 'The creation of posts for men who could not otherwise afford to play is a silly subterfuge,' *Truth*, a London weekly, stated in December 1901. 'Those who hold the posts are professionals pure and simple. They are paid to play just as much as any pro. A man is no more nor less of a gentleman, if that is his real social standing, because he takes money for playing.' The *St James's Gazette* referred to MacLaren in one of its reports in 1902 as a 'somewhat amateur'.

Jessop once termed himself a 'limited-income amateur', who could really only afford to play the game regularly in one of two ways, assuming that turning professional was not a realistic option – taking the assistant secretaryship route, or working as a journalist, which was also regarded as an acceptable occupation for a gentleman. Jessop would work extensively as a journalist, though not seriously before 1902, and towards the end of his playing days with Gloucestershire he became club secretary on a salary of £200; this, though, was not a sinecure, but a proper job that had to be combined with playing.

There was considerable disquiet about sham-amateurism and some of the leading professionals were vocal in their criticism of payments to amateurs. Several, believing they were actually less well rewarded than amateurs, threatened strike action ahead of the Oval Test of 1896 unless their own pay was increased, and two of them did not play as a consequence. Subsequently, match fees for professionals were doubled from £10 to £20, though by 1902 even Pelham Warner, another of the leading amateurs, was arguing it was time this figure was raised to £25. The authorities well knew who the true 'shamateurs' were, and disapproved of those such as W. G. Grace, Walter Read, Andrew Stoddart and MacLaren who were considered to have gone too far in lining their pockets.

That said, most amateurs often lost money when they played, which was why few of them could afford to join long tours overseas unless they could haggle their way into securing generous allowances. Towards the end of Jessop's only Test tour of Australia, in 1901-02, he and two other amateurs made a late claim for additional expenses, and secured a £50 supplement each, although not without upsetting their hosts. 'What an ass Jessop must be to talk about letting the public of England know how the amateurs of MacLaren's team have been treated,' one local official wrote to a colleague. 'From what I saw and heard, Jessop himself would have a fine time explaining his position to the MCC authorities.'

Jessop's first move to support himself as an established cricketer saw him take a job on the London Stock Exchange in the autumn of 1899. At the time, the City of London was the hub on which the world's money spun. Its exchange markets set global prices of major commodities and the exchange rates of the world's currencies were adjusted to the price of gold, fixed in sterling. Jessop joined the legions of black-suited, black-hatted men – and they were all men – hurrying to work in the winter months, and in the census of March 1901 he gave his occupation as 'stockbroker', residing as a boarder at 4 Lansdown Place, St Pancras.

By the summer of 1902, though, Jessop's situation was changing. He was engaged to be married and, perhaps a little fancifully, the papers reported that his fiancée had 'inherited a good income'. As most amateurs rarely had long careers, there was regular speculation about how long they might carry on playing, and things were no different with Jessop. On the very morning of his great Test innings, there appeared in the *Uttoxeter New Era* an unsigned profile which stated: 'I have heard it said that Mr Jessop, who is only 28, contemplates early retirement from first-class cricket for reasons respecting his professional status in life.'

*

By his own admission, Jessop was in his early years more interested in bowling and fielding than batting. He enjoyed the thrill of bowling fast, and bowling short-pitched balls from round the wicket, although it was accepted that he never did so with the intention of hitting the batsman. But he was inclined to overwork himself as a bowler, or be overworked by his captains, and a back strain during his Test debut against Australia at Lord's in 1899 was the start of fitness problems that would result in him becoming a fast-scoring batsman who occasionally made an impact with the ball, rather than a genuine all-rounder. By the summer of 1902, his fast-bowling days were almost over.

At 5ft 7in, he was hardly built for a career as a speedster, though he had a sturdy physique and weighed around 11 stone. A low centre of gravity must have been useful when it came to bowling skiddy bouncers, but would have been more helpful still with agile ground-fielding and nimble-footed batting.

In order to become a more effective batsman, he had to make a number of technical changes. This process began in earnest in 1897, his third full season of first-class cricket, and was essentially complete by 1899. When he started out, his approach towards batting was rustic. This was how others, and how he himself, described it. He would stand outside his crease, eager to attack the bowling, and then indiscriminately run at fast and slow bowlers alike. Charles Townsend, who regularly played alongside Jessop for Gloucestershire from 1894 until 1901, provided this graphic description of the young Jessop:

When he first played he was what I would call a mere slogger, and used to dash wildly down the wicket and miss the ball, and we were all rather sceptical about his ever making a bat ...

He continued to be a slogger for several years but gradually cultivated his batting, and from 1899 onwards he was the finished article. I do not mean that before 1899 he did not play many extraordinary and marvellous innings, but there was always an element of chance about them; from then on I always looked upon his batting as a great art. He played every shot as he wanted to and knew exactly where he was going to hit the ball. Unless he was going to hit it out of the ground, he hit it along the ground or hit it sufficiently high to clear mid-off.

Jessop would have agreed with such an analysis. It was only through playing county cricket week in, week out, and gaining the opportunity to study at close quarters how the best batsmen went about their work, that he appreciated just how crude his methods were. 'In those days I knew next to nothing about batsmanship,' he wrote. 'Whatever success I did gain in making runs I owed entirely to a good eye and a total disregard to where the ball went, so long as it did not go into a fieldsman's hands or my wicket.' Hours at the nets had failed to make him realise that 'there were other methods of making runs than by sheer slogging'. A seminal moment came at The Oval in June 1895 when Tom Hayward of Surrey batted beautifully for a century and Jessop was a member of the Gloucestershire attack labouring to stop him. He actually got through 61 five-ball overs and returned his best bowling figures to this point of six for 124.

The way Hayward hit straight with a vertical bat made a deep impression on someone whose own method of scoring relied heavily on risky cross-batted strokes. Changing his game was a slow process, though. Jessop said that after watching Hayward he began to concentrate on straighter driving but conceded, 'I cannot truthfully claim that the idea was immediately put into action.' He also admitted that it was not until his second year at Cambridge in 1897 that he was able almost to cure himself of the 'suicidal propensity' to charge down the wicket.

It is not that Jessop gave up advancing down the pitch altogether, rather that he chose his moments to step out better – and certainly not before the bowler had released the ball, which would have given the bowler the chance to adjust his line or length. Jessop's 'advance' remained a central part of his game.

He made other important refinements at around the same time. He was originally quite upright in his stance, but now decided to get lower in readiness to scurry down the wicket when the time felt right. He said that he developed this crouching position – which gave rise to Jessop's most famous nickname, 'The Croucher' – after practising starts for sprints on the running track. He found that he could launch himself more quickly by first crouching.

As a starting position, he also dropped his grip down the bat handle. Whereas he had previously placed his right (lower) hand halfway down – the orthodox thing to do – he put his left hand there while moving his right hand lower still. This helped ready him for late adjustments according to which shot he chose to play. G. L. O. Jessop, his son, wrote: 'He had ... his hands apart. But for any hard shot he closed them up. When driving, to obtain power, the right hand came up, but when hooking or cutting, to obtain more control, the left hand went down.' Sydney Santall, who bowled at Jessop many times for Warwickshire, also noticed this fine-tuning: 'He slipped his hands up and down the handle of his bat in proportion to the pace, length and direction of the ball delivered. His biggest drives were made with his hands at the top of the handle.'

What was most unusual was that he would pronate his left hand and forearm (that is, rotate his left hand and forearm so that they faced downwards) in a grip that most players would have found unnatural but which worked for Jessop and would later work for Sir Donald Bradman, the greatest run-scorer the game has known. C. B. Fry, who played with and against Jessop many times and closely studied his technique, said that this grip ought to have meant 'drives would be impossible'.

Jessop found that when he advanced down the pitch the more intelligent bowlers would pitch the ball further up, while 'the other kind sees his remedy in a shorter length'. To take advantage of the shorter ball, Jessop developed a stroke he did not really possess when he started out at Gloucestershire – the cut. He had originally thought that any kind of ball, of any length, could be driven, but again he learned from watching how more experienced batsmen went about things. An innings of 92 not out by Timothy O'Brien for Middlesex at Clifton in August 1895 showed him the possibilities of square-cutting a ball 'which eventually failed to turn into a drivable one'.

Henry Leveson Gower, who played against Jessop for Surrey and alongside him in Gentlemen-Players matches, said: 'The cut was his best stroke; because of his character as a hitter bowlers were afraid to pitch the ball up to him, and so he got a great deal of practice at the cut. Another of his strokes was the pull right over his left shoulder; many captains were almost driven to despair by this stroke. No sooner had they posted men for it than the same sort of ball was cut or driven and the fieldsmen had to be moved again.'

Crucially, his reworked method allowed him to score off many sorts of balls in many different ways, even when convention and logic suggested this ought not be possible. George Hirst, the great Yorkshire left-arm swing bowler who had many duels with Jessop, said: 'He was one of the few great cricketers who could murder the correct theory of the game and get away with it. His wonderful eye and feet made him so confident that he could cut, pull, or at times drive the same length ball. I know, because he has done it to me.' A number of witnesses observed that no one could bowl to Jessop a ball that he could not score off. This was his key to scoring so fast, allied to the speed and clarity of his decision-making.

Fry believed that Jessop's power came from the freedom and speed of his arm swing and a full use of the wrists – what today would be called 'quick hands' – and an ability to put 'every ounce of body-weight' into his strokes. The free swing came from his exceptionally loose joints. He was, Fry added, 'double-jointed all over'.

The improvement in Jessop's batting was dramatic. In 1897, when Jessop 2.0 first emerged, he scored his maiden first-class century in his 84th innings, and a month later followed up with three more hundreds in the space of fifteen days, culminating in his 40-minute blitz against Yorkshire at Harrogate (off what was also calculated to be 46 balls). Having averaged 20.29 across his first three seasons, his average rose to just shy of 30 in 1897.

He struggled the next year due to his health issues but in 1899 touched new heights by scoring almost 1,500 runs;

an early season 171 not out for Cambridge against a strong Yorkshire attack was reckoned to be his finest innings yet. Whereas he had often batted at No 6, No 7 or No 8, he was now more often going in at No 5, the position of a front-line batsman, and fully justifying the additional responsibility.

His determination to be more careful about going down the wicket paid dividends. Whereas he was out stumped in more than 15 per cent of all his first-class innings in his first three seasons, this figure fell to just 5.4 per cent from 1897 to 1900, when he topped 2,000 runs for the first time. Although his stumpings jumped up again in 1901, this was actually the most prolific season of his career, with 2,323 runs at an average of 40.75 – almost double the number of runs, and up by just over a third of the average, of his breakthrough season four years earlier.

In the process, he became established as a great entertainer, the biggest attraction in cricket since W. G. Grace was in his pomp. Crowds thrilled at Jessop's mighty hits and the exhilarating speed at which he scored his runs. At a time when the preparation of pitches was improving, and the game was turning in favour of high-scoring batsmen, Jessop broke the mould by making runs as fast as he did. As *Wisden* wrote in its Cricketer of the Year profile of him for 1898: 'We have had harder hitters, but perhaps never one who could, in 20 minutes or half an hour, so entirely change the fortunes of the game ... To hit fast bowling as he hits it is scarcely given to half a dozen batsmen in a generation.'

The not knowing what was going to happen next when he was batting was the thing that made watching him so compelling. Gerald Brodribb wrote: '[He] provided spectators with an almost hysterical excitement. When he came in to bat the whole crowd broke into an "audible grin", a fever of expectation which made many spectators almost afraid to look in case something went wrong.' W. J. Ford, writing a year or so after Jessop's feat at The Oval, described how news that he was going well would lead to a rush to the cricket ground: 'Placard a town or send a "tape" to the clubs ... "Jessop not out 40 – hitting hard" will make the luncher forgo his coffee and the hansoms will rattle up to Lord's.'

Jessop was modest to a fault and rarely spoke or wrote about his great deeds, but he did once reflect on the nature of the hitter:

> With him goes the sympathy of the great majority of spectators. A few old-fashioned theorists still shake their heads sadly, and endeavour to look disgusted, when the ball crashes into the pavilion clock or disappears into the neighbouring gardens, but ... even those in their hearts are not especially saddened by the sight, while for the more ordinary sportsman, the men who have just come to see some fun, and the younger people of both sexes, the spectacle causes unqualified enthusiasm ... It cannot be denied that there is some satisfaction in feeling that you are giving pleasure to the vast throng.

Even after racking up more than 6,000 runs in three seasons from 1899 and 1901, Jessop was still regarded in some quarters as too unreliable to be trusted in Test matches. Such theories were only given sustenance by his performances in Australia in the winter of 1901-02. The team assembled by Archie MacLaren was not as strong as it might have been, some key players being blocked from touring by their counties, and Jessop batted in the top five in every game, even opening the batting alongside MacLaren on one occasion, but he never managed more than 35. The best place for him was probably at No 7, but the decline in his bowling made it hard to balance the team this way. He produced just one spell of note with the ball, taking four wickets in an opening nine-over burst in the fourth Test at Sydney.

He continued to divide opinion. Around the time of the Oval Test of 1902, the *Westminster Gazette* described him as 'a player who often proves absolutely useless', while V. A. S. Beanland, writing as 'Flaneur' in the *Leeds Mercury*, described him as 'A happy-go-lucky batsman who is never dependable ... If he played steadily for a few overs [at the start of an innings] he would be the most dreaded batsman in the world.' Even Fry, an admirer, said 'he takes huge risks', but also reckoned Jessop 'gambled on a system, a careful system'.

In truth, there was a limit to how much Jessop could change his personality, or his outlook. He never lost his boyish enthusiasm for wanting to hit a cricket ball as far as he could.

2

THE STATE OF TEST CRICKET IN 1902

THE BUSINESS OF TEST CRICKET AND HOW THE GAME OPERATED ON THE FIELD

ONE REASON why Gilbert Jessop's great innings resonated down the ages was because it encapsulated the English relationship with Test cricket, a game that tests mental and physical resilience as much as it does skill.

Jessop scored his runs in a desperate situation: when he walked out to bat, his team looked beaten. Defeat was only a matter of time. Spectators began leaving the ground, thinking all hope was lost. Yet Jessop and Stanley Jackson, who partnered him for most of his innings, and later the Yorkshire pair of George Hirst and Wilfred Rhodes, refused to give up. They could see a path to victory, even if others could not.

Englishmen pride themselves on rising to a crisis, and Test cricket provides scope for just such backs-to-the-wall heroics. Every generation has its favourite moments: Jack Hobbs and Herbert Sutcliffe scoring centuries in fiendish circumstances at The Oval in 1926 to set up a series-clinching win over Australia; Willie Watson and Trevor Bailey batting for hour after hour to save a Test at Lord's in 1953; Mike Atherton and Jack Russell doing the same to defy South Africa in Johannesburg in 1995; and Ben Stokes and Jack Leach turning certain defeat into barely believable victory at Headingley. But, on home soil, in the games that were thought to really matter, Jessop was the first to so outrageously defy the odds. In the process, he cemented Test cricket's capacity to thrill crowds in a way no other sporting occasion could.

Test cricket was still in its infancy in 1902; it had only recently passed its 25th birthday, but it was in the best health it had been in. A pattern of English and Australian cricketers exchanging tours had been in place ever since what was recognised as the first Test match took place in Melbourne in March 1877; indeed, so frequent were these tours that this was the 21st series between them during this quarter-century. The impact the games had on the public imagination had grown significantly; one of the major triggers was an English visit to Australia in 1894-95 which produced an enthralling series settled 3-2 in favour of Andrew Stoddart's touring side after an epic fifth match.

Improved submarine communications meant that for the first time the basic facts of a day's play appeared in an evening paper in England the same day, creating extraordinary interest in events more than 10,000 miles away. Even Queen Victoria was said to have kept an eye on the unfolding drama. The 1902 series provided further excitement. Australia's win by three runs in Manchester was the closest result there had then been to a Test in terms of runs, and The Oval would provide the narrowest outcome in terms of wickets remaining.

The Test game was to all intents and purposes made up of England versus Australia, but South Africa were emerging as a third force. South Africa was hardly yet a country in its own right, more an area over which adventurers – including many Britons – rushed to get gold, diamonds and other resources out of the ground. One of the more minor consequences of the British military victory over the Boers on 31 May 1902, which ended a war of annexation lasting more than two years and finally provided some stability to the region, was that it allowed organised social activities such as cricket to bed in.

There had previously been a few English tours there – playing what are now regarded as eight official Tests between 1888 and 1899 – but they did not involve representative XIs; from now on, though, more effort was made to assemble teams equipped with strong talent on both sides. In fact, during the Oval Test of 1902 it was confirmed that the Australian touring team – despite some misgivings about their safety given that 15,000 Australians had recently fought the Boers – had accepted an offer of £2,000 (more than £300,000 in today's money) to break their long sea voyage home and stop off for three Tests in South Africa. In 1905-06, Pelham Warner led an England team in five Tests in South Africa, and in 1907 South African cricketers played Tests on English soil for the first time, games Jessop would play in.

Test cricket thrived in part because it was seen as a test of national virility, but nationhood itself was an evolving concept. Australia formally became a single political entity only on 1 January 1901 when its six colonies signed an act of federation, while the Union of South Africa was not formed until 1910. Driven partly by South Africa's desire to be treated as equals, England, Australia and South Africa formed the Imperial Cricket Conference in 1909 and agreed to a three-way reciprocation of tours. Test cricket's family was not expanded further until West Indies, New Zealand and India were admitted in the late 1920s, but by then England had already played Australia more than a hundred times and their rivalry was cemented as first among equals.

England and Australia teams hardly entered the field as national flag bearers. Everyone regarded themselves as belonging to the same British Empire. The Australian team were often referred to as 'colonials' and most Australians felt a close emotional bond to the 'mother country'. That said, 'national' caps for the players were coming into fashion, as much as anything to reinforce to the players themselves that they were part of a common enterprise. The Australian players had been wearing touring caps with what was effectively a national coat of arms since the early 1890s. England players first wore caps with three lions and a crown on them in 1909. Jessop's England cap is still in the possession of his family.

With radio and television still far in the future, let alone broadcast rights deals worth millions of pounds, Test cricket relied almost exclusively on gate receipts for revenue. Major cricket tours therefore involved as many matches as possible in as many parts of the host country as might attract significant numbers of spectators. Apart from the five Tests, the 1902 Australians played 35 other matches between early May and mid-September, each typically scheduled to last three days, which left few days off from playing or travelling. Every day's takings added to the coffers but the Tests – staged at the largest venues in the cities with the largest populations – were the main earners. And the more people that could be accommodated, the better.

Test cricket was increasingly big business. The deciding match of the 1894-95 series in Melbourne drew 100,000 spectators and the next English tour of Australia in 1897-98 saw the five Tests watched by more than 330,000. The first day of the Lord's Test of 1896 was attended by 30,000, the most for a single day's international cricket to that point, and the gates for that series were almost double what they had been when Australia toured three years earlier. Several of the Tests in England in 1899 and 1902 had total gates of around 60,000–65,000. This growth reflected the public appetite for Test cricket but also the steps taken by the major venues to expand their capacity: Trent Bridge, Headingley, Lord's, Old Trafford and The Oval all constructed new pavilions between 1886 and 1898.

So highly prized was Test cricket that a Board of Control governing Test matches in England was set up in 1898. Previously, tours had been arranged by groups of enterprising players or financial backers, and in Australia by the Melbourne or Sydney clubs, but there was a desire on both sides to put arrangements on a more stable footing. The idea of a Board of Control was initially championed by Yorkshire, but in the event the board had a majority presence from the Marylebone Cricket Club, based at Lord's and the leading amateur voice in the English game. Once the board was in place, a panel of selectors for home Tests was appointed; previously, each England Test squad was picked by the committee of the club hosting the game – an open invitation to back local players rather than the best players. Lord Hawke, the Yorkshire captain, chaired the selection panel.

Australian teams visiting England received half the gross gate receipts of all matches, but no share of any takings in the stands such as food and drink. In respect of the 1902 tour, this meant that despite much bad weather they took away £4,258 (around £650,000 today).

The view was growing among various stakeholders that the MCC was the best body to organise English tours overseas, with any profits shared between the MCC and the counties. The 1901-02 tour of Australia led by Archie MacLaren in conjunction with the Melbourne club was poorly resourced and proved the last of its kind; when England returned there two winters later it was under the aegis of the MCC, and that was how it stayed until the late 1960s. An Australian Board of Control came into being in 1905.

The MCC takeover made for more smoothly run tours, but capped the financial rewards to professionals, in terms of tour fees, and amateurs, in terms of expenses. English amateurs had previously been generously kept in champagne. The likes of MacLaren and Jessop never made a Test tour under the MCC, and only three amateurs joined the first MCC-led tour of Australia. The management of Test cricket was undergoing profound rationalisation, but there was no question that the product itself was the jewel in the sport's crown.

*

Test cricket in England in 1902 looked different from the modern game in a number of ways, but in respect of Jessop and his record there was one vital distinction.

At that time in English cricket, hits over the boundary line were typically worth only four, not six. For a six, local rules – which sometimes counted more in such matters than the Laws of Cricket – usually (though not always) required the ball to carry beyond the limits of the whole ground, a rare event. And because local rules varied, crowds were often unsure of which hits should be awarded four and which ones six, and as we shall see this led to spectators attempting to persuade an umpire to award six when one of their favourites was batting. Had all over-the-boundary hits counted for six in 1902, Jessop would have reached his hundred even faster than he did, because three of what were recorded as boundary fours would now be taken as sixes.

The out-of-the ground 'six' was partly designed as a means of limiting how many runs could accrue in the event of the ball being lost after a big hit. The most recent code of the laws, dating from 1884, stated: 'If a ball in play cannot be found or recovered, any fieldsman may call "lost ball", when the ball shall be "dead"; six runs shall be added to the score; but if more than six runs have been run before "lost ball" has been called, as many runs as have been run shall be scored.'

The boundary line itself was a relatively recent innovation. Not until the 1884 code was there any mention of boundaries, and even then it stated that the umpires shall arrange boundaries 'where necessary'. The main purpose of the demarcation was to keep at bay the growing numbers of spectators at a time when there were fewer big stands and more open spaces. Nor was there a minimum or maximum distance as to how far from the wickets a boundary line should be. In fact, The Oval was one of the biggest grounds in the country, with one of the biggest playing areas.

The Australians had their own rule that a hit clearing the boundary was worth five runs inside the ground, with the stipulation that the batsmen then change ends, and six runs for an out-of-the-ground hit. These regulations were in force when England played in Australia between 1891-92 and 1901-02, and there were 35 recorded hits of five or six in these Tests, including three by Jessop during his only tour there in 1901-02.

Joe Darling, who captained Australia on three tours of England including in 1902, was an advocate of six runs for every hit over the boundary, believing it would produce more attacking cricket. Darling himself was one of the cleanest ball strikers in the game and in the Test that preceded Jessop's match he twice hit balls from Wilfred Rhodes out of Old Trafford – the first known sixes in Test cricket in England. The Board of Control turned down Australian requests to change things on the basis that 'owing to the different arrangements on the different grounds, it would be inexpedient to lay down any hard and fast rule that a hit to the boundary should count four and a hit over the boundary six'.

It was not until April 1910 that an alteration was made following a proposal from Kent at a forum for county captains, among them Jessop as Gloucestershire's representative, that six runs be awarded 'for all hits that drop over and clear of the boundary line or fence'. Jessop was then thirty-five and would play only five more seasons of first-class cricket, and only twice more for England. Gerald Brodribb estimated to me that Jessop struck '600 or 700' over-the-boundary hits in the course of his first-class career, but the vast majority of these brought him only four runs.

Another handicap was that bats were then much less powerful than the leviathans of the twenty-first century. They typically weighed around 2lb 10oz, not dissimilar to those of today, but modern bats are much deeper, front to back, and as a result more powerful (in spite of the extra wood, their weight is kept down through drying processes that remove moisture). Technology enables modern bats to hit the ball farther, more often; even mishits can carry big distances. Jessop sought to find more power by using bats that were slightly heavier than the norm.

There were other respects in which the game was different. The ball was essentially the same in its dimensions but the seam sat flusher than on modern balls, though not completely flat because the likes of Monty Noble and George Hirst, who played in the Oval Test on opposing sides, were early pioneers in the art of 'swerve', or swing bowling, and without a seam to act as a rudder through the air such movement would have been hard to achieve; Hirst said that he tended to make the ball swerve only when the ball was new and he held the seam upright between his fingers. Unless the original became damaged, one ball had to suffice for a whole innings; there was no second new ball after 80 overs as there is now.

Mystery spin was not yet a feature of international cricket, although Bernard Bosanquet of Middlesex was in the early stages of developing the googly and would first use it to help win England a Test in Australia in 1904. Jessop was not the only cricketer pushing the limits of what was possible.

A set of stumps were an inch narrower at eight inches wide and an inch shorter in height at twenty-seven inches. The leg before wicket law operated to a narrower remit: for the batsman to be given out, the ball had to pitch solely in line with the stumps rather than either in line with the stumps or outside off stump. It was therefore a much rarer form of dismissal: only 6 per cent of wickets fell to lbws in Tests up to 1914, compared to 16 per cent in the 2020s. Jessop was out lbw in only 2.6 per cent of his first-class innings. An over consisted of six balls, as is the case now, although this was a new feature of Test cricket in England in 1902; since 1890, Test matches on English soil had involved five-ball overs. In Tests in Australia they had been using six-ball overs since 1891-92. There were no coaches to help the players prepare and the toss was a small – though crucial – ceremony usually conducted within a few yards of the pavilion, with only the two captains in attendance.

The main activity before the start involved ground staff readying the pitch. The rolling of the 22-yard strip required the services of a horse harnessed either to a light or heavy roller, depending on the wishes of the batting team's captain. In order to protect the surface from hoof marks, horses would be shod in special leather boots. Sam Apted, The Oval groundsman, endorsed the 'Pattisson Horse Boot', describing them as 'The best boots I have ever used'. A maximum of ten minutes was set aside for rolling, but this could mean the overall gap between innings might be around 15 minutes rather than the modern ten-minute turnaround; much depended on whether the horse was obliging or not.

Another key difference between cricket in 1902 and the 2020s was the requirement that the pitch be left uncovered in the immediate build-up to the game and during the game itself. Were it to rain during this time, it could be transformational: once wet turf began to dry under the sun it would become sticky, and the ball would grip and deviate sharply, making batting extremely difficult. The possibility that rain might alter conditions mid-match meant that every team had to pick batsmen with the skill to deal with the turning ball and select spin bowlers capable of exploiting these changed conditions – 'wet-wicket specialists'.

Many men born in the North of England could bat on any kind of wicket and Johnny Tyldesley, of Lancashire, was England's finest in these circumstances, and Stanley Jackson, of Yorkshire, was also very good. Rhodes, a left-arm spinner, was the likeliest to take advantage with the ball. It made for a more varied and skilful game, but luck played a much larger part. The captain who won the toss and batted first enjoyed a big advantage if the weather was fine at the outset and there was rain later. In such a wet summer as 1902 bad weather had a big impact, including on how the Oval match unfolded. The batting average of the two sides combined across the series was 20.7, compared to 32.1 for the Ashes series in England in 2023, a fair reflection of how much harder life was for batsmen. Full covering of Test pitches in this country did not arrive until the late 1970s.

A final note: barring a handful of exceptions, Test matches in England until the 1930s were played over only three days (unlike in Australia, where they were played to a finish). If this seems short to modern minds, two things have to be remembered. The first is that if the pitch was affected by rain, the game could move forward fast. If the weather stayed dry, achieving an outright result might be harder, but this is where the second point comes in, which is that over-rates were then much faster. In the modern era, when there is a steady stream of interruptions for drinks breaks, on-field treatment for injuries, reviews of umpiring decisions and the like, typically teams fall well short of even the expected 15 overs per hour. The Oval Test of 1902 saw a rate of 20.4 overs per hour across the whole game, and this was normal for the time. Despite the loss of more than an hour's play to rain and bad light, the match saw 311.4 overs bowled across three days. Around half of all the five-day Tests played by England between 2022 and 2024 were completed in fewer overs than that.

Whatever regulations pertained, the England and Australia teams contesting the 1902 series rank among the finest of all time. England's XI for the first Test was reckoned by many to be one of the strongest they have ever put into the field – every member of the side scored a first-class century – and the Australians played 39 matches on their tour and were beaten only twice (including the one-wicket defeat in the Oval Test). The series they played out rates among the best, and most dramatic, in history.

3

THE FIRST FOUR TEST MATCHES

JESSOP LAYS DOWN A MARKER

JOE DARLING and his team arrived in England on 25 April after a five-week sea voyage from Adelaide. They shared the journey on the *Omrah* with the English players – among them Gilbert Jessop – whose last match of their long winter tour of Australia ended on 18 March. The Australians opened their programme with a fixture against London County, led by W. G. Grace, at the Crystal Palace, with Jessop in the opposition. No doubt still elated by his whirlwind engagement to Millicent Osborne aboard ship, Jessop struck 47 in 40 minutes, sharing a partnership of 93 with England team-mate Len Braund. It was one of seven matches the Australians played before the Tests began.

The Australian party consisted of only 14 players, which was typical for the time despite the lengthy fixture lists. It was a means of keeping costs down and shares of the spoils up. However, the size of the group led to problems during the wet spring when several of the side, including Darling himself, went down with influenza. Hugh Trumble, the leader of the bowling attack, sustained a dislocated thumb and did not take the field until 9 June, missing the first two Tests. Jack Saunders, who would later open the bowling with Trumble, his fellow Victorian, also missed the start of the series.

Darling was an experienced, battle-hardened cricketer and captain, square-jawed and born for a crisis. As a batsman he could play conventionally and sedately, but was also responsible for some of the most attacking Test innings of the period, hence in part his support for awarding six for all over-the-boundary hits. In the final match of the 1897-98 series in Sydney, he raced to a 91-minute hundred, the fastest Test century then recorded in terms of time, to speed his side to a six-wicket win. In his first assignment as a Test leader, he marshalled Australia to a 1-0 success in England in 1899, proving himself, in *Wisden*'s verdict, 'one of the very best captains that ever took a team into the field'. His situation was complicated by his father, a grain merchant, demanding that his son help run the family farm in South Australia and then, after the 1899 tour, manage a newly acquired sheep station in Tasmania. This led to Darling missing almost two years of cricket before he returned to lead Australia in the first three Tests of the 1901-02 series, and then bring the team to England for a second time, a trip that ultimately kept him away from home for eight months.

The Australians were fortunate that rain allowed them to escape with two draws when they were most inconvenienced by illness and injury. Once their side was settled they became a different proposition. Over the course of the last three Tests, the first two of which were won, the side was unchanged; in these, Trumble took 26 wickets, Saunders

18, Monty Noble 13 and Warwick Armstrong one (that of Jessop, to bring an end to his innings of 104).

C. B. Fry, a multi-gifted sportsman and polymath, who would take part in the first three Tests of the series only weeks after playing for Southampton in the FA Cup final, was also a prolific journalist, and before the series wrote an assessment of Australia's principal bowlers in the *Strand Magazine*. Of the 6ft 5in Trumble, who was making his fifth tour of England, he stated:

> On a sticky or crumbled pitch he can make the ball talk as loudly as any bowler ... Being very tall, he can cause the ball to rise a trifle abruptly; he is very steady and keeps an excellent length ... [He] knows every move in the game. Not only does he quickly discover any weakness in your defence, but sets about using your very strongest points as means of getting you out ... The field is always placed in such a way that if you make the least mistake you are bound to be caught. His plans may not always succeed, but they are nearly always the best suited to the man and the occasion. Consequently, Trumble is a great bowler.

As the man widely thought to have developed swing bowling – or 'swerve', as it was called – Noble, another big man, was also of particular interest.

> His bowling is right-hand, rather above medium pace, and its virtue, besides good length and – on favourable pitches – a smart off-break, consists in its peculiar flight. This peculiarity is not invariably present; but when it is his bowling is very difficult. The ball sometimes swerves in the

air inwards, either from the off or from leg, and sometimes seems to duck downwards. Perhaps batsmen are inclined to exaggerate the amount of this swerve, but no one who has played Noble with a slight wind blowing can doubt its existence.

Much less was known about Saunders, who had never previously played outside Australia, and Fry did not include him in his analysis. Saunders featured in one Test against Archie MacLaren's team in the winter and did well, taking nine wickets. He bowled slow left-arm from a good height and could make the ball break dangerously on the sort of pitches he now regularly encountered in England. He had a novel way of approaching the wicket from behind the umpire which batsmen found disconcerting, and there were mutterings in some quarters about the legitimacy of his quicker balls, but despite some inconsistencies in length he was a great foil to the probing accuracy of Trumble and the swing of Noble.

Ernest Jones, who was reckoned to be the fastest bowler yet seen in Test cricket, was expected to feature prominently but needed hard surfaces to be really effective and dropped out of the reckoning after the second Test. Others whose bowling Jessop faced during the series were Armstrong, who bowled leg-breaks and was often used as a defensive weapon, and Victor Trumper, Australia's champion batsman who purveyed medium-pace and was called on by Darling in five separate innings in the series.

MacLaren was appointed England captain with little debate. That he had been Lancashire's captain since 1894 and had led England in the last home series three years earlier following W. G. Grace's resignation after the first Test, and then again in Australia, was not in itself a guarantee that he would carry on; this was an era when Test captains were routinely and unceremoniously changed. In truth, it was something of a surprise that MacLaren had been appointed when he was in 1899. Then, Stanley Jackson, the Yorkshire all-rounder, was arguably the better choice. Jackson and MacLaren were contemporaries at Harrow, where they had played in the first XI together, but Jackson was the older by a year and had preceded MacLaren into county and Test cricket, playing for England while in his final summer at Cambridge, and immediately proving himself a superb big-match player. For MacLaren to be running things while Jackson was also on the field must have felt contrary to both of them. But MacLaren knew the game and knew tactics.

What complicated things for Jackson was that he could not give as much time to the game as MacLaren; he was destined for a career in business and politics and even during the 1902 Tests was spoken of as a prospective Member of Parliament (in the event, he first became an MP in 1915). His father, William Jackson, was an MP, a former financial secretary to the Treasury and chief secretary of Ireland, and was raised to Baron Allerton of Chapel Allerton in the Coronation honours of June 1902. Unlike MacLaren, Jackson never had time to go on overseas tours, and his military service in South Africa in 1900-01 meant that he had only returned to cricket three weeks before the first Test. Theoretically, Fry was another option, but he was younger still and the least experienced in terms of captaincy, and temperamentally uncertain under pressure.

Lord Hawke's selection panel, consisting of himself, and Gregor MacGregor and Herbert Bainbridge, respectively captains of Middlesex and Warwickshire, typically co-opted two amateurs likely to be involved in the game, and MacLaren and Fry were invited to do so ahead of the first Test. This was good news for Jessop, because both were supporters of his.

The XI that England put into the field both at Edgbaston and for the second match at Lord's was redolent with star quality, and much stronger than the team that had just returned from Australia. The Yorkshire trio of Jackson, Hirst and Wilfred Rhodes, and Bill Lockwood of Surrey, had all missed that tour. But later in the series the team went through several changes due to injuries, loss of form and the whims of Hawke's selection panel, especially when for various reasons MacLaren and Fry were not directly involved in discussions. Jessop would be among four players selected, dropped and re-selected.

MacLaren was regarded as a good judge of a player and a decent tactician, but had no real history of success as a Test captain, and he struggled to find any here. He was not helped by cruel luck with the weather, but at crucial times players failed to gel, or hold their nerve, and it ultimately cost England the series before they got to The Oval. MacLaren often appeared weighed down by responsibility, and W. J. Ford would write in *The Times* at the point of MacLaren's removal in 1903: 'There are those who do not consider Mr MacLaren an ideal captain.'

On the face of it, a sports team drawn from a population of 37 million and playing at home ought to have got the better of one relying on barely one-tenth of that number, but as the *Pall Mall Gazette* reflected: 'It is just possible that this very restriction [in numbers] tells in favour of the Australian players. It tends to bring about a greater cohesion. [An England team] looks uncommonly powerful on paper, but when all is said and done it is a scratch team and is the more vulnerable as a consequence.'

Certainly Darling brought a steeliness of purpose that would be the hallmark of Australian teams down the years. 'No travelling team ever strove harder for victory or more completely subordinated all personal considerations to the prime object of winning matches,' Sydney Pardon wrote. But Darling's tactics and his team's qualities would be found wanting at the last big hurdle.

FIRST TEST

Edgbaston, Birmingham, 29–31 May: England 376-9 dec (Stanley Jackson 53, Johnny Tyldesley 138, George Hirst 48, Bill Lockwood 52 not out); Australia 36 (Wilfred Rhodes seven for 17) and 46-2. Match drawn.

The expansion of Test cricket meant a need for more big venues in more big cities. Leeds and Nottingham staged their first internationals in 1899, and 1902 saw the introduction of Birmingham. The ground at Edgbaston was specially fitted for the occasion; new stands were erected and freshly painted, and flag-decked marquees pitched around the boundary. Trains brought people from surrounding towns and from an early hour the public arrived at the ground in a continual stream by foot, tram, charabanc or bus. The first day was watched by 15,000.

England took advantage of MacLaren winning the toss on an easy-paced pitch, scoring 351 for nine by stumps against an attack missing Trumble and Saunders. After the loss of three early wickets, Johnny Tyldesley's superb 138 formed the backbone of the innings, and he was well supported by Jackson and Hirst. The Australians did not help themselves by dropping him three times on 43. Jessop, who had been vying for a place in the side with the Kent all-rounder Jack Mason, went in at No 8. Darling immediately spread his field, putting men on the boundary to frustrate him. Having hit a four and two singles and played, in the words of *Wisden*, 'very wild cricket', Jessop failed to get hold of a wide ball from Trumper and was easily caught at deep point. The correspondent of the *Leeds Mercury* shook his head: 'Thus far, Jessop has again failed signally.'

In a unique development for a home Test series at this time, Fry as an active participant was recruited to file reports for the *Daily Express*. He found writing easier than scoring runs and was obliged in his first despatch to relate being dismissed by Jones, bowling fast and short, without scoring. 'We started ill,' he stated gloomily, '[when] I was caught at the wicket off my third ball.' Fry's scouting report on Jones before the tour proved all too prescient: 'His speed is so great that his very shortest ball is liable to prove difficult. He is reported to have lost the extra pace which has hitherto constituted his excellence, but in all probability most of our batsmen will find him quite fast enough.'

Rain delayed the start of the second day until almost 3 p.m. and threatened to transform the pitch. MacLaren thought it would play all right for an hour, so he let Lockwood and

Rhodes bat on before declaring at 3.30 p.m. His call proved spot-on. In 23 overs, all bowled by Hirst and Rhodes save for one over from Braund to allow Hirst to change ends and harness the breeze, Australia were routed for 36. This still stands as their lowest score in Test cricket. It was a singular triumph for Hirst and Rhodes, both of them born in the same Yorkshire village of Kirkheaton, on a hill east of Huddersfield, both of them right-handed batsmen and left-arm bowlers, and both destined for greatness. They were never buddies, though, even after their famous last-wicket partnership which would end the 1902 series. Their characters were simply too different. Hirst was extrovert and genial, with a wide smile; Rhodes was wiser, cannier and less expansive.

Fry praised Hirst's ability to get a sure footing and achieve full pace on damp turf, and both bowlers struck perfect lengths, Rhodes turning the ball away from the right-handers. But without a hot sun to dry it, the pitch was far from a classic 'sticky dog'. The light was poor, but Australia batted badly. Fry thought 120 a par score. The Yorkshire pair were given good support in the field: Braund held a superb catch and Jessop was typically brilliant with his ground-fielding and would have run out Trumper, who top-scored for Australia with 18, had Dick Lilley gathered cleanly. Rhodes picked up six of the last seven wickets in 37 balls. Australia followed on but had not been batting long when the rain returned.

It again rained torrents on the second night, leaving the ground 'a complete lake' in the words of Warwickshire secretary R. V. Ryder. While the players kicked their heels in the pavilion, Ryder dispensed with the services of half his gatemen and half the police, and kept the gates closed. By afternoon, though, the sun was shining bright, raising hopes of a genuine 'sticky dog', and people hurried to the ground. Fearing disorder if spectators paid for admission only to be denied play because the ground was unfit, the Warwickshire committee continued to bar the gates, but with insufficient police on hand a large crowd on Calthorpe Road grew impatient and rushed the gates. It was estimated that 600–700 people gained free entry but more seriously several people were thrown to the ground and trampled on. One person received a badly cut face and another suffered a broken collarbone. To compound matters, some of the gates and railing were still wet with paint and tar, meaning that in the crush 'many persons had their clothing irretrievably ruined', according to the *Birmingham Daily Post*.

To assuage another crowd estimated at 15,000, it was decided to resume the match at 5.15 p.m., the players battling to keep their footing on sodden turf sprinkled with sawdust. 'The pitch was not fit,' Fry wrote. 'The hour and a quarter of play was a bit of a farce.' Australia lost two wickets but secured the draw.

SECOND TEST

Lord's, London, 12–14 June: England 102-2 (Archie MacLaren 47 not out, Stanley Jackson 55 not out); Australia did not bat. Match drawn.

So severe was the illness in the Australian camp that there was speculation that the second Test might be delayed, but it went ahead as planned even though several players were scarcely up to the task. The team's spirits had taken another hit three days after the first Test when they were bowled out for 23 by Yorkshire at Headingley, the lowest score they ever made against a county side, Hirst and Jackson each taking five wickets. It would be their only defeat until the Oval Test.

Using a half-sovereign lent him by Jessop, MacLaren won the toss, condemning the Australians to time in the field when they would rather have been sheltering from more bleak weather. The match started late at 2.45 p.m. and England quickly lost Fry and Ranjitsinhji, the Indian-born batsman who had settled in England as a teenager, to Bert Hopkins for ducks. Fry offered a tame catch to short leg – 'I hope to forget how to play the stroke I invented for that ball' – and Ranjitsinhji was bowled off his pads. There were two more rain breaks and, with the Australians hampered by a wet ball and greasy footholds, MacLaren and Jackson scored freely. Saunders, half blinded by an ulcerated eye, got through only three overs. By stumps, a partnership of 102 had put England in a promising position and the batsmen were cheered in by a crowd of around 6,000.

Steady rain put paid to play on the second day and on the third morning, with the ground virtually under water, the game was abandoned at 11.15 a.m. This was the last of the lengthy rain interruptions in the series, but the weather was rarely good; 1902 had fewer dry days than any English summer in the twentieth century except for 1912, and with an average temperature of 17.8 degrees it was the third coldest summer behind 1907 and 1954.

THIRD TEST

Bramall Lane, Sheffield, 3–5 July: Australia 194 (Monty Noble 47, Sydney Barnes six for 49) and 289 (Victor Trumper 62, Clem Hill 119, Bert Hopkins 40 not out, Wilfred Rhodes five for 63); England 145 (Jack Saunders five for 50, Noble five for 51) and 195 (Gilbert Jessop 55, Archie MacLaren 63, Hugh Trumble four for 49, Noble six for 52). Australia won by 143 runs.

England were well beaten in Sheffield, which, like Edgbaston, was staging its first ever Test match, but for the purposes of our story there was a particular significance to the game. Jessop, having persuaded his captain to let him open the batting after MacLaren expressed tiredness after a long day in the field, went after the Australian bowling so ferociously as England set off in pursuit of 339 to win, that he revived hopes that his team might actually achieve their daunting task. Scoring at faster than a run a ball, he reached 53 out of a score of 73 for one at stumps in under an hour, putting English supporters in better spirits than they had been for the previous two days. The view of one morning newspaper that 'Nothing is impossible to such a batsman' reflected the opinion of many.

As it happened, the dream quickly died. Jessop drove his first ball of the final morning for two off Trumble, who had been unable to bowl the previous evening after taking another blow on his thumb, but to his second he was given out lbw to a ball that hit him on the top button of his shirt as he attempted to sweep. Jessop was clearly unhappy as he walked off and umpire Walter Richards later apologised for a bad decision. 'Trumble's appeal was half-hearted whilst Richards' arm was long in going up,' the *Nottingham Evening Post* reported.

Trumble followed up with the wickets of Tyldesley and Fry to all but put the match out of England's reach, but Jessop's performance had put down a marker. It must have persuaded him that, for all his recent struggles in Tests, he could have success sticking to his usual methods, and it showed the Australians what a dangerous adversary he could be – perhaps not quite the pushover they had thought. Jessop had meted out hefty punishment on Saunders, whom he cut for four during his first innings of 12, and hit for 15 from eight balls in the second. It must have been chastening for Darling to have to withdraw Saunders from the attack after only two overs, and even Noble, who took 11 wickets in the game, was unable to halt Jessop's progress as he had in the first innings, when Jessop skied a catch to mid-on after scoring 12 off nine balls.

Although his team had eventually prevailed, Darling had been given pause for reflection. Directly before the game, the Australians had played in Edinburgh and Darling had told one of the Scotland players, William Sharp, that they were 'always glad' when Jessop was selected for England, 'as they knew how to get him out before he got set'. Well, perhaps. 'Mr Jessop, despised as he has been in certain quarters, cut his critics to ribbons by his display in the second innings on Friday night,' the *Sheffield Daily Telegraph* stated. '[He] showed that he could play the game as well as hit.'

Thanks to Trumble and Noble, England lost nine wickets for 122 on the last day, both bowlers getting the ball to break several inches off the pitch and kick awkwardly. For all Australia's brilliance with the ball, and resourcefulness with the bat after slipping to 73 for five on the first day in the face of a superb spell from Sydney Barnes, there was a sense that England had let things slip at key moments. They allowed Australia to get too many runs second time around, when Trumper and Clem Hill played brilliant, attacking innings, but Lilley missed two chances at the wicket, and Rhodes and Fry also put down catches. Several England batsmen failed to fire in both innings. 'Jessop, Lilley and Fry,' one observer noted, 'were deeply affected over the reverse.'

The contest had been quite even until late on the first day when England lost three wickets in poor light caused in part by the smokestacks of Sheffield's local industry. The game was watched by 41,000 across the three days, but a good turnout was not enough. Sheffield was to lose out to Headingley as Yorkshire's long-term Test venue; it never staged a full England international again.

FOURTH TEST

Old Trafford, Manchester, 24–26 July: Australia 299 (Victor Trumper 104, Reggie Duff 54, Clem Hill 65, Joe Darling 51, Wilfred Rhodes four for 104, Bill Lockwood six for 48) and 86 (Lockwood five for 28); England 262 (Stanley Jackson 128, Len Braund 65, Hugh Trumble four for 75) and 120 (Trumble six for 53, Jack Saunders four for 52). Australia won by 3 runs.

Despite his brilliant fielding and an important contribution with the bat in Sheffield, Jessop was surprisingly dropped for the fourth Test, a game England needed to win if they were to win the series and regain the Ashes. He was one of four changes: Ranjitsinhji replacing Fry and Lockwood being preferred to Barnes were uncontentious decisions; the selection of two uncapped players in Fred Tate and Lionel Palairet was altogether more surprising. Admittedly, Hirst was not in his best form and Jessop had just had a poor game for Gloucestershire against the Australians in Bristol, where he scored 13 and 21 and, according to the *Sportsman*, 'proved easy prey'. Nor did he bowl. But their absence weakened the fielding – 'no English team can ever have been picked with less regard for its fielding capabilities', Jessop would later claim – and Tate's batting was not remotely comparable to Hirst's.

MacLaren, tied up with Lancashire matches in the north, was not directly involved in selection but provided Lord Hawke with a list of players he wanted and it included Jessop. Who pushed for Jessop's exclusion is unclear, but with Fry sure to be dropped he was also absent from the meeting, meaning Jessop had lost his strongest advocates. Co-opted in their absence was Jackson, whose presence may well have been pivotal.

Jessop's relationship with Jackson had never been easy, but the gulf between them only grew with time for reasons both sporting and social. As a batsman, Jackson was as measured as Jessop was mercurial; unlike Jessop, he would never try to gamble his way out of trouble. His innings of 128 in this fourth Test was a classic of its kind: on a difficult pitch, England slumped to 44 for five in reply to Australia's

299, but thanks to the fighting qualities of Jackson and Braund the situation was painstakingly turned around and the deficit kept to 37. When England then dismissed Australia for 86 – which could have been even less had Tate not dropped Darling – they were left only 124 to win and after reaching 68 for one really should have won. But whereas Darling's men raised their game, their opponents again faltered. MacLaren got out when set and Jackson could not repeat his earlier heroics.

Jackson viewed the way Jessop batted as needlessly reckless and ill-suited to the cauldron of a Test match. Nor would he have forgotten how Jessop, in a skittish start to his debut innings for England at Lord's in 1899, had nearly run him out before they went on to add 95 in their contrasting styles. He had no doubt heard, too, of how Jessop had run out MacLaren, and then got out himself, at a crucial stage of the final Test in Australia the previous winter. Jackson's blue-blood background further highlighted their dissimilarity. Not for him a grammar school upbringing; not for him journalism for the popular press (although the Jackson family held a stake in newspapers). As Jessop's son reflected many years later, their personalities were 'chalk and cheese'. The Oval Test of 1902 would bind the names of Jackson and Jessop together forever, but as with Hirst and Rhodes they were never close – in fact, anything but.

England did well to come as close to winning as they did because Australia gained a vital advantage batting first. After yet more rain, the pitch just needed a hot sun to become treacherous, so Australia's openers, Trumper and Reggie Duff, set about making runs as fast as they could, taking advantage of Jessop's and Hirst's absence on the off side to steal singles and plunder 135 in 78 minutes. Confirming his reputation as the world's best batsman, Trumper reached his century before lunch, despite the two-hour session starting 13 minutes late, before falling for 104 – what would prove to be the second most famous score of 104 in the series.

Trumble and Saunders were the architects of England's dramatic late collapse, Saunders bowling last man Tate with four runs needed, something that may have influenced Darling's thinking in sticking by these two bowlers when the final Test was also on the line. The Australian players ran from the field shouting with delight before celebrating in time-honoured fashion with a few drinks, resulting in a few sore heads the next morning. For England, such an agonisingly narrow defeat was almost too much to bear, especially as it sealed a fourth straight series loss to Australia. After two Tests in the north of the country, the series was set for its conclusion in the south. Might a return to London bring a change in fortunes?

4

LONDON AND THE OVAL

LONDON AT THE start of the twentieth century was the first city on the planet in terms of size, wealth and grandeur. It sat at the head of the largest empire the world had ever seen and at 6.5 million people its population was greater than Berlin, Moscow, Paris and St Petersburg combined. It had more inhabitants than the next 20 cities and towns in Britain taken together. It boasted not only the greatest financial institution in the Bank of England, but the greatest port. Its economic life was built around the River Thames: the produce of the world came upriver and the nation's goods sailed down it on their way to all parts of an empire that would soon cover more than a quarter of the world's land surface. Wharfs and factories lined its edges.

The city was vibrant – and growing. The population had risen by one million during the 1890s alone. The number of workers in the City of London – where Gilbert Jessop spent some winters – stood at around a third of a million. It housed armies of accountants, auditors, barristers, solicitors, clerks and conveyancers, while numerous large printing firms served the bankers, lawyers and newspapers based around Fleet Street. If London's nightlife was not yet as racy as that of Paris, that would soon change once Edward VII, the playboy prince, ascended the throne. Except on Sundays, the capital's pubs rarely closed.

What could not be conveyed by water was mainly drawn by horse. Motor buses and motor lorries were starting to make an appearance, but most vehicles were horse-drawn, whether it was public trams, cabs or omnibuses, or wagons delivering coal or other commodities to businesses and homes. There were estimated to be only 800 private cars in the entire country. But the explosion of people heading to London had created an urgent need for new means of transport, and trams and the fast-developing underground system were seen as the likeliest solutions.

The Oval cricket ground in Kennington sat close to the heart of London's teeming life. It was surrounded by streets whose noises provided a constant backdrop, while the river itself – and the sounds of boats and their fog horns – was less than half a mile away. At the Vauxhall End of the ground – also known as the Baths End in reference to the Crown Baths, a public bathing facility – sat five mighty gasometers in wrought-iron frames of the South Metropolitan Gas Works. These had a combined capacity of six million cubic feet, the first of them built only a few years after the ground itself was created out of a market garden in the mid-1840s. A short walk from the Pavilion End was the Oval underground station, opened in 1890 as part of the City & South London Railway. A ride on the electric railway – 'trains every four minutes, fare 2d' ran the adverts – was still a novelty, but it was a crucial means of ferrying tens of thousands of spectators to and from the ground.

On a clear day, the highest vantage points inside The Oval offered views of Westminster Abbey and the Houses of Parliament, where Arthur Balfour's new administration had been in power for a month following the retirement of his ageing and exhausted uncle Lord Salisbury.

Not that clear days were particularly common, owing to the relentless smog caused by dozens of factory chimneys operating six days a week, and thousands of domestic coal fires. Figures issued by the Registrar General on 20 August 1902 put deaths from respiratory diseases for the previous week in London alone at an above-average 159. On cloudy days, visibility could be particularly poor, if not quite as bad as around Sheffield's Bramall Lane. At around this time, Claude Monet made repeated visits to London, staying at the Savoy hotel and painting scenes of Waterloo Bridge, Charing Cross Bridge and the Houses of Parliament in which fog, along with industrial chimneys and commuter trains belching black smoke, were key features. 'Without the fog, London would not be a beautiful city,' Monet once wrote. 'It's the fog that gives it its magnificent breadth.' In the week of Jessop's match, newspapers reported cloudy skies and temperatures below what was usual for the time of year.

Unlike at Lord's, home to the exclusive Marylebone Cricket Club five miles to the north-west in St John's Wood, The Oval was a sporting arena located in the capital's mainstream. Its patrons, in the words of Surrey player

Digby Jephson, encompassed soldiers and sailors, postmen and clerks, tinkers, tailors, City swells and immaculate clubmen. At the end of county matches, this eclectic crowd liked to gather in front of the pavilion to cheer their heroes, something that would have been frowned upon at Lord's. It was a place of the people, and if someone was going to set an England record that would not be broken for generations, there was, frankly, nowhere better.

*

The Oval was as celebrated a sports venue as there was in the country. Apart from hosting major cricket matches, including the first Test played in England in 1880, it had staged many early England football and rugby internationals, as well as 19 of the first 21 FA Cup finals. This was partly because Surrey's long-time secretary Charles Alcock, an Old Harrovian and former footballer of note, was a leading sports administrator and an indefatigable innovator, organiser and publisher. He did more than anyone to create the FA Cup, and instinctively saw the attraction of arranging England–Australia Test matches when the MCC was too sniffy to treat the 'colonials' as equals.

The Oval also had an advantage of space. It was a large enough piece of land to put on football codes as well as cricket, and even after members of the Surrey cricket club, which leased the ground from the Duchy of Cornwall, voted in the mid-1890s against the continuation of other team sports due to the damage it was doing to the field, the large playing area remained. The length of the boundaries at the Vauxhall End were especially long, and remained as such until the modern redevelopment of the stands in that part of the ground. There were a number of cases of all-run sevens and in the 1880 Test George Bonnor, batting at the Pavilion End, was caught by Fred Grace, W. G.'s younger brother, inside the boundary off a hit measured at 115 yards. No other first-class ground in the country was as big; Jessop himself wrote in 1913 that 'the Oval is almost twice the size of Taunton'.

Once the club had settled on its future as a cricket venue, Alcock and Richard Webster, Surrey's president and the Lord Chief Justice of England, oversaw the commissioning of a new pavilion, built in the winter of 1897–98 at a cost of £38,000 (about £4.2 million in today's money). The building, of red brick and Bath stone, was designed by the same architects employed by Lancashire for the new pavilion at Old Trafford, but was equipped with state-of-the-art extras that put it ahead of both Old Trafford and Lord's, where a fine new pavilion had been constructed in 1890.

As was the case with England's other Test grounds of the time, The Oval was structurally far less imposing than now. By the standards of the day, though, it was well out of the ordinary. What was additionally impressive about the new pavilion complex was that the main building, fronted by seats and a wooden fence abutting the playing area, was adjoined on either side by stands with upper and lower tiers, creating a grander sweep of seating than anything Lord's could offer. Elsewhere in the ground were more modest roofed stands on the east side and at the Vauxhall End, as well as large swathes of asphalt steps and wooden terraces open to the elements – the cheap seats, costing around a shilling per person and mainly consisting of banks of wooden benches several rows high. Behind some of these seats were large refreshment stalls, and in front of them areas where spectators could sit on the grass around the edge of the boundary, marked by a rope. There was therefore no run-off for fielders chasing the ball in the deep in the way there is in the modern game.

There was thus accommodation for plenty. The last FA Cup final held at the ground in March 1892, before the redevelopment, was watched by 32,810, and the 1902 Test would be seen across the three days by more than 49,000 paying spectators – so, not counting members sitting in the pavilion – or around 16,500 per day. Audiences were overwhelmingly, though not exclusively, male; many venues, including The Oval, had a ladies' seating area.

The only part of the ground not given over to spectators was the Vauxhall End, where a sightscreen consisting of large white sheeting attached to five giant poles, the whole thing measuring about twenty yards wide, was situated. No venue had yet devised a means of providing batsmen facing bowling from the Pavilion End the same assistance, as this would have meant obscuring the view for many of the most important clientele. Picking up the ball against such a dark backdrop as a full pavilion was problematic; C. B. Fry had referenced the difficulty of seeing the ball out of the pavilion backdrop at Bramall Lane.

There were no advertising hoardings inside the ground, but the neighbouring Clayton Arms, which afforded patrons a handsome square-on view of play from its upper floor and roof, carried prominent signs, promoting Bovril ('Bovril Always Scores'), the *Sporting Life* newspaper and Claymore whisky, all the more powerful for their exclusivity. On the same side of the ground, in front of the gasometers, was situated the ground's main scoreboard, the principal means for the thousands of spectators being appraised of the state of play.

The best views of all, of course, were afforded those in the pavilion, through a long series of large arched windows on the ground floor, and an array of smaller windows on the first. The central part of the pavilion was made up of a cavernous members' club room – what is now known as the Long Room – with a bar to the rear. The club room was one and a half times bigger than its predecessor in the old pavilion which had been knocked down in the rebuild. To one end of it were members' private and writing rooms; to the other the secretary's offices, separated from the club room by corridors opening onto the seating at the front which could hold 2,000. On the first floor was the committee room, members' dressing-rooms and dressing-rooms for visiting players; in the basement, lavatories and storage rooms.

The west wing contained a large dining hall as well as dressing-rooms for the professional players, an important innovation as previously there had been adequate facilities only for the amateurs, while professionals were expected to change in dingy rooms without views of the playing arena. The east wing – so, to the left of the pavilion as seen from the field of play – housed a press room and adjoining telegraph room, as well as a scorers' box with crescent-shaped windows offering a panoramic view of the field of play on the first floor. Directly below the telegraph room, on the ground floor, was a printing office which provided regularly updated scorecards.

The press gallery was probably the best in the country, though it did not meet with the satisfaction of the *Daily*

Telegraph correspondent because it was not fully in line with the stumps. 'The press box was too much to the side of the wicket to afford a perfect view,' he grumbled the day Jessop went ballistic. But a press box that reporters don't complain about has yet to be built.

Above the first floor in the main part of the pavilion were 2,000 open seats offering magnificent views across the whole playing area. On the tiled roof itself was a large clock, which was not part of the original construction but added during the 1898 season. Umpires ran the game by this clock.

Before the new building went up, Surrey knew they had some catching up to do – 'the fine pavilion at Lord's has been the envy of metropolitan cricketers south of the Thames', stated one periodical – but the development was hailed as a triumph. The *South London Press* was effusive in its praise and highlighted the groundbreaking nature of the facilities:

The new pavilion bids fair to be the best of its kind in England. It has certainly a merit of architectural style and form which is seldom allied with this class of work … The roofs of the central portion of the pavilion and over both wings are constructed with fireproof flooring, and upon these roofs are stepped 'stands', affording an unobstructed view of the whole of the cricket ground … Open fireplaces are provided in the club-room, committee, secretary's, and writing-rooms, and the dressing-rooms, bar, corridors etc, will be heated with hot water. Electric lighting will be arranged for all the principal rooms, lavatories, and corridors, supplemented by gas. The fittings to the lavatories and bath-rooms will be of a character suited to the purposes of a building which it is intended shall be essentially a club house, and as perfect in its accessories as it is possible to make it.

The pavilion would stand the test of time. Although it has been much modified, with the players' dressing-rooms moved into the adjoining Bedser Stand and the media relocated to the other end of the ground, the main structure still stands, with a handsome edifice recognisable from the original. The roof clock still serves its purpose.

In 1902, the players taking part in the final Test match, the people working at it and the members watching it, wanted for nothing.

5

THE RUN-IN TO THE FINAL TEST

JESSOP'S RECALL

THE ENGLAND selectors had endured a bad few weeks. The nature of the defeats in Sheffield and Manchester left plenty of room for the what-might-have-beens. MacLaren's strategic failings did not escape criticism; a letter-writer to one of the popular prints condemned him as the worst captain in the country. At the heart of the problem was that MacLaren and Lord Hawke had been at odds over the teams for the third and fourth Tests, not the last time a Lancastrian and a Yorkshireman would clash in such a way.

The two men had history. Hawke, who had inherited his barony on the death of his father in 1887, and thereafter felt it was his duty to play cricket all year round, had captained Yorkshire for almost 20 years and was the presiding force at the most powerful county club in the country.

Yorkshire cricket was his fiefdom, but he was also a prime mover in putting the organisation of Test cricket in England on a better footing. He had tried the previous year to arrange an MCC-led tour of Australia, but the plans had fallen through, creating an opening which MacLaren had opportunistically filled with a scheme of his own. Both were stubborn; they wanted what was best for England provided it suited their own needs. As the 1902 series unfolded, their relationship creaked under the strain.

Both were at fault. MacLaren's late call at Bramall Lane in summoning Sydney Barnes – the bowler he had plucked from obscurity to take to Australia with such notable success – backfired when Barnes's long-standing knee problem resurfaced, reducing his effectiveness in the second innings. Hawke, for his part, erred in two respects ahead of Old Trafford.

He allowed the views of a co-opted member of the selection panel, Stanley Jackson, regarding Jessop to supersede those of the captain under whom Jackson would be playing. That Jackson was a Yorkshire team-mate, and the person to whom Hawke often handed the county captaincy when he himself was unavailable, may have been a factor in this. Hawke, it was suspected, also put the interests of Yorkshire first when he sent Fred Tate of Sussex to Manchester as a wet-wicket specialist rather than Schofield Haigh. Had Haigh been despatched, it would have left Yorkshire four players down for their championship match at Worcester. MacLaren, who had supposedly said, 'My god, look what they've sent me', then picked Tate anyway ahead of George Hirst, with disastrous consequences. MacLaren tried to distance himself from these blunders, but he was every bit as culpable as Hawke, or Jackson.

Happily, the two men came to their senses ahead of the fifth Test. It must have helped that MacLaren was co-opted onto the selection panel again, along with Jackson, so that his views were better heard when the panel met to pick the team – probably in London on Sunday 3 August.

In part, Jessop forced the selectors' hands. Unwanted by England for the fourth Test, he had played instead for Gloucestershire at Trent Bridge and taken out his frustrations on the Nottinghamshire bowling by hitting 126 in just over an hour and a half. It was a perfectly timed riposte given that England were then fighting an uphill battle in Manchester. A few days later, he took his Gloucestershire side to Old Trafford itself to play a Lancashire side led by MacLaren, and gave the England captain another reminder of what he had been missing by striking 68 in 55 minutes in the first innings (batting higher than usual at No 3) and 68 not out in 43 minutes in the second. Outplayed, Lancashire hung on grimly for a draw.

Jessop was a man on a mission and MacLaren must have known it.

The following week, on Tuesday 5 August, Hawke wrote to Jessop from the Sports Club in St James's Square:

Dear Jessop,

Selection committee will be pleased if you will play at the Oval next Monday. They however wish me to tell you that Archie MacLaren has guaranteed that you will bowl for at least half to three-quarters of an hour at a stretch, and they sincerely hope that this is correct as it materially affects the bowling strength of the side. [Tom] Richardson [of Surrey] has given me a very nasty right thumb and I can't play this week.

Kindly reply to 107 Jermyn St. Yours sincerely,
Hawke

The demand that Jessop must be capable of bowling spells of a decent length may offer a clue as to why he was left out of the previous Test. In the lead-up to that match he had not bowled at all for almost a fortnight. Jackson – and others – may have argued that if Jessop was not bowling England might be better off selecting a specialist batsman, which was precisely what they did. An additional point was that if Jessop *could* bowl a good number of overs, it would also mean less was asked of Jackson himself with the ball; in Sheffield, Jessop had sent down only four overs while Jackson got through 22.1 overs.

Jessop promptly replied to Hawke that if this stipulation really mattered then the selectors had better choose someone else because his fast bowling days were over, but curiously Hawke then informed him that the condition was not important – a swift climbdown after such a firm opening communiqué. The likely conclusion to be drawn from this is that Hawke and MacLaren were not really that bothered about Jessop's bowling, but others in the selection meeting had been, and therefore the demand needed passing on, even if it was not going to be acted upon come the Test match.

It is possible that Hawke and Jessop even spoke on the telephone about the matter, with Hawke stressing the need for Jessop to look like he was readying himself to bowl overs in the Test match, because Jessop certainly gave himself plenty of overs in Gloucestershire's two championship games that week. On the second and third days of Gloucestershire's match with Sussex at Hove, and across the three days of their game against Middlesex at Bristol, Jessop got through 58 overs, including 22 unchanged on the final afternoon at Hove. This was more overs than he had bowled in the whole of the previous month. He was giving the appearance of a man demonstrating he could bowl, even if privately he was saying he was not the bowler he had been when it came to the higher standards of performance required in Test cricket.

By the second evening of the Bristol match on Friday 8 August, Hawke released the team to the press. He could hardly have left it any later, with the Test starting three days later. By this stage, in any case, everyone's thoughts were focused on the King's Coronation the next day, not least Jackson who in his soldiering capacity was required for duty for the royal procession, and had pulled out of Yorkshire's match at Leicester as a result.

Perhaps in an attempt to avoid further misunderstandings about the best XI, Hawke's committee named a squad of only 11 players. Apart from Jessop, it was also agreed that Hirst would return and Tom Hayward come in for his first game of the series. The players to miss out were Ranjitsinhji, Bobby Abel and Tate. After the turmoil of recent weeks, the team had gone back to nine of the players who had featured in the opening contest in Birmingham, and one which many people including Jessop felt should never have changed. Of Jessop and Hirst's recall, the *Athletic News* declared: 'The committee have virtually admitted that they erred in leaving them out at Manchester.' Jessop himself was eager for battle, as he always was when it came to Test cricket. 'I enjoyed every minute of Test matches,' he once said. 'They were keen – deadly keen – but none the less pleasant on this account.'

*

The Coronation had been due to take place in late June but was postponed at the eleventh hour after the King developed an abdominal abscess requiring immediate surgery. Many of the foreign delegations who came to London for the original ceremony did not return for the rescheduled service on Saturday 9 August, but even so the event did not lack for grandeur. Nor did it fail in its aim of celebrating the vast scale of the British Empire. The 30,000 servicemen called on to march or line the procession route from Parliament Square to Buckingham Palace included 2,000 from overseas territories such as Australia and India. The formal part of the day culminated in Edward VII and Queen Alexandra appearing on the palace balcony to salute the crowds (thereby setting a precedent for future coronations), after which the streets of central London were thronged with people admiring the scores of illuminated buildings and sharing in the carnival atmosphere.

The Australian cricketers were as keen as anyone to watch the procession and requested that their match against Hampshire be reduced to two days so that they could leave Southampton early for the capital. As it happened, they still managed to win the shortened game comfortably, Joe Darling hitting 116 in 80 minutes with five out-of-the-ground sixes. They then headed to their usual base of the Inns of Court hotel in High Holborn. Manager Ben Wardill had arranged for the players to observe the parade from a vantage point high in Piccadilly as guests of the octogenarian Baroness Burdett-Coutts, a banking heiress and philanthropist, who gave them lunch and afterwards presented each with a Coronation Medal. 'Good view of show,' Trumper wrote in his diary.

Most of the England players chosen for the Test on the Monday were less fortunate as they were wanted by their counties for a round of championship matches ending on Coronation Day. The weather was foul around many parts of the country in the lead-up to the weekend, hampering efforts to get in any meaningful play. Hirst and Rhodes kicked their heels at Aylestone Road before Yorkshire's fixture with Leicestershire was abandoned shortly before noon on the final day without a ball being bowled. The game in Birmingham only began on day three and meandered to a draw, Dick Lilley keeping wicket for Warwickshire while Johnny Tyldesley batted serenely for Lancashire for 70 not out. MacLaren was missing for Lancashire due to a knee problem that had been troubling him since the fourth Test and for which, it was reported, he had undergone 'electrical treatment'.

At Canterbury, where the weather was drier, Hayward and Bill Lockwood were part of a Surrey side that sank to an innings defeat to Kent, who captured the last nine wickets for just four runs. The game was over by 12.25 p.m., leaving the crowd at the St Lawrence ground to gather in front of the pavilion and sing the National Anthem in fealty to the monarch.

Jessop's Gloucestershire also went down to an innings defeat, losing to Middlesex despite rain wiping out most of the second day. Jessop's lengthy bowl in the Middlesex innings served its purpose, and he fared relatively well batting at No 3 again, scoring 32 in the first innings and top-scoring with 25 in the second, the game finishing at 4.30 p.m. Lionel Palairet and Len Braund were in action even later at Taunton where Somerset tried in vain to force a win over Sussex.

Jessop may have stayed the Saturday night with family in Cheltenham rather than attempt to navigate the crowds back to his home in London. Players who required accommodation during a Test match were normally only provided with hotels by the Board of Control from the night before the game, so most players selected for The Oval would have spent Saturday at home before catching their trains on Sunday. Had Jessop not been selected for the Test, he would have spent the Sunday heading north to Perth with the Gloucestershire team for a two-day match against the Scottish Counties; in his absence, his younger brother Osman went instead.

Apart from Jessop, the only member of the team who lived in London was Lockwood, who, according to the 1901 census, resided as a boarder at 18 Offley Road, Kennington, a short walk from The Oval. Lockwood, thirty-four, was a widower, his wife Betsy and young son William having died a few years earlier. Although Hayward was also a Surrey player, the same census showed him living in Cambridge with his parents. The Haywards were a great cricketing dynasty, Tom's uncle, also Thomas, having been the finest batsman in England before the arrival of W. G. Grace. Tom's father had once run a cricket outfitting business but was now a publican, and another uncle had coached Ranjitsinhji while he was at Cambridge. Only a week earlier, Tom's benefit match from Surrey had taken place against Yorkshire at The Oval and it could scarcely have gone better: the weather stayed fair and 27,000 turned out over the three days, leading the *Sportsman* to predict that Hayward's takings from the gate receipts would be around £1,500. A good benefit was fundamental to a professional cricketer's long-term wellbeing and this was a handsome windfall which must have put Hayward in good spirits heading into the Test.

He was more fortunate than Lockwood, whose benefit match for Surrey the previous year had been spoiled by rain, although it was estimated that he still received around £1,000. Senior professionals such as Lockwood and Hayward earned around £300–400 per year at a time when only about 15 per cent of the population lived in households with earnings above the income tax threshold of £160 per annum, or the 'gentility line'. But this could be misleading as the careers of sportsmen were short and precarious. For many of them, a second line of work was vital.

Tyldesley, who lived in Eccles near Manchester with his wife and young daughter, termed himself a professional cricketer and sports outfitter in 1901, and Braund, who had originally played for Surrey before settling in Bath and joining Somerset, would also become an 'athletic outfitter'.

Lilley, at thirty-five the oldest man in the team, had set up as a publican, and lived at the Prince of Wales hotel in Moseley with his wife Kate, two daughters and three servants, two of whom worked as bar staff.

MacLaren had recently moved to Basingstoke with his wife Maud, whom he had met on his first tour of Australia and married in Melbourne on his second. Maud's father was a wealthy landowner but not much money appeared to filter MacLaren's way. His move to Hampshire had prompted an offer to play for the county rather than his native Lancashire, with the paid post of assistant treasurer part of the deal but, in the midst of the Test series in Australia, MacLaren had issued a panicked statement turning it down, insisting he received no salary from anyone. Palairet's amateur credentials were more authentic; he lived in Cheddon, Somerset, with a wife, two children and five servants and worked as an estate agent.

Rhodes, the most junior member of the XI, described himself only as a professional cricketer. He was satisfied with the title, if not the rewards, believing that, despite the scope for Yorkshire's players to supplement their match fees with performance bonuses, he was effectively 'a hired servant on a low wage'. Rhodes had married Sarah, a local Kirkheaton girl, at the age of twenty-two and they had set up home in a nearby farmhouse at Bog Hall.

Hirst still lived in the heart of Kirkheaton with his wife Emma and a young son and daughter. On the day before the game, Hirst shared a train to London with James Stainton of the *Sheffield Evening Telegraph*, who recalled the following day: 'As we came up in the train last night, Hirst had quipped, "If I can get nine wickets in the match I shall be quite satisfied".'

Meanwhile, in their offices the daily newspapers and weekly journals were putting together their preview pieces for Monday morning and giving their verdicts on Jessop's recall. The *Sportsman* had already provided its view on the Saturday, saying: 'Possibly the reappearance of Jessop will give rise to a little controversy, but here we are entirely on the side of the selection committee. Unparalleled as a fieldsman, Jessop is worth his place in any team.' Stainton approved of Jessop's return as much as he did that of Hirst – in Jessop's case for the positive effect his presence would have on the spectators, 'for he is essentially a man beloved of the crowd'. The most prescient comment appeared on page 11 of the *St James's Gazette*: 'As a batsman he [Jessop] is uncertain; but the unexpected in the shape of a century from his bat may be realised.'

6

HOW THE PRESS OPERATED

REPORTERS, PHOTOGRAPHERS, ILLUSTRATORS

THE TEST MATCHES were attended by record numbers of reporters. This was partly a reflection of the mounting interest in international sport but also evolving means of communication which meant that it was ever cheaper, faster and simpler to send messages. An overflow area had to be created to accommodate the 70 pressmen who attended the series opener at Edgbaston, and around 50 were present at Bramall Lane for the third match. These totals would certainly have been exceeded for the two games in London, or at least would have done at Lord's had the weather been better. Many journalists who planned to attend may have stayed away. Not so for the fifth Test.

The Oval, with its specially designated press box, scorers' box, telegraph room and printing room all in close proximity, was perfectly designed to meet the demands of this fast-changing world.

There was an extraordinary plethora of daily and evening newspapers in London at the start of the twentieth century, as well as in major provincial cities. By 1900, there were estimated to be around two hundred daily papers alone across the country. London itself had nine evening papers. At least a dozen evening papers and more than twenty dailies sent their own representatives to provide eyewitness accounts of the match, publications that typically ran to eight to twelve broadsheet pages made up almost wholly of the printed word, photographs being essentially the preserve of specialist illustrated weeklies. In their stead, line drawings made up the main pictorial content, but were used sparingly.

How up to date a publication's coverage was with a big, unfolding event like a Test match was an obvious way in which it could measure itself against rivals. A 'live' story of this sort reflected the skill of the journalists, the reliability of communications and the speed of typesetters, printing presses and delivery men. The Stop Press section of a newspaper was guaranteed to include the cricket score, and many evening papers would have 'Cricket Special' or 'Cricket Edition' stamped at the top of their front pages.

The newspaper industry was undergoing great change through a combination of technological advances and the recent entry into the market of a new player, Alfred Harmsworth, later Lord Northcliffe. Harmsworth had bought his first daily paper, the London *Evening News*, in 1894 and created his first morning paper, the *Daily Mail*, two years later. He sold his papers at aggressively cheap prices, often at a halfpenny against the penny of some competitors, and well below the threepence of the ailing *Times*, which was read by the Establishment but few others. Harmsworth built vast presses in Whitefriars Street that could print 600,000 papers a day and a cutting-edge distribution network using motorised vehicles. He would have multiple transcribers working on one political speech to rush it into print faster. Both titles were hugely successful: by 1898, the *Evening News* was selling 800,000 daily and the *Daily Mail* sold one million copies at the height of the Boer War and beyond. One of Harmsworth's tactics with the *Evening News* was to greatly increase its football and cricket coverage, but the *Mail*'s coverage of the 1902 Tests was trumped by the *Daily Express*, owned by Harmsworth's great rival Arthur Pearson, because of their signing of C. B. Fry as correspondent. It was a defeat Harmsworth would later address.

With England winning the Oval Test at around 4.25 p.m., the result came much too late for those editions of the London evening papers which went to press in late morning or early afternoon, and presented a major challenge for the big provincial ones anxious to incorporate the closing stages in their final evening editions. But some of them did scramble the finish into their final print runs, and did so in some style.

The evening papers were actually the ones that covered the story in most detail, and best. Correspondents for established national dailies such as *The Times*, *Daily Telegraph* and *Morning Post*, and newcomers to the morning market like the *Daily Mail* and *Daily Express*, could wait to see how most of the day's action unfolded before starting to compose their pieces, and by the time they were read the story had been in evening publications for 12 hours. Although the daily reports might seem a little long by today's standards – R. H. Lyttelton's report in *The Times* of the final day was some 1,300 words – they were around half the length of those in some evening papers.

Provincial newspapers covered the Test in almost unimaginable detail. James Stainton's report in the *Sheffield Evening Telegraph* of England's win ran to around 2,800 words and a substantially reworked piece the following morning for the *Sheffield Daily Telegraph* filled four columns on the back page and topped 5,000 words. Cricket was a quasi-religion in Yorkshire, so the breadth of the coverage in the Sheffield and Leeds papers should be no surprise, but publications in Birmingham and Manchester were scarcely less magisterial in their sweep of events.

One reason why the pieces were so long is that, in the nature of newspaper coverage at the time, most publications carried only one account of the game, which was intended to provide not only run of play but also broader analysis. For example, the report in the *Sportsman* consisted of around 1,750 words of overview followed by a more prosaic account under the cross-heading 'The Play', and this was a pattern commonly repeated elsewhere. Nor were 'quotes pieces' common, although a few correspondents alluded to conversations they had had with players during lunch breaks or after play. The *Sportsman* was alone in sending a reporter to speak to the Australians at their hotel after the Test had finished and ran a piece the next morning containing direct quotes from Joe Darling and Hugh Trumble under the heading:

WHAT THE AUSTRALIANS THINK
A CHAT WITH THE COLONIAL CAPTAIN

There were reflective pieces on the game in the evening papers the day after the Test had finished, but otherwise the press in the main quickly moved on to other matters, in part because the players themselves were immediately in action again, often in a different city from the one where the Test had taken place. There was subsequently fresh analysis from specialist weeklies such as *Athletic News* and *Cricket: A Weekly Record of the Game*, as well as some interesting insights from other periodicals which had sent feature or 'colour' writers to the game, or were furnished with some of the few photographs taken at the match.

An important role was played by agency reporters. The Press Association began operating in the early 1870s to provide news from around the country to subscriber publications, but within a decade its sports coverage had been subcontracted to the Cricket Reporting Agency (CRA), run by the Pardon family who were for many years involved in producing *Wisden's Cricketers' Almanack*. This arrangement continued until the 1960s. The Cricket Reporting Agency's running copy on play at The Oval was picked up by numerous national and regional papers. Those who had not sent their own reporters to the game would simply take CRA's account but others, who had sent their own men, might still use the agency copy as ballast, particularly in the case of evening papers for whom time was short. Many run-of-play reports, therefore, contained similar wording because they came from the same source. An agency's version of events was amplified by repetition, even though it might not be correct in every particular. In any analysis of what happened, it is important to bear this in mind.

Exchange and Telegraph was another major agency, set up in 1872 chiefly to distribute financial and business information emanating from the City of London. By the late

1870s, though, it was also providing a general news service and would rival the Cricket Reporting Agency as a source of sporting news. It was ExTel that established telegraph machines in offices, banks and gentlemen's clubs, and in all likelihood cricket pavilions such as those at Lord's and The Oval. Cricket scores from around the country that came through via the agency 'ticker-tapes' were still being posted on noticeboards in the Oval pavilion in the early 1990s.

The agencies and most of the capital's principal papers were based in Fleet Street or its environs – Whitefriars Street, St Bride Street, Stonecutter Street and Shoe Lane to the north, Tudor Street to the south, all within a few hundred yards of each other. The workloads of agency men and those servicing daily and evening newspapers were onerous, as H. V. Jones of the Cricket Reporting Agency described in 1899:

> His [the cricket reporter's] work has increased enormously in importance in recent years [and] demands absolute accuracy and promptitude, and his labours by no means cease when stumps are drawn for the day. During a long day he has perhaps been attending to the requirements of evening papers, and after play is over he has to despatch his reports for the morning journals. He has very little leisure time to himself; indeed, I have been more than once hard-pressed to find time in which to get my hair cut. The pursuit of his calling frequently necessitates long, tedious railway journeys, often made during the night.

At least the conditions in which they worked had improved. Jones recalled a time at Edgbaston when reporters and scorers were squeezed together in 'a miserable little shed' affording inadequate accommodation: 'It had not even the merit of being rainproof, it being necessary, in the event of wet weather, to open umbrellas inside the box.' A photograph in the *Sketch* in the week following the Test at Edgbaston in 1902 shows a press box situated alongside the main scoreboard that looks luxurious by comparison. Leicester's press box, however, had yet to enjoy an upgrade, Jones said; it remained a wooden structure 'only fit for a rabbit run or fowl's house'. Trent Bridge's press box was a tent in the 1880s. The Oval must have seemed wonderful indeed.

Most newspaper articles went unsigned, although regular correspondents were often given abstract noms de plume such as 'Mid On', 'Astral' or, as in Stainton's case with the *Sheffield Telegraph* titles, 'Looker-On'. Other papers simply put at the head of their reports descriptors such as By Our Special Representative or By Our Special Correspondent. In any case, long-serving cricket reporters became well known to their audiences, and among the most respected and authoritative were Stainton, Alfred Pullin of the *Yorkshire Post* ('Old Ebor') and Jimmy Catton ('Tityrus'), editor of *Athletic News*.

Those amateur cricketers who supplemented their income through journalism were generally keen to keep their identities hidden. The prolific Pelham Warner, for instance, rarely wrote under his own name. He attended the 1902 Tests when his commitments with Middlesex allowed, which meant every match except the fourth, and the pieces written for the *St James's Gazette* and more especially the *Westminster Gazette* – for whom Warner occasionally wrote around this time and would file regular despatches from Australia when he led an England team there in 1903–04 – bore the hallmarks of an establishment insider. Circumstantial evidence strongly points to him contributing to the *Westminster Gazette*: a reference in the match report for the final day at The Oval, to holes in the pitch being repaired with sawdust during the morning rain break, 'as the new MCC regulations permit', was a classic Warner-ism. No one else referred to this point in their pieces.

The *Daily Express* was altogether less shy about C. B. Fry, whose reports were relentlessly promoted and given pride of place on the paper's front page, to the tut-tutting of the game's establishment that never uttered a word against Warner. Both were Oxford-educated future England captains, but the shrewder, more political Warner was always more discreet, and destined to the life of service to the MCC that escaped Fry. The latter was not only frowned on from above, but also below, with Catton saying that the professional reporters regarded him as 'a poseur'. Neither Fry nor the *Express* cared a jot: he was the paper's star act and he – and they – made the most of it. Fry had to work hard at learning to write at speed, and often wrote having just left the field of play, but by 1902 he was a capable wordsmith. The evening papers often provided some of the most vibrant and immediate match reports, but Fry's copy was up there with the best, and required reading.

What serviced this legion of writers was the telegraph system. This wonder of the Victorian Age had burst into life in Britain half a century earlier and been under national ownership for more than 30 years. It was reasonably inexpensive and the established lifeblood of the up-to-date newspapers; only a few country papers were still using homing pigeons to relay urgent copy. The telephone was coming into fashion and taking business away from the telegraphic companies, but only slightly – during the fiscal year 1902-03 the number of inland telegrams in Great Britain fell by 2.5 million but still totalled 90 million. Some newspapers had begun to put their telephone number below their mastheads ('Telephone 1303 Holborn' stated the *Evening News*) and when Archie MacLaren persuaded Lord Hawke to allow him to summons Sydney Barnes for the third Test he did so via telephone rather than telegram. But old habits died hard and there was a reluctance to embrace the new technology. When an attempt was made to introduce a telephone into The Oval press box in the early years of the twentieth century, it was resisted by reporters who did not want to suffer the distraction of hearing a colleague dictating copy.

In 1902, the telegraph system remained king. For the Sheffield Test, the ground authority laid on 18 specialist telegraph operators for the use of pressmen, and sent almost 10,000 telegrams on their behalf across the three days at a rate of 300 words per minute. The bigger newspapers made special arrangements to ensure their correspondents' copy was transmitted as smoothly and as swiftly as possible by setting up their own personalised service: the words 'By Our Private Wire' often featured at the top of reports. It was a proud boast.

The full benefits of the telegraph were still something of a novelty to cricket reporters, according to Jones, who wrote:

At the present time [1899] there is a telegraph office on nearly all of the important county grounds, but not many years since such a boon was almost unknown, and telegrams had to be entrusted to messengers to deliver at the head office, a mile or two miles away from the ground.

The use of these messengers filled most reporters with dread, he added:

The average boy, I am afraid, has not the bump of responsibility very largely developed, and is very prone to loiter on the way. One young scoundrel once calmly dropped a batch of messages in a brook, while another youngster deposited the telegrams in a pillar-box.

The mother of another messenger refused to allow him to return to work at the ground in Gloucester when she learned that the pressmen had bottled beer in their tent. For The Oval to have its own telegraph room adjoining the press room represented cutting-edge technology. Things were less conveniently arranged at Lord's, where the telegraph office was situated at the Nursery End, while the press were accommodated at the opposite end of the ground.

Those following the match in Australia were reliant on cables from the Reuters agency, an international news service created in London in the 1850s by Paul Reuter, a German baron. A massive cable-laying programme had seen 'submarine cables' reach Australia by the 1870s, and by the start of the twentieth century news from Britain could be received within hours (provided the cable didn't go down, as sometimes happened). Australian newspapers relied heavily on Reuters, bulletins for first news of the Tests as no Australian journalists accompanied the team to England.

Former Test cricketers such as Jack Worrall and Frank Iredale wrote occasional comment pieces from home, based on their assessments of cables. Additionally, one unnamed member of the Australian party, writing under the byline 'From Our Correspondent', provided sporadic eyewitness accounts from the tour for the Melbourne *Argus*. However, these were despatched by mail rather than telegraph, leading to lengthy delays before publication. The article that appeared on the day the Oval Test began, for instance, was one that dealt with Australia's first victory of the series almost six weeks earlier.

*

If this was a boom time for newspapers, and the arrival of the *Daily Mail* and *Daily Express* had enlivened the market, it was also a period in which images of various kinds played an increasing role in the consumption of news. Photographs, sketches and cartoons, and moving film, all of them monochrome, had walk-on parts in our story.

Most striking to a modern audience are the surviving photographs. It was not yet possible to get news photographs into daily newspapers because printing them was too slow for the needs of the mass market, so until a solution was found by the *Daily Mirror* (initially the *Daily Illustrated Mirror*) in 1904, photographs were the preserve of specialist publications such as *Black & White*, *Country Life Illustrated*, *Illustrated London News* and its sister paper the *Sketch*, and the *Illustrated Sporting and Dramatic News*, which as weeklies had time to produce and print images. Due to the Coronation, their focus was chiefly elsewhere, but *Country Life* sent a photographer to the Oval Test on the second day, and ten days after the match their issue of 23 August carried four images shot from in front of the pavilion. *Country Life* was set up in 1897 by Edward Hudson, the head of Hudson & Kearns, an established printer based in Southwark that specialised in photographic reproduction. Hudson used new printing presses invented in Germany in the 1880s and, later, ones imported from the United States, and turned *Country Life* into one of the first commercially viable illustrated periodicals. The quality of images was high.

Country Life did not quite have things to themselves. George Beldam, thirty-four, an amateur cricketer with Middlesex, was in the early throes of what became a pioneering interest in sports action photography. As a player, he was fascinated by the technique of batting and studied the methods of great players such as Trumper, Fry, MacLaren and Jessop. He knew he could not be as good as them and jokingly blamed Jessop for making him feel under pressure to score faster and entertain the crowds. 'I told Jessop once that he was responsible for this sort of thing, and that if he hadn't set such a shocking example of making a hundred in a few minutes, we methodical players would have been left in peace,' he said in 1901.

Ultimately, Beldam would produce several ground-breaking volumes of sports photographs which dissected the techniques of batsmen, bowlers and fielders, as well as athletes from other disciplines such as golf and lawn tennis. The slogan 'Their Methods at a Glance' featured in a number of the titles and summed up the scope of the work.

Fry, another student of sporting mechanics, provided the text in some instances. But in 1902, Beldam, armed with a Videx camera equipped with a Zeiss lens, was just setting out on his journey of exploration. He lived in Brentford, and when he had time off from Middlesex commitments took his equipment to Lord's and The Oval, where the new, multi-storey pavilion offered excellent vantage points. He and his camera were certainly present on two if not all three days of the Oval Test. He was not operating commercially but one of his images appeared in *Cricket: A Weekly Record of the Game* on 21 August. His pictures were not as sharp as those in *Country Life*, but he was mostly operating from further away, capturing panoramas of play whereas *Country Life* took its shots from closer quarters. The zoom lens was an innovation that lay in the future.

In the absence of news photographs, daily and evening papers often employed illustrators, who must also have been present on the ground, to produce line drawings and cartoons. These were quick to produce and relatively easy to publish, and a number of artists made names for themselves as regulars at big sporting events, among them Roland Pretty Hill, or 'Rip' as he was known, whose drawings became a fixture in the London *Evening News*, and Alfred Bryan and Thomas Downey in the *Illustrated Sporting and Dramatic News*. Downey was at the Oval Test and produced eight cartoons, including one of a bowler charging towards a batsman: 'Jessop v Trumble, Irresistible Force v Immovable Object'.

Early filmmakers also took a close interest. Jasper Redfern, a Sheffield-born photographer, had captured images of the 1899 FA Cup final at Derby and made a short film of an

FA Cup tie between his two home-town teams of United and Wednesday the following year. The first Test match played in Sheffield in 1902 was a timely event for him and he not only shot film of the action on the second day but that evening hosted a screening at a packed Empire Theatre in the city that was attended by all the Australian players and seven England players (all professionals: none of the four amateurs, including Jessop, went along). He showed several cinematograph pictures of the match, including a film, 300-feet long, shot as the Australians left the pavilion for England's second innings late on the second afternoon. '[It was] developed in record time,' the *Sheffield Evening Telegraph* declared proudly. 'The likenesses of the players came out very clearly, and the house was loud in its applause.'

Tantalisingly, it appeared that some of Jessop's great innings, and several other passages of play, all probably from the final day of the match, were filmed by the British Mutoscope and Biograph Company, based in the West End. The company had been founded in 1897 by William Kennedy-Laurie Dickson, a British inventor born in France and a key figure in helping Thomas Edison invent movie film. He made a name for himself capturing newsworthy events such as Queen Victoria's Diamond Jubilee, the Henley Regatta, the Boat Race and the Grand National, and often had his short films ready for screening at the upmarket Palace Theatre of Varieties in Cambridge Circus the same evening. They would appear on a large screen between live performances, billed as 'an act by itself and without rival'. His biggest coup was taking his bulky camera to South Africa and shooting scenes of the Boer War, the earliest surviving footage of a British war. A screening programme that appeared at auction a few years ago alluded to five items shot by the company of the Oval Test, one of which was described simply as 'Jessop batting'. Researches have failed to find evidence that the footage survives, despite an appeal by Rodney Ulyate on YouTube in 2021.

*

Taken together, the words and images produced on 11, 12 and 13 August 1902, and the days shortly afterwards, provide us with our clearest window onto what happened in Jessop's match. Only the 16,000 or so fortunate spectators in the ground on the final day saw events with their own eyes. Everyone else was hungry for news of the drama and an array of reporters strove to give them what they wanted. Theirs were highly impressive, if naturally flawed, first drafts of history. But even they were beholden to two men sitting nearby in the adjacent scorers' box for the details that would inform their accounts, and provide the basis for Jessop's record.

7

HOW THE MATCH WAS SCORED

ONE OF THE photographs that appeared in *Country Life* showed play in the Test underway directly after lunch on the second day, with a large wooden scoreboard in the background, nestled between packed rows of spectators and the mighty gasometers in the distance.

This scoreboard was the main one on the ground and was another recent addition to The Oval's architecture. It was made by Marshall Brothers of Nottingham, who also provided boards for Trent Bridge, Headingley and Old Trafford, and was installed the previous year. It would stay in position for half a century – and keep tally of Len Hutton's England record score of 364 in 1938. The information it carried was limited by the standards of modern computerised scoreboards, but standard for its era. It showed the runs scored and wickets lost by the batting team, the scores of the two not-out batsmen and the score made by the last batsman dismissed; it also identified which bowlers were in operation. This was done by a system that numbered the players on each side from one to 11, with the key provided on the scorecards that could be purchased inside the ground for a penny. The not-out batsmen were similarly identified by numbers above their scores.

The mechanised nature of the board was relatively new, with the numbers that changed most readily such as the team total and individual batsmen's scores operated on rotating wheels, which made updating easier and faster. The main rival to the Marshall Brothers was the Sam Deards board, which, according to its advertisements, had 'nine sets of movable figures on rollers' and was so well designed that 'a lad of 16 can easily work [it]'. The same adverts carried a pointed footnote: 'In answer to many inquiries I wish to state the Scoring Board lately erected at the Oval is not of my make.'

These boards were an improvement on what English crowds had been treated to before, but they were not easy to comprehend and paled in comparison to what was on offer in Australia, as N. J. Mack, an Australian visitor, spelled out in a letter to the *Pall Mall Gazette* shortly before the Test:

It [the new scoreboard] was a subject for comment in the Australian onlookers' enclosure, during a recent match at the Oval, that better facilities were not afforded for spectators to keep in touch with the play. True, cards indicating the progress of the game, and affording a key to the complicated scoring-board, are offered for sale at intervals, but it would be much more pleasing to that portion of the public who cannot distinguish all the men in the field to see the cause of a player's retirement distinctly and officially recorded before their eyes at the fall of each wicket, instead of waiting till the printer turns out his cards, the howling newsboy wends his way thither, and the game progresses.

There was additionally a second, much smaller scoreboard located on a balcony to the left of the pavilion as seen from the playing area. It provided less information than the main board – total runs, wickets lost, last man out's score, and the numbers corresponding to the two bowlers, but not the scores of the not-out batsmen.

The operation of these two scoreboards was fundamental to the game. They were the only means available to players, umpires and spectators as to the state of play. It would also have been the simplest way for the many pressmen covering the match to track the score. The speed at which the scoreboard men worked, and how accurately, was vital, and when a batsman such as Jessop was running amok it must have been hard for even the most experienced operators to keep up. In this respect, the location of the smaller scoreboard was vital because it was situated next to the scorers' box. If those running the main board were unsure if their details were correct, they could check what the smaller board was saying, except in respect of the scores of the 'not-out' batsmen. It is unclear how these last details could be verified, if the need arose; it is possible there was a telephone line between the scorers' box and main scoreboard, but no evidence has been found that this was the case.

Ultimately, the most important people in recording the progress of the game were the official scorers: Fred Boyington, the Surrey scorer, who for many years had worked on Tests at The Oval, and Bill Creese, who travelled with the Australians throughout their tour as scorer and baggageman.

Boyington was fifty-three and had been Surrey scorer for more than twenty years. In his youth he was a good cricketer in Nottingham but business interests took priority. He went into boot-making and invented an early form of spike; the 1882 Australians had their boots fitted with Boyington's spikes. He was a cheerful, popular figure, and something of a celebrity for his sheer longevity of service. A photograph of him in the scorers' box at The Oval in 1924, aged seventy-five, is captioned 'the oldest chronicler in first-class cricket'. When he retired the following year it was said he had not missed a Surrey match for 42 years. He also looked after Surrey's travel arrangements and when he died in 1927 the Surrey players took the field wearing black armbands.

In an interview in *Cricket: A Weekly Record of the Game* in December 1902, four months after Jessop's match, Boyington recalled some of his most memorable days. He referenced the drama of the recent Test – 'the last three overs of the match I shall never forget' – but did not admit it was unusually difficult. He cited the 1884 Test as a challenge due to a large, restless crowd impeding the view from the old scorers' box, with the result that a Mr Irving, scoring for the Australians, threatened to walk out and appeal to Charles Alcock and William Murdoch, the Australia captain, 'to do something to make it easier for us'. Boyington comes across as an unflappable character, experienced at scoring in front of some of the largest and most boisterous cricket crowds in England.

Unlike Boyington, Creese was not a scorer by trade and Australia's tour is the first time he is known to have been employed in this capacity. That said, if he had scored every match since early May he would have done 78 days of play going into the final Test, so should have been well versed in his duties. Of the many participants in the drama, Creese's story would be among the saddest. Born in Monmouthshire, he appears to have spent most of his life in the UK, save for a trip to South Africa in 1898. He made a handful of appearances for Monmouthshire between 1899 and 1901. How he came to be appointed to Joe Darling's team is unclear, but, when it was arranged that they would play three Tests in South Africa on the way home, he went with them. He continued as baggageman and scorer, but actually served as umpire in the final Test at Newlands, Cape Town, in which South Africa's Jimmy Sinclair scored a hundred in 80 minutes.

When the Australians then sailed for home, Creese chose to stay on and start a new life in the Cape. He remained involved in cricket, occasionally umpiring provincial matches, serving as baggageman and possibly also as scorer to Johnny Douglas's England team that toured South Africa in 1913-14, before becoming groundsman at Newlands. He also set up as a sports outfitter in Claremont. His son Len moved to England and became a useful player for Hampshire, but for some reason darkness descended and Bill took his own life in August 1931, aged sixty-one, 'found shot dead with a rifle beside him'.

By 1902, the system of scoring cricket matches in England was well established, had changed little in many years and would remain substantially unchanged for many years more. In a handwritten scorer's book, designed to be broad enough to accommodate a whole innings on one page, a batsman's scoring strokes would be listed along a line next to his name, while each ball of every over was recorded in a series of boxes alongside the bowler's name. This practice created a fundamental imbalance, one which Charles Davis, a statistician and researcher into early scorebooks, explained thus:

> There is a basic anomaly in the traditional reporting of cricket scores, which derives from the way scores have been recorded. This is: since the very beginning, the number of balls bowled by each bowler, and even the number of maiden overs, have been assiduously recorded, counted and reported, yet the balls faced by each batsman was not. It took almost 100 years of Test cricket before it was widely accepted that the latter was at least as important as the former, as a tool for understanding the progress and quality of play.

However, around the turn of the twentieth century, a few scorers, in England and Australia, were developing systems by which 'balls faced' for each batsman was recorded in a manner very different from the traditional English scorebook – what became known as the 'linear method', in which each over was given a single line sequentially, with a whole team innings running down several sheets from which it was possible to readily calculate how many balls each batsman faced, and from which bowler.

An Englishman, John Atkinson Pendlington, developed a system along these lines in the late 1880s. Born in South Shields in 1861, Pendlington was an accountant and engineer, and keen club cricketer. How much scoring he did is unknown, but he certainly used a linear scoring system at least once in a high-profile match, a three-day game at Scarborough involving a touring Australian team and Lord Londesborough's XI that included W. G. Grace. It was reported at the time of Pendlington's death in 1914 that the match in question took place in 1893, but Grace's participation makes it more likely it was in 1886, 1888 or 1890. Pendlington's obituary in the *Newcastle Daily Chronicle* stated:

> He conceived the idea of a scorebook which would record the result of every ball bowled. With this ingenious book he took the score at Scarborough in Lord Londesborough's match against the Australians in 1893 [sic]. The record showed the number of balls each batsman received from each bowler and what runs he made from them, and revealed some strange facts which the keenest observer could not describe till they were recorded. Dr W. G. Grace and his friends were greatly amused with the book when they were presented with it after the match.

Pendlington lived in Hampstead from at least 1901 to 1903, and as a keen cricket enthusiast must surely have attended matches at Lord's and probably The Oval during that time, possibly even Jessop's match, but there is no evidence that he made extensive use of linear scoring or passed it on to others to use. There is a plaque to him on the site of former West Turnpike Cricket Ground where Pendlington's club of Benwell CC once played.

Davis identified Johann Gottlieb Jackschon as an early Australian pioneer. Born in Bavaria in 1846, Jackschon moved to Australia with his family at the age of six. He became fascinated by the statistics of cricket and by 1886–87 had risen to be scorer for the New South Wales team and for all the main matches in Sydney, including Tests. When England played Australia at Sydney in 1892, Jackschon was for some reason the sole scorer, contrary to the normal practice of both teams providing a scorer. Newspaper accounts of the game contained allusions to the balls received by individual batsmen, with the *Referee* showing the number of balls faced by every batsman in the match.

Jackschon went into even more depth for a Victoria–New South Wales match in 1906, beyond compiling tables for the head-to-heads between each batsman and bowler, as the *Referee* noted: 'Mr Jackscohn [sic] has compiled a table of each innings ... showing how each batsman scored off each bowler, how many balls he received and played from each bowler, and how many he missed.' Recording whether a batsman played at or missed a particular ball was extremely rare at this time, although this is a point to which we shall have cause to return in connection to Jessop's innings.

Jackschon was not alone. The Melbourne *Argus* published the runs scored by each batsman off each bowler for two England Tests at the MCG in 1898. The most important figure in popularising this system (which also became known in some quarters as 'the Australian method') was Bill Ferguson, who as baggageman and scorer would record most of Australia's Tests home and away between 1905 and 1953, as well as accompanying several tours involving other countries. But Ferguson used the system intermittently to start with and 'balls faced' data was published only sporadically.

Crucially, though, there is no suggestion that Boyington or Creese were disciples of such innovative methods. Boyington was an old-school scorer in a job he had been doing, and doing well, for 20 years; he was unlikely to see the need to change. Any ball-by-ball analysis would have to have come from others.

*

No one was more in need of fast, accurate information than the pressmen. They required up-to-date details of how batsmen were dismissed, and at what score, the running scores of team and not-out batsmen, and end-of-innings bowling analyses. Their particular demands might depend on deadlines and their newspaper's demand for 'running copy', but the collective appetite for 'data' would be almost insatiable. As they could hardly be interrupting the scorers every few minutes (even if they might want to), for the most part they probably relied on the main scoreboard for information, but it is likely that occasional messages were sent into the scorers' room. Even in the 1980s and early 1990s, before computerised scoring and online ball-by-ball coverage became common, pressmen routinely interacted in this way with official scorers. Their respective work stations were usually located in the same part of the ground for just this reason.

That said, anecdotal evidence from the 1902 Test makes clear that reporters had their own practices for keeping statistical track of the game, including the kind of details probably not readily available from the scorers such as balls faced or minutes batted.

Scoring was far from a perfect science. The purpose of having two scorers rather than one was to ensure that a tally was kept without favour to either side, and as a means of checking for errors. Boyington recalled the relief he and Irving felt during the 1884 Test when their bowling figures tallied for an Australian innings totalling 551 runs and spanning 311 four-ball overs. An article in the *Sportsman* in 1904 about close finishes cited a case of a county match at The Oval in 1876 in which Middlesex were originally declared winners by one run before members of the press, including Charles Alcock, then working for the *Sportsman*, produced their own running scores – called 'a dotted note' – which proved that the scorebook must have been wrong and the result was declared a tie. The article went on:

> It is astonishing in what a slipshod manner the important duties of scoring have in the olden days been fulfilled in first-class matches – much the same as now obtains in club matches ... it is level money that at the close of an innings the scorers will differ as to the total, to say nothing of discrepancies in the analysis. The same inaccuracies are often evident in the copies forwarded to the Press for insertion.

This last point suggests that it was routine for copies of a completed innings with bowling figures to be handed out from the scorers to journalists. That reporters had devised their own means of keeping track of the score is important to our story; as we shall see, a number of reporters and statisticians appeared to keep their own detailed notes in relation to Jessop's innings.

Davis has written that accounting errors in the official scorebooks of early Test matches were not uncommon:

> As information sources or resolvers of anomalies, they [original scorebooks] are not always the cure-all that might be hoped for, especially for very early Tests. Some of these scores lack timing information, for example, and some (it should be whispered) just do not tally. (If Victor Trumper scored 185 not out at Sydney in 1903, why do his scoring strokes add up to 187?) The available copies of others are unclear and ambiguous in places.

It has also been noted that the two scorebooks from the Oval Test of 1926 did not tally on the number of overs bowled by Australian spinners Clarrie Grimmett and Arthur Mailey. Gerald Brodribb concluded that original scorebooks could contain errors, 'especially when some hectic innings has got out of hand'.

Another area of potential confusion and discrepancy concerned timings. The main clock at The Oval was situated on the pavilion roof. It was therefore clearly visible to players and umpires on the field of play, and spectators at the Vauxhall End of the ground, but not easily seen by anyone in the pavilion itself, and certainly not by scorers or reporters. How they measured how long a particular batsman was at the crease, or a partnership or team innings lasted, is unclear, but the reported figures for the 1902 Test varied widely, suggesting no clear-cut method, such as a press box or scorers' clock, existed. Perhaps everyone used their own watches or timepieces, and were not minded to obtain a consensus.

With newspaper competition hotting up, innovative use of statistics was another way rival publications could show themselves one step ahead of the opposition. The *Daily Express* was among the most adventurous in this respect. When Johnny Tyldesley scored 138 in the first Test, the *Express* listed the runs he made and the balls he faced against each of the six Australian bowlers, suggesting someone was keeping a Jackschon-like record of head-to-heads. Other papers simply referred to Tyldesley facing 304 balls. The *Sheffield Daily Telegraph* gave a similar head-to-head breakdown of Jessop's quick-fire 55 in the third Test at Bramall Lane. The *Express* was also a frontrunner in the development from 1905 of 'wagon wheel' charts, showing to which part of the field a batsman's scoring shots went.

Whatever the imperfections, the scorers' books were regarded as the final word. At the end of the Oval Test, the full details of the game were passed to the in-house printers – Merritt & Hatcher Ltd, headquartered at 168 Upper Thames Street – and a complete match-card produced for sale. The words 'printed on the ground' were intended as a guarantee of accuracy.

*

Sadly and frustratingly, both scorebooks for the Oval Test match of 1902 are lost, their fates unknown. Unfortunately, this is not uncommon with early scorebooks; indeed, many of them are missing.

The largest single physical archive for historical Test match scorebooks is held by the MCC at Lord's. The emphasis in this collection is understandably on the England tours abroad administered by the MCC itself from 1903-04 onwards, as well as home Tests played at Lord's, but even here there are large gaps for the early years. Where scorebooks survive for Tests at other grounds in England, these are typically held by the host county, with Yorkshire alone boasting a set of scorebooks for county matches and England Tests at Headingley dating back to the nineteenth century. Lancashire also has one of the better collections covering Tests at Old Trafford. Surrey have in their possession the scorebook of the first Test played in England at The Oval in 1880 and also Boyington's book for the 1884 Test. 'Unfortunately the whereabouts of most other early scorebooks for Tests in London are unknown,' Davis wrote in an article surveying surviving scorebooks for early Tests.

It is thought that the loss of some collections was a result of them being moved during wartime, and, given its location, nowhere was more vulnerable than The Oval during the Second World War. The pavilion was damaged more than once by German bombing raids on central London, one bomb that landed on the terrace in front of the pavilion bringing down part of the balcony and roof, as well as damaging doors and windows.

Later, the ground was readied for use as a prisoner-of-war camp. Such was the extent of the restoration work that Surrey launched an appeal to raise £100,000 (about £1.6 million today). When author and journalist Richard Streeton researched a biography of Percy Fender, who scored a 35-minute century for Surrey against Northamptonshire in 1920, he was told that Surrey's scorebook had disappeared during the war (the Northamptonshire one survived).

The Australians' scorebook from the 1902 tour presumably travelled with them to South Africa and was used to record the matches played there. It is possible that Creese might have kept it with him when he remained in the Cape while the team sailed for Melbourne in mid-November, but there is no evidence, or particular likelihood, that this happened; nor was he actually the scorer for the final match of the tour as he was umpiring. It appears that the usual practice when the Australians toured at around this time was for the book to be placed in the keeping of the manager or captain. The scorebook for their 1893 tour of England, which survives, contains a written request to 'kindly return to the team manager', while the one for 1905, also extant, is inscribed, 'Presented to Joe Darling by his fellow players of the Australian XI after their tour of England in 1905'.

The scorebook from Australia's tour of England in 1882 was still in the possession of Tom Horan, a rank-and-file member of the team turned journalist, more than 25 years later. Cricket New South Wales possesses the best collection of pre-war Test scorebooks in Australia, but even this does not include the one from 1902.

The absence of either scorebook complicates research into the game, and handicaps attempts to construct a timeline of Jessop's innings. Without them, we must rely on other sources such as newspaper reports – based in part on information provided by the scorers – and eyewitness accounts.

PART TWO

THE MATCH

8

MONDAY 11 AUGUST: DAY ONE

AUSTRALIA GAIN THE INITIATIVE

THOUSANDS FLOCKED to Kennington Oval early. They came by hansom cab and bus, by electric railway and on foot. For once in this benighted summer, the scene was bathed in sunshine, even if it was still cooler than usual for the time of year. It was a good ground for gathering, with space to mill, and well before 10 a.m. great masses had come through the gates. The chat among the spectators was about the toss, the weather and England's selection; also, that it did not matter who would win as the series was already decided, but even as people said this they hurried to get to their seats. Deep down, it was felt that an England win would heal some of the hurt of Manchester, and allay the fear that English cricket might be in terminal decline. And it was a long time since Australia had been beaten on home soil.

The Coronation had put everyone in good spirits. This was a Bank Holiday, as well as the first match of the series to start on a Monday rather than a Thursday. There were more day-trippers than normal, and fewer aficionados. There were also an unusual number of clergymen among those jostling through the turnstiles, and more City workers at this early hour than there would have been had their offices been open. Had that been the case, they would have been obliged to visit their desks first, and discreetly put up notices saying, 'Out on important business – back at five o'clock.' The mood was festive. People were ready to cheer their heroes.

The England and Australia players arrived punctually for net practice at the Vauxhall End and by 10.30 many hundreds of people had gone across the playing area – for only the pitch itself was sacred territory – to watch them prepare. On their way over from the pavilion, the Australian team in their dark green blazers stopped to survey the pitch. When the two captains tossed the coin, the outcome was displayed on large blackboards paraded at both ends of the ground, with a capital 'A' denoting that Darling had been successful for the third time in a row, an innovation introduced for this match.

Naturally, Darling elects to bat. There had been rain around in the build-up but with the weather set fair for the day, it is an uplifting moment for the Australians, and a bad one for the luckless MacLaren.

People continued to get into their seats and prepare for the last round of a duel that had spanned almost 11 weeks. The crowd was different in character from usual because among them were colonial troops from Australia, New Zealand, Ceylon and South Africa, some wearing jauntily cocked feathers in their broad hats, fresh from their part in the Coronation pageant. There were, too, large numbers of home troops recently back from the front. There were ladies dressed in the amber and green of Australia, and the seats reserved for families and friends of the cricketers – where Jessop's fiancée would have sat – were filled to overflowing. In the pavilion there were bigwigs aplenty, peers and wealthy commoners rubbing shoulders, as well as an unnamed 'royal personage'. As people settled, some noticed a flag above the pavilion flying at half-mast. It was for Arthur Webster, the son of Lord Alverstone, the Surrey president, who had died suddenly of appendicitis, aged twenty-eight. He was a month younger than Jessop.

By the time the ten-minute bell rang at 11.20 a.m., there were reckoned to be around 12,000 people inside the ground. The umpires, Charles Richardson and Archie White, walked out. Both had been regular first-class umpires for several years, Richardson having previously played cricket for Leicestershire. White had accompanied some English tours abroad as travelling umpire. He had stood in three of the Australians' matches already and Richardson in two, including the Lord's Test. Richardson had just umpired the championship game at Bristol that Jessop had been involved in, while White was at Canterbury for Surrey's thrashing by Kent. One of the Yorkshire newspapers reported that White was thinking of quitting umpiring at the end of the season.

In fact, play did not get underway on time because, no sooner had the England players taken the field than Braund, the tall Somerset all-rounder, returned to the pavilion to sort out some problem, probably an issue with his bowling boots. It was almost 11.40 by the time everyone was finally ready. Before a crowd so large yet so quiet, Bill Lockwood's first ball was a yorker, which Reggie Duff did well to dig out. The game was underway.

*

Australia were given the brightest of starts by Victor Trumper, the stylist, and Duff, the utility man. Both knew how to attack, as they had shown at Old Trafford. Both were largely untroubled by Lockwood and Wilfred Rhodes as England opened up as usual with pace at one end and spin at the other. Trumper batted beautifully, amazing in his mastery and almost absurdly confident in his ability to survive. After half an hour, the score had skipped along to 45 without loss, and English spectators were fearful of a repeat of the explosive opening session that set the Manchester Test on its fateful course. Then the thick-necked, broad-shouldered George Hirst entered the attack and with the sheer energy of his bounding 16-yard approach to the crease, which began with a peculiar hop, he confirmed what early strike capability MacLaren had been missing in the previous match. With his sixth ball Hirst had Duff caught down the leg side by Dick Lilley, the England keeper who had pioneered the method of standing back to faster bowlers. Lilley anticipated the stroke and made a couple of yards to his left to intercept a ball that was going away from him. He told people later that it was the best catch he had ever taken. It was an electric moment.

Clem Hill, Australia's new batsman, moved quickly to 11 and was then bowled while Darling was smartly caught by Lilley, again standing some yards back, to give Hirst all three wickets. His return to the team was already a remarkable one. In the 21st over of the innings, Lockwood bowled the game's first maiden and a few moments later Hirst, having conceded only four singles to Trumper, bowled him with a slower ball, making Australia 82 for four. Monty Noble narrowly escaped playing on against Hirst, who was making the ball swerve in distinctive fashion, but he and Syd Gregory settled in to add 44 in an hour either side of the break for lunch. When Hirst eventually bowled Gregory, the Yorkshire left-armer was more than halfway to the nine wickets he had jokingly told James Stainton was his target for the game, and Australia were five down for 126. To the delight of a crowd now approaching its day's peak of 25,000, England were on top.

Unfortunately, the second half of their day was to be much harder work, and English spirits dipped along with the thermometer as the skies began to dull. The Noble–Gregory stand had blunted the bowling and Hirst in particular was starting to fatigue. Noble, the tall dentist from Sydney, who had played such a valuable innings on the first day in Sheffield, had come to Australia's rescue again, grinding out 52 precious runs in just over two hours. Warwick Armstrong, at twenty-three the youngest member of the team, took over from Gregory by assisting Noble in a stand worth 48 in 40 minutes. Alfred Pullin of the *Yorkshire Evening Post* had spoken to an England bowler during the lunch interval, probably Hirst or Rhodes, who had told him that the pitch was playing 'as easy as pie', and so it now proved.

Pullin mentioned this in a bulletin for his paper at 3.05 p.m. in which he also expressed surprise that Jackson had not yet been asked to bowl by MacLaren. Soon after, though, Jackson was brought on and in his second over accounted for Armstrong with a ball that kept low, and in his third held onto a red-hot, shoulder-high return from Noble with the utmost sangfroid, drawing gasps of amazement from the crowd. Australia were 175 for seven and English hopes briefly revived of restricting them to a score of not much more than 200.

Jackson's reflex catch was indicative of England's excellence in the field. Like Hirst, Jessop was justifying his recall by bringing off one fine stop after another from the hardest drives, earning rapturous applause. In fact, Hirst's early bowling and Jessop's fielding at extra cover were among the standout features of the day. Jessop transmitted vibrancy with every move, from his lightning dashes to the ball to his clean gathers and bullet-like throws. One of Thomas Downey's cartoons shows a row of spectators applauding, above a caption: '"Oh, well thrown", "Why wasn't he picked?" Talk about Jessop.'

But, remorselessly and excruciatingly, Australia rallied again. Hugh Trumble was not only a champion bowler, but a stubborn, resourceful batsman, and he enjoyed many narrow escapes to finish unbeaten on 64 and oversee the addition of 149 runs for the last three wickets. When he had scored just 9, he appeared to be dropped by Lilley standing up to the stumps – most onlookers thought it a missed chance – but Trumble actually hit the ball into his leg from where it flew up and struck Lilley on the shoulder, giving the keeper no real prospect of a catch. Trumble was helped in a stand of 81 for the eighth wicket by Bert Hopkins and then in one of 68 for the ninth by James Kelly, Australia's keeper. Rhodes was convinced he had Hopkins lbw for 3 but the appeal – practically the first of the day – was turned down and Hopkins survived to contribute 40 before Lockwood went round the wicket to have him caught at slip.

Trumble's partnership with Hopkins was the only one of value they would share in ten Tests together, but he and Kelly, who were born nine days apart in 1867 and would die on the same day in 1938, had a history of putting on runs when they were needed, most famously to win a tight Test at Old Trafford in 1896. This was their biggest ever stand together and it appeared to leave English hopes of a win looking very remote. Kelly had made only seven runs in the series before this and started shakily before hitting out confidently later, at one point taking Jackson for three fours in an over. There was nothing eye-catching about the batting; it was just the steady accumulation of runs and highly frustrating to England and their followers. Trumble's stonewalling particularly infuriated one young spectator, the fifteen-year-old Ben Travers, the future playwright, who was able to graphically recall this match in memoirs published almost 80 years later. Travers was not alone.

Exasperation mounted. In the press box, there was annoyance once more at MacLaren's captaincy. The correspondent from the *Birmingham Daily Gazette* felt the England captain showed too much faith in Lockwood, who looked out of sorts all day and was punished for his bad lengths, going for 65 runs in his first 17 overs. The *Manchester Evening News* reckoned the bowlers lacked inventiveness, betraying a weakness from which Australian cricketers were seemingly exempt: 'All our best bowlers are professionals who are the mainstays of their county teams, and are forced to bowl un-numbered overs in every match. The result is that they become entirely mechanical instruments, and when once collared seem to have no fresh enterprise left.' Nor were many onlookers happy when a 20-minute break was taken for tea. The tea interval was still a novel concept and had been taken only sporadically during the earlier Tests, sometimes simply by drinks being taken out to the players on the field. Many in the crowd thought it an absurd practice.

If Jackson had been expecting Jessop to play a full part with the ball, he, too, must have been disappointed, because Jessop was given only six overs, and only because at the time MacLaren was stuck for ideas during the Trumble–Hopkins stand. Jackson himself got through 20 overs, although after his two early wickets that was perhaps unsurprising. Jessop kept a fair length and only conceded 11 runs.

As Australia's score continued to mount, the tension was palpable, a tension captured by the French writer Henri de Noussanne, who paid his first (and in all likelihood only) visit to a cricket match during this Test. The experience left him baffled at the Englishman's obsession with sport and the vast colosseums he had built to watch it, as de Noussanne wrote in an article in the *Daily Mail* entitled 'A Frenchman on Cricket, A Visit to Kennington Oval':

> I pay down my shilling and enter with the others. On the left is all that is necessary to drink to one's fill; opposite all the requisites for writing or telegraphing. At the side are heaps of newspapers, a mountain of *Evening News*. Overshadowing everything a huge brick building. I direct my steps towards the arena. No sound whatever; there is doubtless nobody there … What is this I suddenly discover? Round an immense lawn a whole people is assembled,

seated, standing, or lying down on the benches and on the ground. There are even people on the neighbouring roofs.

The reference to the piles of copies of the *Evening News* should come as no surprise; this was the *Daily Mail* promoting its sister evening paper, a classic trick on the part of Alfred Harmsworth.

Finally, Braund had Kelly caught at short leg and Jack Saunders trapped lbw in quick succession and Australia were all out for 324 at 6.25 p.m., only minutes before the scheduled close. England had laboured for five and a half hours, and got through 123.5 overs, and seen Australia lift themselves from 175 for seven to their highest total of the series. They had not done a huge amount wrong; their opponents had just been their usual resourceful selves, and taken advantage of an easy pitch that improved as the day went on.

Reflecting on the day, the England players thought their chances of winning had gone, as Jessop recalled in his autobiography in 1922: 'That [Australia] innings must have appeared to them – as it most certainly did to most of us – to have placed them in a position [that] though they might not win, they could not lose.' Many of the journalists were not hopeful either. The *Manchester Evening News* concluded, 'it is now practically impossible for the Australians to be beaten'. This view was shared by the *Sportsman*, who thought Australia 'extremely unlikely to lose'. Even the normally sanguine Stainton could see nothing better for England than avoiding defeat: 'Already they [Australia] are possessed of a lead which nothing within the narrow confines of this match looks like overturning ... Unless the rain comes and completes the shipwreck of the Englishmen, a draw is already assured.'

AUSTRALIA: FIRST INNINGS

Victor Trumper	b Hirst	42
Reggie Duff	c Lilley b Hirst	23
Clem Hill	b Hirst	11
Joe Darling	c Lilley b Hirst	3
Monty Noble	c and b Jackson	52
Syd Gregory	b Hirst	23
Warwick Armstrong	b Jackson	17
Bert Hopkins	c MacLaren b Lockwood	40
Hugh Trumble	not out	64
James Kelly	c Rhodes b Braund	39
Jack Saunders	lbw b Braund	0
Extras (byes 5, leg-byes 3, no-balls 2)		10
Total (123.5 overs)		**324**

Fall of wickets: 47-1 (Duff), 63-2 (Hill), 69-3 (Darling), 82-4 (Trumper), 126-5 (Gregory), 174-6 (Armstrong), 175-7 (Noble), 256-8 (Hopkins), 324-9 (Kelly), 324-10 (Saunders)

Bowling: Lockwood 24-2-85-1, Rhodes 28-9-46-0, Hirst 29-5-77-5, Braund 16.5-5-29-2, Jackson 20-4-66-2, Jessop 6-2-11-0

9

TUESDAY 12 AUGUST: DAY TWO

ENGLAND'S GREAT FIGHTBACK

SURE ENOUGH, rain came in the night and an English shipwreck became a distinct possibility. It did not just rain but it rained a lot, leaving the pitch drenched, and when the game resumed at 11 a.m. – play begins at 11.30 on the first day but half an hour earlier on subsequent days – it was predictably soft. Even then, the light was barely good enough. All talk of England beating Australia's score was abandoned. It quickly became clear that batting at the Vauxhall End was even harder than at the Pavilion End; the ground was softer there for Hugh Trumble, who knew exactly how to exploit the advantage he had been given. Bowling into the pitch from such a great height, he had been known before to cut pieces out of the turf when it was as yielding as this.

Coming so soon after what happened at Old Trafford, this turn of events was hard to take for the many Englishmen who poured through the gates and into their seats. 'The stars in their courses seem to be fighting against the England team,' Alfred Pullin wrote in the *Yorkshire Post*. 'What happened at Manchester has occurred at Kennington Oval. England bowl and field on an easy pitch, rain comes during the night, and prepares a bowler's wicket for them to bat upon. It is all in the game, of course, but one cannot get away from the fact that luck has been dreadfully one-sided throughout this series.' The *South London Press* said: 'The hopes of Englishmen fell to zero.' The Australians could scarcely have stage-managed things better.

In fact, although no one would have appreciated the point at the time, a rain-affected pitch actually opened up the prospect of an outright result, one way or the other. Had the weather stayed fine, it was probable that England would have batted too long in their first innings in an effort to match Australia's score, and there would have been insufficient time left after that for either side to force a win, especially with Australia no doubt content to play out a draw.

The one blessing for England as they began batting was that there was not a hot sun to turn the pitch to glue. By the time MacLaren and Palairet followed the Australian players out to the middle, the skies were actually bright and it encouraged the England openers to try to get on with things before the surface became tackier and batting even trickier. Palairet took nine off Saunders' first over, but caution soon got the better of both batsmen. Trumble was hitting a perfect length and getting the ball to break and fly alarmingly; every delivery needed careful attention. The crowd looked on in dead silence as the England captain and his partner anxiously consulted between overs as how best to go about things.

Playing back seemed the best option but, as one observer noted, 'back or forward, there was no royal road to scoring'. After five maiden overs in a row, MacLaren appealed to the umpires about the light, which had deteriorated dramatically. The players went off with England 20 for no wicket.

The heavens were behaving strangely, in a way that might have fascinated Claude Monet, but worried Englishmen bent on survival. A copper sky was a strain on the eyes, then gave way to a curious brown haze which hung over the ground, meaning that the stoppage lasted around 35 minutes. Eventually, the *Westminster Gazette* reported: 'The air cleared, and the day settled down into the ordinary summer day that we have become accustomed to – cold and dull, with never a trace of blue sky, and with a possibility of rain at any moment.' But the rain did not come and England's top order were left to their fate.

Palairet and MacLaren played skilfully but eventually both were undone by Trumble – Palairet bowled by a quick ball that nipped back and MacLaren taken at slip playing back to a delivery that jumped on him.

Johnny Tyldesley then played a brilliant attacking innings, confirming his reputation as England's finest wet-wicket batsman. Quick on his feet, he mixed powerful drives and square cuts with deft placements into the leg side. He took nine runs off an over from Trumble and 14 off two overs from Saunders, and the extent to which he was in a class of his own in these conditions was demonstrated by the fact he scored 33 of the 37 runs added while he was at the crease. Tom Hayward, who was more at ease on faster wickets against faster bowling, was batting twenty minutes but contributed nothing towards their 26-run partnership.

Both were rather unlucky to be bowled dragging balls from Trumble into their stumps. Between these two dismissals, Stanley Jackson walked out to great applause in recognition of his century in the previous Test, but soon played rashly at a bad ball from Saunders and was well caught one-handed above his head by Armstrong at second slip. England had lost five wickets in less than an hour for 36, four of them to Trumble.

Tyldesley's departure brought in Jessop to join Braund. Jessop's entrance created a familiar scene: there were predictable cheers from the 20,000-strong crowd for their favourite, from whom they urgently needed some heroics, but also field changes from Darling as he despatched his safest catchers into the deep. 'Astral', in the *Morning Leader*, took in the moment:

> Jessop represents at once the uncertainty and splendid possibilities of cricket. As the Australians beat a strategic retreat towards the terraces and pavilion rails, a low murmur of expectation went through the mighty crowd. Duff, Trumper and Hill waited with eager hands. When he then cut Trumble's first ball for three past slip there was laughter. It was unlike Jessop, but finely diplomatic.

After that opening shot, Jessop drove Saunders twice for two before cutting him for four. He then took another two off Trumble to move on to 13. C. B. Fry reckoned that Jessop had not yet quite achieved his freest state, and frustratingly for England before he could do so he was beaten by a ball from Trumble that went on slightly with the arm rather than broke back. 'Joy was strangled at birth,' bemoaned 'Astral'.

England were 83 for six and in a desperate plight. Thankfully, Braund and Hirst managed to get through to lunch without further damage, although it was a close-run thing. Hirst had an early swing at Trumble but the ball bounced higher than expected and he was lucky not to get an edge. In the following over, Braund, with only a single to his name, also swung and missed at Saunders and gave what looked like a stumping chance to Kelly. Hirst went into the break on ten, and Braund on 1, with the home side 94 for six, still 230 adrift of Australia's score. The game looked lost.

*

Jessop's dismissal shortly before lunch marked England's lowest point in the game. They were so far behind that they were in grave danger of being made to bat again, the follow-on being available to teams with a lead of 150 on first innings. In order to avoid this fate, and almost certain defeat given that Australia would be bowling again in favourable conditions, England had to get their total up to 175, and when Jessop was out they were still 92 short of that target with only four wickets left.

Their task might have been even harder, because the last time Australia toured England in 1899 the follow-on could be enforced with a lead of only 120 (and was actually compulsory, rather than optional), but in recognition that scoring levels in the game had risen the law relating to the follow-on had been changed. If the old law had still been in place, England would have needed to score 205.

That Braund and Hirst managed to get through the last few overs of the morning session was vital because it gave them a chance to regroup, gather their thoughts and devise a plan of attack to get themselves up to 175. The situation was desperate, many would have said hopeless, but it was actually from this point onwards that England fought with every sinew, as though the fate of their country itself depended on it. They refused to be disheartened by their misfortune, and to accept what seemed inevitable. Even MacLaren would not yet be bowed.

It was at around this tense period of the game, before and after lunch on the second day, that the *Country Life* photographer took his images. One portrayed Saunders about to bowl from round the wicket to Braund with the scoreboard showing England 89 for six, perhaps very close to the time of the stumping chance. Others were taken as the afternoon session was about to begin: one showed the Australians taking the field and another, revealingly, Hirst and Braund, the two professionals, emerging from the pavilion gate to resume battle. Though it is a cool day, both men have their sleeves rolled to their elbows and their expressions are set; Braund, the taller, is looking straight at the camera while the sturdily built Hirst, his Yorkshire cap with its white rose emblem pulled firmly down, its peak just above his eyes, is surveying the distance.

It was decided that Braund would continue to play the anchor role while Hirst and others took their chances and attacked. Braund survived only with luck, because he was repeatedly beaten by Trumble. Hirst set himself to hook or pull anything pitched short, although he would make runs off good-length balls as well, and in little more than half an hour he raised his score to 43, his hits including six fours and five threes. He made all but 11 of a 54-run partnership. Eventually Trumble drew him into giving a return catch but Lockwood, who walked out with 38 still needed to save the follow-on, took up where Hirst left off. One of the most critical moments in the entire game occurred when Hill, inexplicably for such a good fielder, missed a straightforward catch at long-on when Lockwood had scored 11 and England were still 19 short of their follow-on target. Hitting vigorously, Lockwood survived to score 25, a leg-side four off Saunders taking England's deficit below 150 to a great roar from the crowd. Braund and Lockwood actually added 42 in just over 20 minutes, their plucky resistance marking a shift in the mood of the game according to Stainton in the *Sheffield Daily Telegraph*:

> As the score rose, with four following four, the cheers of the crowd rang out triumphantly. For the first time in the match the Colonials were o'er-mastered. England forced her way through the excellences of the Australian attack, and renewed in the game an interest which, prior to the association of Hirst and Braund, had been sadly wanting.

The England innings did not last much longer, Lockwood, Braund and Lilley all falling in quick succession, but Lockwood's was a fine effort after enduring a tough first day with the ball. Braund's effort, too, was remarkable, as he batted with extreme restraint for an hour and a half while seeing the score raised by 116, of which his own share was a mere 22.

Trumble had bowled unchanged for 31 overs from the Pavilion End and taken eight wickets, the best haul by any bowler in a Test match in England to this point, but he had not been particularly well supported by Saunders or Noble at the other end, neither of them being as threatening as they might have been. This was to count against Noble when it came to England's run-chase the next day.

'It was of great importance to save the follow-on, so as to have a go at the Australians before the wicket had completely recovered,' C. B. Fry wrote in the *Daily Express*. 'It would have been a bad job had England been obliged to bat again. The only chance of making a match of it was to work a good hole in the Australians' second innings.'

*

England had batted spiritedly to add 89 in an hour and ten minutes after lunch, the innings ending at 3.25 p.m. This meant that the change of innings, which lasted around 20 minutes with the rolling of the pitch, was taken as the second break rather than one of the new-fangled tea intervals. The consequence of this was that the final session of play would be very long, lasting around two hours 45 minutes through to 6.30 p.m. If this was a long time for England to bowl, it was also a lengthy period for Australia to bat. Darling's team still held a big lead of 141 and were in a very dominant position, but they now faced the task of trying to put the game out of England's reach on a pitch that was still drying steadily – it was now brown rather than black in colour – and not yet hard. Jimmy Catton in the *Athletic News* described it as 'unreliable, though recovering'. There seemed to be little in it for Hirst or Jackson, who would bowl only nine overs between them, and nothing for Jessop, who was not called on at all. There was some debate among the Yorkshire correspondents as to whether Hirst should have been used more, but in the event others got the job done.

The best weather of the day briefly accompanied the start of the Australian innings. High up in the pavilion, George Beldam took some photographs which showed Lockwood bowling to Trumper from the Vauxhall End, with sawdust around the footholds a legacy of the sogginess of the turf earlier in the day, and players' figures casting clear shadows on the ground.

Things began badly for England when Hirst missed Duff at mid-off in Rhodes' opening over, but then a moment of brilliant athleticism from Jessop, combined with a little luck, delivered the prized wicket of Trumper with only six on the board. Trumper hit the ball between point and cover, and ran, only to be urged back by Duff who saw Jessop converging on the ball. Trumper slipped as he turned, as did Jessop as he gathered, but Jessop recovered to fire in a powerful throw to Lilley, who swept off the bails with Trumper still yards short of his ground. Many years later, MacLaren would claim that he had noticed during the tour of Australia that Trumper was willing to risk a single when the ball went in the direction of Jessop in the covers, and felt that it would one day cost him his wicket, and now it had happened. C. B. Fry later wrote that Trumper's run out was a feat that no English cricketer other than Jessop could have achieved, 'for no other would have got to the ball'. To MacLaren's mind, this incident was the chief cause of the remarkable events that followed.

Moments later, Duff played on against Lockwood, and although Darling twice hit Rhodes into the pavilion, the rejuvenated Lockwood soon had him caught at slip for 15 as well, leaving Australia tottering at 31 for three.

There followed the one real partnership of the innings of substance as Hill and Noble put on 40 through steady play, but a collapse followed. Noble was bowled off his pads by Braund and Hill brilliantly caught low to his left by MacLaren at wide slip off Hirst, Hirst's one wicket of the innings. Hill's was a particularly big wicket as he had been playing patiently and looking very solid. The crowd was now abuzz. Everyone sensed that the contest was coming back to life and the electric atmosphere transmitted itself to the Australian players. Gregory and Armstrong retreated into their shells, anxious not to surrender more ground, but Gregory was unable to survive long and nor could Hopkins. When Darling then sent out Saunders, who had only ever batted No 11 before, in an effort to shield Trumble and Kelly until the next morning, it was clear the Australian captain feared his side's lead was not yet big enough.

Saunders did his job insofar as no one else needed to bat that evening, but in the final over of the day he had a brain fade and tried to hit Rhodes down the ground, only for Tyldesley at long-on to cling onto a brilliant catch. Initially Tyldesley misjudged things and ran in before realising his mistake and tracking back to the boundary edge, where he managed to knock the ball up with both hands before taking it in his right. This cool piece of work gave Rhodes his first wicket of the match in his 47th over – a poor return for much good work – and left Australia labouring on 114 for eight, a lead of 255. They had scored at just over two runs per over.

The dramatic revival of English hopes was conveyed by the frantic Stop Press traffic between reporters and their offices. The *Manchester Evening News* managed to get the wickets of Noble and Hill into its Last Edition Extra, while London's *Echo* pulled out all the stops to get the close-of-play score into its 7 p.m. edition, which went to press only 30 minutes after Tyldesley took his catch. In his match report for the *Sheffield Daily Telegraph*, Stainton described the desperate turn the battle had now taken: 'All the afternoon the cricket remained terribly keen, the fielding was superb, the bowling well changed and always fine, and the batsmen, far from finding themselves in a safe position, began to realise that, after all, England is not easily beaten, and that the situation had been wholly changed.' The *Sportsman* further gauged the mood by snatching a word with one of the players: 'As one of the English XI observed last night, it [the situation] is not hopeless.' C. B. Fry's front-page piece for the *Daily Express* also concluded on a note of optimism: 'Provided the weather holds fine and the two remaining wickets do not add many runs, England may still make a good show.'

ENGLAND: FIRST INNINGS

Archie MacLaren	c Armstrong b Trumble	10
Lionel Palairet	b Trumble	20
Johnny Tyldesley	b Trumble	33
Tom Hayward	b Trumble	0
Stanley Jackson	c Armstrong b Saunders	2
Len Braund	c Hill b Trumble	22
Gilbert Jessop	b Trumble	13
George Hirst	c and b Trumble	43
Bill Lockwood	c Noble b Saunders	25
Dick Lilley	c Trumper b Trumble	0
Wilfred Rhodes	not out	0
Extras (byes 13, leg-byes 2)		15
Total (61 overs)		**183**

Fall of wickets: 31-1 (Palairet), 36-2 (MacLaren), 62-3 (Hayward), 67-4 (Jackson), 67-5 (Tyldesley), 83-6 (Jessop),

137-7 (Hirst), 179-8 (Lockwood), 183-9 (Braund), 183-10 (Lilley)

Bowling: Trumble 31-13-65-8, Saunders 23-7-79-2, Noble 7-3-24-0

AUSTRALIA: SECOND INNINGS

Victor Trumper	run out (Jessop-Lilley)	2
Reggie Duff	b Lockwood	6
Clem Hill	c MacLaren b Hirst	34
Joe Darling	c MacLaren b Lockwood	15
Monty Noble	b Braund	13
Syd Gregory	b Braund	9
Warwick Armstrong	not out	21
Bert Hopkins	c Lilley b Lockwood	3
Jack Saunders	c Tyldesley b Rhodes	2
Extras (byes 7, leg-byes 2)		9
Total (8 wickets, 52.5* overs)		**114**

Fall of wickets: 6-1 (Trumper), 9-2 (Duff), 31-3 (Darling), 71-4 (Noble), 75-5 (Hill), 91-6 (Gregory), 99-7 (Hopkins), 114-8 (Saunders)

Bowling: Lockwood 16-5-39-3, Rhodes 18.5-5-37-1,* Hirst 5-1-7-1, Braund 9-1-15-2, Jackson 4-3-7-0

*It is not known to which ball of Rhodes' 19th over Saunders was out, but the over was not completed until the next morning.

10

JESSOP'S BET

DINNER AT THE GREAT CENTRAL HOTEL

IN THE AUTUMN of 1922, when his playing days were far behind him, Jessop wrote a book of memoirs, *A Cricketer's Log*. As an autobiography it could have been more revealing, but he was always reluctant to talk about himself, or his great feats, and in any case the years after the trauma of the First World War were not a time for self-aggrandisement. 'He keeps himself always in the background, referring with almost slighting briefness to his own great performances,' observed a review of the book in the *Western Daily Press*. But Jessop did tell one interesting tale in connection with his most famous performance, and he dates it to the second evening of the game.

Jessop recounted how he and some team-mates gathered for dinner at the Great Central hotel, which had been recently built to serve Marylebone station and still stands today as the Landmark hotel, where England teams sometimes stay when they are playing in London. They had made the hotel their quarters for the match, he said. At the start of the evening the skies were cloudless, but as darkness fell the rains that had so blighted the summer blew up again. 'We had sat down before an open window from which could be perceived a cloudless sky giving hope of a welcome change in the weather,' he wrote. '[Then] pitter-patter, pitter-patter, the change came. It rained harder. And then the floodgates … were let loose.'

Clearly, this would have been very bad news for England's prospects of making the runs they would need the next day when the Test match reached its finale; Australia were already 255 runs to the good, which even without more rain to further liven up the pitch was going to present a challenge. Jessop described how when the rain eased he attempted to lift the spirits of his team-mates by offering odds of 10-1 on anyone in the team scoring a fifty, and 20-1 on anyone scoring a hundred. The sums suggested were only small but, Jessop explained, 'as this seemed such a clear case of money for nothing the offer was snatched up immediately'.

The next morning the weather broke fine, but the ground in Kennington was still wet from the previous evening – or so the account ran. This story has been often repeated, and seemingly accepted without question – one account in later years, feeding off Jessop's version, stating that 'it was nothing short of a miracle that play was possible before lunch', and that in the early stages of day three the pitch was 'saturated'.

But contemporary accounts simply do not support the suggestion of heavy rain in London on the night of 12 August. On the contrary. The early editions of the London evening papers the following day, some of them probably drawing on agency bulletins but some also using eyewitness accounts, reported favourably on conditions at the start of play. The *St James's Gazette* described the weather as a great improvement on the day before, adding: 'No further rain having fallen during the night, the wicket had dried up considerably and should play much better.'

Not many reporters shared the view that the pitch would play much better, but there was a general consensus that the absence of rain overnight was a blessing, at least as far as England were concerned. The *Daily News* alluded to the 'ground being drier', while the *Echo* stated that 'the rain had kindly held off during the night'. Stainton in the *Sheffield Evening Telegraph* noted, 'The weather was dull but the night had been quite fine', though he thought a heavy dew had done the pitch no good. C. B. Fry in the *Daily Express* on the day after the game agreed with him on this point: 'Although no rain fell overnight, the pitch yesterday morning, owing to a very heavy dew, was wetter than at close of play on the second day, and it remained a damp-affected pitch.' The *Halifax Evening Courier*'s reporter said, 'a fine fresh night had been succeeded by a heavy dew'.

Admittedly, Marylebone is five miles north-west of the Kennington Oval, so it is possible that it might have rained there but not south of the river, but this seems unlikely. Had this been the case, surely Jessop and his dinner companions would somewhere have expressed relief that while it had rained heavily where they were the previous evening they had arrived at The Oval to find conditions far better than expected. Newspaper reporters alluded to several exchanges with the players during and after the match, but there was nothing along these lines.

Jessop would hardly have made up his story, but it is possible that he misplaced the evening, and that the dinner at the Great Central hotel actually took place on the Monday, the first evening of the game. There is no question that it rained heavily that night; all witnesses agree on that. It is also the case that, had the dinner occurred that evening, the England players who were present would have still viewed the rain with foreboding because Australia had just completed their first innings that day and England were due to start their own innings the next morning. Jessop's proposal of a wager would still have made sense.

Given the contrasting weather on the Monday and Tuesday evenings, Jessop's account makes far more sense as a description of the first night of the game, but is a better story when attached to the second. At a remove of 20 years, Jessop may have quite innocently confused the one for the other.

11

WEDNESDAY 13 AUGUST:
10 A.M. TO 11.38 A.M.

ENGLAND SET A RECORD 263 TO WIN

BY TEN O'CLOCK the next morning there were already large numbers of people inside The Oval. England's fightback meant that interest in the game was intense. As on the first and second days, the public availed themselves of the opportunity to walk across the outfield and inspect the pitch. The *Evening News* representative was among those who took a close look at the surface. 'The question uppermost in the minds of the thousands who turned up to see the first ball bowled was, "How will the wicket roll out?"' he wrote. 'To the eye it appeared all right except at the end where Trumble's accurately-pitched deliveries had worn an unmistakable "spot".'

Although the weather was dry, the skies were dull and there was clearly the possibility of rain returning at some point.

Darling considered not having the pitch rolled at all, but in the end asked for the light roller to be applied briefly before Australia resumed batting, no doubt conscious that when the Australian innings ended, as it might do quite soon, MacLaren would be able to request for it to be rolled again, probably with the heavy roller. Darling did not want the pitch dulled by two protracted rollings close together ahead of England's run-chase. The Reuters man noted in one of his early despatches that the roller was used for only three minutes. Reports vary on the size of the crowd before the resumption, but several put it at around 8,000 – with more still coming in – just before the 11 a.m. restart, and as the day unfolded this would grow substantially. As MacLaren leads out the England players, they are greeted by loud cheers.

*

MacLaren again started with Rhodes and Lockwood. Rhodes, in fact, had an over to complete that he had begun from the Pavilion End the previous evening and, the batsmen having crossed in the process of Jack Saunders being caught in the deep, Warwick Armstrong was the man on strike. He was beaten first ball but Rhodes' appeal for lbw is turned down by umpire Richardson. However, Armstrong did not escape for long because in Lockwood's first over, after Trumble had taken a single into the leg side, he was bowled by a quick, full-length delivery that sent the off bail flying 15 yards. It was a sight that sent up a great shout from the gathering throng.

This brought in Kelly to join Trumble, and while they had caused England problems in the first innings, batting was now less straightforward.

Trumble was immediately in difficulty against Rhodes, and nearly popped up a catch to Braund at point. He then managed a quick single to Jessop, whose throw almost beat Kelly home, and then put Lockwood away through square leg for four before taking a nasty blow above the knee as Lockwood continued to make the ball skid. Trumble thought he had beaten the ring again in Lockwood's next over but Rhodes made a brilliant left-handed stop at point to save four runs. This electric piece of fielding helped Rhodes and Lockwood string together three successive maidens.

Australia's score was going nowhere.

Finally, Trumble managed a single but this merely exposed Kelly for the first time to Lockwood, who needed only one ball to clean him up, stone-dead lbw to a ball that struck Kelly full on the foot. Australia for their last two wickets had scraped together just seven runs, all scored by Trumble, which meant that since Noble was fourth out the previous evening their last seven wickets had tumbled for 50. On a pitch that was too slow to really suit him, Lockwood had taken five for 45 from 20 overs in what would turn out to be his final effort with the ball for England.

Delighted though England and their supporters would have been to restrict Australia to 121, the way the pitch behaved during this 20 minutes of play did not bode well. 'There was suggestion of trouble for the English batsmen,' Alfred Pullin noted in the *Yorkshire Evening Post*. 'Balls do not pop about in the same way [as they had here] on an easy wicket.' The *Daily News* was no less concerned: 'The pitch did not roll out well; indeed, considering that there were clearly some awkward spots on it on Tuesday, such an improvement was not to be expected. The ground being drier, the ball came faster off the pitch, so with bowlers skilful enough to find the worn places, the prospects for batsmen were far from hopeful … it was regarded as distinctly ominous for England's chances that he [Rhodes] two or three times made the ball get up awkwardly.' The next Reuter bulletin stated simply: 'There are spots on the pitch.'

*

England's target was thus 263 to win. While this represented something of a triumph, because they would certainly have taken in advance keeping their target as low as this, it nevertheless left them facing a major challenge. No team had ever scored so many to win a Test match in England. As if this was not enough, England had failed in all of their last three run-chases against Australia, so they were going to have to lay a few ghosts to rest along the way if they were to succeed this time.

Quite apart from the defeats in Sheffield, when they were left to score 339, and Manchester, where they went in pursuit of a more manageable 124, they had blown a great opportunity to win the fifth and final Test of the tour of Australia five months before this. There, they needed 211 in the fourth innings. Moreover, Jessop's name had become inextricably linked with these doomed enterprises. In Melbourne, England were going well at 87 for two with MacLaren and Jessop at the wicket when in the final over of the day Jessop had run out his captain declining a second run. He then compounded the offence by getting out to Trumble first ball the next morning, offering up an easy catch to mid-off. Similarly, England's hopes rested on Jessop going into the final day at Bramall Lane when, again, he was out to Trumble almost immediately, albeit to an unfortunate lbw decision. Although he was not selected to play at Old Trafford, it had been said repeatedly since that England would have won had Jessop and Hirst played. Could England – and could Jessop – finally change the pattern?

MacLaren duly summoned the biggest available roller in the hope of further quietening the pitch, and asked that it be used for almost the full ten minutes permitted. 'Will England get the runs? Can England get the runs?' observed the *Pall Mall Gazette*. 'These two questions were the only subjects discussed during the interval between the innings.' In the England dressing-room, the mood was not upbeat. 'I don't think that there were a great many of us who really fancied our chances before the commencement of our second innings,' Jessop wrote years later.

AUSTRALIA: SECOND INNINGS

Victor Trumper	run out (Jessop-Lilley)	2
Reggie Duff	b Lockwood	6
Clem Hill	c MacLaren b Hirst	34
Joe Darling	c MacLaren b Lockwood	15
Monty Noble	b Braund	13
Syd Gregory	b Braund	9
Warwick Armstrong	b Lockwood	21
Bert Hopkins	c Lilley b Lockwood	3
Jack Saunders	c Tyldesley b Rhodes	2
Hugh Trumble	not out	7
James Kelly	lbw b Lockwood	0
Extras (byes 7, leg-byes 2)		9
Total (60 overs)		**121**

Fall of wickets: 6-1 (Trumper), 9-2 (Duff), 31-3 (Darling), 71-4 (Noble), 75-5 (Hill), 91-6 (Gregory), 99-7 (Hopkins), 114-8 (Saunders), 115-9 (Armstrong), 121-10 (Kelly)

Bowling: Lockwood 20-6-45-5, Rhodes 22-7-38-1, Hirst 5-1-7-1, Braund 9-1-15-2, Jackson 4-3-7-0

12

WEDNESDAY 13 AUGUST: 11.38 A.M. TO 1.08 P.M.

ENGLAND COLLAPSE TO 48 FOR FIVE

AS ARCHIE MACLAREN and Lionel Palairet walked out to start the England innings, large drops of rain began to fall. They were isolated and did not last. In the press box, word had got around among reporters that Hugh Trumble had said rather gleefully the previous evening that he had found a patch at the Vauxhall End that was giving him a lot of help. But while both opening bowlers promptly made the ball talk, it was Jack Saunders who created the early havoc.

Three confident strokes brought five runs in Trumble's opening over – two singles to MacLaren and a three to Palairet – but in the space of the next five balls English hopes took a grievous hit. First MacLaren shaped to drive at Saunders, only to change his mind, defend, and see the ball spin back into his stumps off an inside edge; then three balls later Tyldesley, having been startled by his first ball and not known much about his second, was bowled playing forward. It was a fine delivery which C. B. Fry reckoned pitched on leg and hit the top of off, luring Tyldesley into attempting to clip into the on side. Given his ability to score runs on difficult pitches, Tyldesley's was a particularly big wicket, and was greeted by raucous shouts from the Australian enclosure.

Stainton had just been looking up the biggest successful run-chases in Test cricket and now felt the futility of the exercise. 'Five minutes' cricket took the edge of the interest clean away, and all this looking up of the records seemed so much wasted time,' he wrote. 'We never know, but the sight of that awful [score]board which told the story of MacLaren and Tyldesley, both out for five runs, and with only 11 balls bowled, was too sad for mere words.'

Palairet survived a torrid examination from Trumble as the beanpole Australian probed away at the spot that had been proving so beneficial to him, but he could not keep out Saunders when he faced the left-armer for the first time. This was another terrific ball, which nipped back sharply to take the stumps. This left England 10 for three in the sixth over and, as the *Manchester Evening News* correspondent noted, 'the faces of the spectators wore the most disconsolate expressions'.

To add to the drama, it quickly became evident that in the process of Palairet being bowled, Australia's wicketkeeper James Kelly had taken a blow in the face; one of the bails had flown up and struck him full in the eye. Kelly had thrown up his hands to his face and sunk to the ground in agony as his team-mates ran to his aid; Clem Hill then rushed off to the pavilion to seek assistance. 'In an instant, all was confusion in the Colonial camp,' one report said. Hill returned with brandy while a frock-coated doctor and colleague hurried out to attend to the stricken player; for several minutes Kelly lay on his back, dazed and sick from the blow, while he was checked over. There was speculation that Hill, who had kept wicket for South Australia in the past, though not recently, could deputise if needed, but in the end Kelly was able to continue behind the stumps.

All the while, Stanley Jackson, the new batsman, stood by waiting to receive his first ball. When the moment finally came, he was comprehensively beaten by Saunders. England were floundering.

Over the next 25 or so minutes, Tom Hayward and Jackson fashioned something of a recovery, but they needed luck to survive even this long. Jackson unfurled a handsome off-drive against Saunders to bring the first boundary of the innings amid great applause, but Hayward found life altogether tougher. He had scored only three when Trumble got another ball to climb and Hayward popped it up at head height to forward short leg where Syd Gregory, astonishingly for such a good fielder, spilled the chance. Jackson survived his own scare when he just managed to stop a delivery from Trumble trickling back into his stumps, but then roused the crowd for a second time with a delicate late cut to the long Vauxhall End boundary which resulted in an all-run four. Moments later the players were forced from the field by a light shower which persisted for half an hour and necessitated fresh sawdust being put into the footholds.

Within minutes of the resumption, Hayward, on the front foot, was smartly caught behind off Saunders by Kelly, a good effort for a fielder nursing a bruised eye. Having caught the ball, Kelly turned to umpire Richardson at square leg and appealed for a stumping, creating some confusion as to how Hayward had been dismissed, but the umpires confirmed during the lunch break that he had been given out caught. Hayward's comeback game on his home ground had been the dampest of squibs. England were 31 for four and in his seventh over Saunders had the remarkable return of four wickets for 9 runs.

Saunders – described by the *Morning Leader* as 'a dark-featured Spanish type of Colonial' – had played his part in Australia's wins in Sheffield and Manchester but he had not made an impact like this before in the series.

He, like Trumble, had found a spot on the pitch to help him, and – again like Trumble – was tall enough at 6ft 2in to generate troubling variations in bounce. Even so, there was some debate as to quite where his mystery lay. 'He varies his pace so well without indicating it to the batsman, [so] that all his deliveries are a puzzle,' the London *Echo* suggested. Stainton in the *Sheffield Evening Telegraph* thought that a strange run-up played its part, with Saunders coming at the bowling crease in a curve from the direction of mid-on and approaching the stumps behind the umpire. 'He has a knack of creeping round to the delivery in a stealthy, horrible fashion, which may or may not make a batsman inclined to go across the pitch and smash him over the head with the bat. It is a worrying sort of action whereby, perhaps, his power over the ball is accentuated. He certainly appears to get a lot of spin and work on the ball.' The *Daily Mail* called it a 'quaint semi-circular run'. Jessop's verdict was that these early wickets fell to Saunders' 'flicky wrist'.

In fact, Saunders' curious run-up had concerned the England batsmen for some time and the previous day, in England's first innings, Braund had asked during his partnership with George Hirst if umpire Richardson could stand further back from the stumps so that Saunders could run in front of the umpire and thereby remain in full view of the batsmen. Previously, with the umpires standing well up to the stumps, Saunders had come into sight only as he was about to deliver the ball. Alfred Pullin in the *Yorkshire Evening Post* thought the change long overdue: 'This course ought, I think, to be insisted upon by every captain as a matter of principle when Saunders is bowling.'

Not that the change greatly helped Braund now. While Jackson was getting into his stride with a series of productive strokes off both bowlers, Braund looked ill at ease, especially against Trumble, and the idea that he and Jackson might repeat their great partnership of Old Trafford always appeared fanciful. Eventually, after labouring 15 minutes for two singles, Braund was adjudged caught behind by Richardson off a quick-rising off-break from Trumble that Braund said later had passed between his gloves without making contact with either.

Not only were England now five wickets down, but the five batsmen who were out had failed to make any sort of impact whatsoever, mustering only 17 runs between them. The only player who had looked remotely comfortable was Jackson, who was playing superbly. The other batsmen had trusted to forward play and come to grief but Jackson, noting their mistakes, was relying on playing back and waiting patiently for his opportunities. 'He watched the bowling most carefully, judged the length of the ball every time, played back like a book, and lost no chance of scoring,' Fry wrote. Jackson even managed to force runs off balls from Trumble that rose into his ribs, and he would have scored more still but for some wonderful fielding. Just before Braund was out, Jackson, having just moved into the twenties, was almost run out by a sharp throw from Gregory. Of England's first 48 runs, Jackson's share was 31 and he had scored all but seven since coming to the wicket.

Fry, in his report the next morning, said these were some of the most difficult batting conditions of the match:

> The Australian bowlers gave it as their opinion that the wicket played more difficult up to lunch than at any time on the previous day. They could make the ball break as much as they liked, and that rather quickly – decidedly more quickly than on the previous day. It was not an absolutely sticky wicket, but it was beyond doubt a difficult one ... Not only did the ball break, but it came along at different paces and heights, and several times kicked up nastily, chest-high.

Jessop in his autobiography would concur. He said that the pitch prior to lunch 'was in its worst stage, the ball not only turning quickly but getting up abruptly at an awkward height'.

Not counting the break for rain, England had been batting for just over an hour, and the way things were going it felt as though another hour of play might be enough to see the game to its grim conclusion. Some delighted Australian spectators sitting in front of the press box certainly thought so. With just over 20 minutes to go until lunch, England's hopes, and their options, were running thin. The next man in was Jessop.

13

WEDNESDAY 13 AUGUST: 1.08 P.M.

JESSOP ENTERS THE ARENA

AT THE FALL of Len Braund's wicket, Jessop made his way through the spacious new pavilion and headed down the steps and onto the field of play. On his way, he encountered Archie MacLaren in the main club room, or Long Room, and a brief exchange between them was overheard by an onlooker, a Mr Gill, whose ten-year-old son was watching outside in the stands and would record the story for posterity. 'I bet you a sovereign you don't make a century!' the England captain said to his friend and team-mate. To which Jessop promptly replied as he carried on walking, 'Done!'

That MacLaren was watching the game from a public viewing area rather than the players' balcony was perhaps revealing of his mood as England appeared to be heading for yet another defeat under his command, but his comment to Jessop also suggested he was able to see the lighter side. Perhaps he was reviving the chat at dinner one or two nights earlier when Jessop had offered odds on anyone making fifty or a hundred. It was a wager which the perennially hard-up MacLaren could hardly afford to lose, but he would not have worried about that when he proposed it to Jessop as he hurried past.

As the spectators caught sight of Jessop emerging from the pavilion, yells went up around the ground. Jessop was always a cause for renewed hope and he always exuded confidence in the way he strode out and the way he set his features; he was ever the embodiment of energy and purpose. He may have been short in build but no one could doubt the physical power that lay within his stocky frame. Leslie Ward's caricature of him in *Vanity Fair* in 1901 showed Jessop with a sturdy backside. The artist James Thorpe, a friend of Jessop's since they first met in South Woodford, Essex, as teenagers, drew a cartoon showing Jessop walking briskly out to bat, his left leg thrust forward, his chin prominent and his sleeves rolled to the elbows. Here was someone who meant business. 'Here he comes with a springy, sturdy stride that suggests what is to follow,' J. T. Bolton wrote, 'this thick-set man of the aggressive chin and square shoulders.' The manner of Jessop's entrance was something many commented upon. Edward Pugh described him as 'stockish, bull-throated, ruddy, his fierce-looking face set grimly'.

Jessop's stern demeanour as he set out on an innings went to the heart of matters with him. He loved to entertain the crowd and not let them down, and wanted to win matches for his team, so he was steeling himself not to fail when he headed for the middle. But he also knew the way he went about batting was so unorthodox that it would never meet with the approval of the purists who abhorred his crouching and his cross-batted strokes on principle. It was another reason why Stanley Jackson would have frowned upon him. Every Jessop innings, therefore, was an act of defiance. If he was reluctant to talk about what he did on the cricket field, it was because he would have shied away from articulating this subversiveness.

Opponents knew what tell-tale signs to look for when Jessop headed for the middle. 'If he emerged from the pavilion flexing his neck slightly to one side, and occasionally giving a tug to the back of his trousers, it was a sign of trouble,' said one. C. B. Fry recalled Jessop walking out to bat in a county championship match at Bristol 'with a big cap on his small head, peak well over his nimble eyes, at a fast pace and with no fears'.

England certainly needed Jessop at his most optimistic now. The previous day he had gone out to bat shortly before lunch with the scoreboard reading 67 for five, but things looked even worse than that now. Shouting support for him was one thing; what everyone truly felt about England's prospects another. Stainton assessed the situation as it stood in his magisterial report for the *Sheffield Daily Telegraph*:

Everyone had reconciled themselves to approaching defeat after Braund had followed Hayward, and half the side was out for 48. It was far too much to expect victory then, and the general hope – and it did not go beyond that – was that even in so desperate a situation England might get enough runs to take away the actual feeling of disgrace. The well-filled reserve enclosure in front of the Press gallery was sounding with cheers from the excited Colonials and their friends. Ladies were waving their handkerchiefs to the players in the field, at the fall of every wicket; the men in the same enclosure were crying their favourite 'coo-ee' in stentorian tones, and there was apparently nothing between England and disgrace but a miracle ... As Gilbert Jessop strode out of the pavilion, taking a snatchy glance at those sad figures on the board, and with determination written all over his face, there was a feeling abroad in the crowd that if only he stayed we might yet have a chance, for there is no man who is more capable of winning a game out of hand than he.

'Astral' in the *Morning Leader* also sensed that the crowd were not yet quite ready to give up, and their defiant mood invigorated the England players who had fought so hard against the odds for so much of the game:

> The big British public is true to its cricket idols, and is not The Croucher supreme favourite with all? It was traitorous even to recall how often he had failed against the Colonials. Supposing he had been a gift for them Down Under, as they said; he was back in England now, and it was about his time to come off. So ran the argument round the ropes as the game was resumed and something of the crowd's steadfast faith in his ability must have strengthened Jessop's arm and steadied the purpose that was revealed in the hard, square jaw, the firm mouth, and the clear bright eyes that never winked at the fastest bowler that ever lived.

Another thing observers commonly noted about Jessop was the size of his bat. It was often mentioned that he used a heavy bat, which was certainly the case relative to the light weights of bats then in fashion, but what was also striking was the thickness and length of the handle. Jessop always used a long-handled bat to give him greater scope to move his hands up and down, and vary his grip, which – as has already been discussed – he would often do from one ball to the next, depending on which stroke he chose to play. The bat Jessop used for this innings, which still survives, was the Crawford's Exceller, produced by John Wisden and Co.; according to advertisements, these bats were 'universally acknowledged the grandest driving bats ever made'. Among contemporaries who endorsed the Crawford were MacLaren, Jackson and Hayward, as well as several of the leading Australian batsmen, including Darling, Gregory and Trumper.

Having examined and picked up this bat, I can vouch that the handle does feel unusually thick and out of proportion with the blade. The handle measures 32cm from the top to the shoulder of the blade. Overall the bat measures 88cm in length by the standard 11cm in width. In February 2025, a bat belonging to Harry Brook, one of England's most powerful players, was at my request measured for comparison. The length of the blade, from shoulder to base, was the same as Jessop's at 56cm, but the handle was 4cm shorter at 28cm, supporting the theory that Jessop's handles were unusually long. The width of the handle was the same for both players at 3.7cm, but the Brook handle was encased in two rubber grips whereas Jessop's was wrapped in just one, made of leather and obviously now very well worn. Another striking difference is the depth front to back: the Brook bat is 3.8cm at its thickest, about twice as deep as the Jessop one. Brook's bat thus has more wood in it – and more power.

Piercy Britten, writing in the 1970s, recalled going to this Test match as a lad of eighteen and one of his brightest memories was the sturdy Jessop strolling out to the middle, wielding a bat 'with a very thick handle'.

Like many batsmen of the time, Jessop wore batting gloves of the flimsiest kind, although in his case he had developed rubberised protection across the top of the knuckles using refashioned bicycle tyres. A pair of these still survive.

Jessop's preparations before receiving the ball – what would in modern parlance be called his trigger movements – were also quite distinctive. His famous crouched stance at the wicket, after he had taken his customary 'centre' guard, could never be mistaken for that of any other batsman, and the way he would peer around the field while the opposing captain put men on the boundary line was also unique to him. As he grounded his bat, he also had a curious habit of clenching and unclenching his hands on the handle, in a kind of restless exploration of the shots he might be preparing to unleash. E. H. D. Sewell, the Essex amateur and journalist, explained it thus:

He was a great little personality with his jaunty, almost cockney air, in almost all he did. As he crouched to address the bowler, both his hands kept on opening and shutting on the bat-handle as though he was uncertain whether he'd got the grip right.

Actually this perpetual motion of handling enabled him the more quickly to secure the grip that was necessary directly he had decided on his stroke. Then, nimble footwork abetting, he was speedily in the right place to attempt that stroke.

C. B. Fry observed the same thing in the technical notes he wrote to accompany George Beldam's photographic books, writing of Jessop that while he waited for the bowler he would constantly 'clasp and unclasp his hands as though fingering for a tighter grip', adding: 'As the ball left the bowler's hands he would make a sudden stoop with his shoulders and head almost down to a level with the top of the stumps, as though endeavouring to get the eyes as much below the ball as possible.' The nearest modern equivalent to this kind of trigger movement was perhaps the left-handed Eoin Morgan, who similarly ducked down as the ball was about to be bowled.

Sydney Santall, the Warwickshire player, gave an idea of what Jessop's presence at the crease felt like from a bowler's perspective. 'All one could see of the wickets when running up to deliver the ball, was the off stump,' he explained. 'There he stood, very unorthodox with jaw stiffened, looking at you from just under the peak of his cap.'

The Australians, of course, were very familiar with what bowling at Jessop was like. They thought they knew how to get him out and Darling now set his usual field for his arrival. The pitch was in the bowlers' favour and so also the match situation. There were singles on offer in certain places if Jessop wanted them, but he would have to take his chance if he was looking to hit boundaries. The *Morning Leader* noted how satisfactory everything looked for the Australians as Jackson and Jessop first came together: 'To all intents and purposes now the Australians had got the match well in hand. Joe Darling smothered a smile with his hand as he remembered that the back of the English team had been broken.'

One other facet of how Jessop started his innings, noted by C. B. Fry, needed to be borne in mind by everyone: '[He] plunges straightaway into play which can only be described as the height and depth of aggressiveness.'

14

WEDNESDAY 13 AUGUST:
1.08 P.M. TO 2.15 P.M.

JESSOP'S WILD START; AN ANXIOUS LUNCH BREAK

JESSOP WAS NEARLY bowled by the first ball he faced. Attempting a drive at Trumble, he got an inside edge which skirted past leg stump and ran away for a single. It was, said one critic, 'a fearful stroke', but he was up and running.

As it was the final ball of the over – the 19th of the innings – Jessop retained the strike. Seemingly unperturbed by his close escape, he swung away to leg the first two balls he received from Saunders, the first time for two and the second time for a boundary. They were both relatively measured strokes. He then took a single to pass the strike to Jackson, who played out the rest of the over in as quiet and unconcerned a fashion as before. When Jessop then took another single off the first ball of Trumble's next over, he had scored 9 runs from five balls since coming in while Jackson had remained on 31, but Jackson then scored 3 and would have added a boundary later in the over but for a fine stop by Hill at third man. Australia's fielding continued to be excellent. The sun had started to shine. It was the best weather of the day.

After a quiet over from Saunders, from which Jessop ran a leg-bye off the only ball he faced, Jessop unleashed his first really aggressive stroke, stepping out to drive Trumble straight and high down the ground, the ball landing on the awning above the seats in front of the pavilion to thunderous applause. The *Pall Mall Gazette* described this hit as going 'onto the roof of the pavilion', which would be a further and higher hit, but most accounts referred to the awning. Next ball, Jessop drove narrowly over the head of mid-off, where Darling 'lifted his hands in a dramatic token of his helplessness', to send the ball running away to the pavilion rails. Jessop then added a single which meant the over cost nine, Trumble's most expensive of the innings so far.

An off-drive against Saunders past cover for four was perhaps Jessop's purest stroke so far, and moved his score to 22, but he then almost came unstuck as he stepped down the pitch to the left-armer and was beaten. Fortunately, the ball went through low and awkwardly to Kelly, who could not take advantage of the stumping chance. Clem Hill many years later said of this incident: 'He [Jessop] should have been stumped off Saunders before he had made 30. He was down the pitch two yards, and did not attempt to get back until he saw that the wicketkeeper had fumbled the ball. He scrambled home just in time.' But no contemporary account supported this claim. This was, of course, the kind of dismissal to which Jessop often succumbed, especially in his early days, but had Jessop really survived such a clear-cut chance it would probably have given him more pause for thought, and resulted in him reining in his approach, at least for a few deliveries, but he continued to hit out fearlessly. He lifted Trumble over mid-on for a single and then cut Saunders uppishly over deep cover point, where Armstrong made a tremendous leap in a vain attempt at an interception.

This was the first real cut stroke that Jessop made in his innings, a stroke that he played perhaps better than any other and the shot he looked to play when a bowler dropped short to avoid being driven. As C. B. Fry explained, Jessop's first tactic was to induce bowlers to pitch short for fear of being driven, and then apply his brutally powerful cuts and square cuts. Sewell said that Jessop was also in the habit of setting himself as though preparing to drive – thereby inviting the bowler to pull back his length – before switching to other options. 'The cut was his best stroke,' he wrote. 'He could cut better than almost anyone [but] he'd also prepare to drive, then stop, and crack past point, a true square-cut. Then he would do something similar only to nudge over square leg.'

Having been cut, Saunders now compensated by going fuller, only for Jessop, his score now 27, to dance into a fierce drive. But he did not quite get hold of it cleanly and the resultant strike went into a low slice to long-off where Trumper, sprinting in, got his hands to the ball but could not cling on. 'It was a terrific skimming hit, and the ball swerved away from Trumper to the right as he ran in full tilt,' C. B. Fry wrote that afternoon as he composed his match report. 'The fielder did well to get to the ball at all. It would have been a most remarkable catch.' But Trumper was furious with himself and threw the ball in with disgust.

By now, everyone's nerves were jangling. The dropped catch gave Jessop a single and later in the same over Jackson was beaten as he lunged forward in defence and had to scramble to ensure his back foot was behind the line before Kelly could whip off the bails. After one more, uneventful over from Trumble, from which Jessop took a single, the lunch break arrived with England 87 for five. Jessop had already raced to 29. Jackson's share of an unbroken partnership of 39 was just eight, but for many his infinitely more measured approach came as a blessed contrast to Jessop's wildness.

Jessop's approach divided opinion. He had survived twice by the skin of his teeth and other aerial shots had left onlookers with hearts in mouths. A number of critics were not best pleased with how hard he had gone before getting his eye in. R. L. Hodgson, who wrote as 'A Country Vicar', described how – as ever – excitement intermingled with fear when watching Jessop. 'Jessop's in,' he wrote. 'The words caused a shiver of excitement, a cold sensation down the spine.' He was watching from the pavilion where, after Jessop had deposited Trumble onto the awning, a long-faced neighbour shook his head in disgust. 'Why in the name of sense can't he go steady for a bit? He'll slog another couple of fours and then give a catch in the deep, and we'll have lost the match.' Then, when Jessop gave the stumping chance a few minutes later, the same man said in exasperation: 'There, what did I tell you?' The *Daily News* thought Jessop's cricket before the interval 'had not been of a description to inspire any confidence', while the correspondent for the *Manchester Guardian*, like Hodgson, came across a disgruntled amateur critic who was of the view that 'schoolboys would play better'.

Many years later, Jessop recounted in a letter how a friend who had watched this innings 'hid his face behind his hands', so afraid was he that Jessop would get out. Stainton wrote that English spectators could only watch Jessop with 'painful zeal'. But for all the alarms created by Jessop's early fireworks, the realisation dawned even during that short passage of play that Jessop had shifted the balance of power in the game. Even his initial flurry of 9 runs in five balls transformed the mood on the terraces according to 'Astral' in the *Morning Leader*:

> The magnetic influence of the man Jessop is wonderful. England had a rare long way to go ... but within five minutes the spectators shook off the melancholia that had been settling down on them, and were laughing as if victory was almost within sight.

Roland Hill, the cartoonist known as 'Rip', and reputedly the first line artist to concentrate on cricket, was in attendance at the game to produce drawings for the London *Evening News*, but he quickly had to abandon an early sketch as he found the game changing before his eyes, as he recounted in the *Nottingham Evening Post* three days later:

> We looked sure losers of the match. So I commenced drawing a picture of a lion grovelling in the mire and weeping copiously into a handkerchief of table-cloth size. But I did not get on far with it, for things brightened up so much that one felt as though our chance was not quite a hopeless one all the time the little Gloucestershire smiter remained at the wickets. I felt so jubilant over the way Jessop immediately set about the bowling that I promptly started upon another picture, which this time took the form of the

lion raising his head and roaring defiance at a very frisky and bounding kangaroo. I had barely traced the outline of it when, with Jessop thumping Trumble on top of the pavilion, and the crowd beginning to throw off the sadness which the downfall of half of the English wickets caused, I forgot all about this second drawing. I joined in the spirit, and cheered, and howled, and shuddered when Trumper almost caught The Croucher from a lusty drive to long-off.

Hill eventually sent the *Evening News* four drawings which were published in the next day's edition under the heading 'Scenes at the Oval, with sketches by "Rip"', including one of Jessop swinging the bat. There were none of lions or kangaroos.

There was also a sense that the Australians were already rattled by Jessop's explosive counter-attack. Trumper's fury at failing to hold onto a difficult chance revealed as much, while Darling was shuffling his fields in an attempt to meet the demands of Jessop's inventive hitting to the places where the fielders were not. During the Tests in Australia the previous winter, MacLaren was asked by a local reporter why Jessop had been unable to replicate the form he showed in England, and he had said: 'I don't agree with those who call Jessop a failure; a hitter is bound to have more small scores against his name than a consistently sound batsman ... but it must not be forgotten that Australian bowlers in Tests keep their heads when bowling against him, which is not always so at home.' But were they keeping their heads now? The *Sportsman* thought that even in reaching 29 not out, Jessop had 'to a certain extent demoralised the field'.

Stainton assessed the situation thus at the end of the morning session in the *Sheffield Daily Telegraph*:

In 20 minutes, Jessop had taken away all the feeling of utter depression from the crowd, and when he and Jackson marched in at lunch they had, in the time I have mentioned, added no fewer than 39 to the total. Even then, naturally, there was no feeling that the game could be won. It was just thought possible that, after all, England might yet make a fair show, and that Jessop might do well enough to make it plain that those were sadly wrong who have so persistently argued that he should have been left out of the teams in these matches.

One observer thought the Australian players went into lunch with a fairly self-satisfied look, but if so had perhaps miscalculated. As the Reuters man stated in his final bulletin for the session: 'Jessop is still going great guns.'

*

The 45-minute lunch interval saw one heavy-hearted young man hurrying away from The Oval. He would dearly have loved to stay, but Pelham Grenville Wodehouse, better known as Plum, had to return to his junior clerk's position at the City office of the Hongkong and Shanghai Bank. Wodehouse was an aspiring author, who had already had some eighty magazine pieces published, with a first novel set to appear within weeks, but as things stood he needed the bank job to pay the rent. He had hot-footed it over Waterloo Bridge to The Oval in his own lunch break and to his delight he had caught the start of the Jessop–Jackson partnership. Wodehouse had developed a passion for cricket during six years at Dulwich College and would never lose his love for the game.

It was jokingly said that his decision to quit the bank a few weeks after this was inspired by his disappointment at not being able to stay and see the conclusion of Jessop's match, but in reality Wodehouse was by then ready to take his chances as a freelance author. 'There were so many morning papers and evening papers and weekly papers and monthly magazines that you were practically sure of landing your whimsical article on, The Language of Flowers, or your parody of Omar Khayyam somewhere or other after, say, 35 shots,' he quipped. But one wonders how much banking activity there was that afternoon as the drama at The Oval unfolded, and whether Wodehouse's bosses would have really missed their junior clerk had he gone absent without leave. The *Daily Express* noted the following morning: 'As will be seen by our City reports, the Test match caused bargains on the Stock Exchange to be few and far between.'

Many years later, Wodehouse recalled: 'I always remember how formidable Trumble seemed that day. One got the feeling that he was unplayable. And the wicket was in a horrible state.'

The state of the pitch was one of the main topics of conversation during the interval. The *Westminster Gazette* report for the afternoon, unsigned but probably written by Pelham Warner, had even managed to acquire the views of some of the players themselves during the lunch break: 'The players themselves maintained that the light shower, instead of making it [the pitch] easier, had caused it to become even more sticky ... This being the case, it seemed almost impossible that England could save the game, even though Jackson was playing the most perfect cricket possible.'

Fry's report at the end of the game actually concluded that this break for lunch was crucial in allowing time for the pitch to dry out, and play slightly easier thereafter.

Everyone around the ground had an opinion on the state of the game. The London *Echo* stated: 'At lunch, the talk gravitated between Trumper's bad miss and the possibility of England obtaining the necessary 176 runs.' Roland Hill had set down his sketchpad and suddenly become infected with optimism: 'All the lunch-time I was discussing the remote possibilities of an English victory. It was true that we then had only 87 runs out of a needed 263 … My stock argument, I can just remember, was, "If Jessop stops there for a little while, he'll give them Australians!" People kept saying, "You've got Jessop on the brain!" And I gave the same answer to one and all of, "And so will you very likely before long."'

A spectator who had come up from Dover reckoned that most English spectators still feared the worst, which had largely been the case since the fall of the fifth wicket:

> Silence, save in the Cornstalks' camp, reigned supreme. We all felt what the patent medicine dealers term a 'sinking sensation'. Rather than be quite overcome, numbers left the ground at lunch time, when our tally was five for 87. Certainly a little better, but very little reliance was placed on the sticking-in powers of Jessop. Jackson we trusted, but no hilarity could be noticed as we undid our sandwich packets.

The youthful Ben Travers recalled: 'During the lunch interval I noticed quite a number of disgruntled elderly members gathering up their belongings in the pavilion and departing home, unable to face the indignity of witnessing England's abasement.'

The accounts tallied with a number of newspaper reports which made mention of spectators leaving after England lost their fifth wicket. The correspondent of the *Scottish Referee* said he had known of friends who went home out of sheer disgust. But the broad evidence showed that overall the attendance rose as the morning went on, and during the lunch interval itself. The fact that Jessop was going well and still not out at the break undoubtedly had something to do with this; it was the classic Jessop phenomenon that was so often alluded to, that people rushed to the ground when they knew the game's biggest hitter was on the rampage. The *Sheffield Evening Telegraph* estimated that by the time the afternoon session began there were 17,000 inside The Oval.

This was not a bad guess: the official attendance for the day was put at 16,000 of which 13,387 paid, making for a total paid attendance across the three days of almost 50,000. The overall receipts for the Test would come in at £3,750, around £600,000 in today's money, which meant a handsome cut for all parties, including the Australians. Jessop might have been threatening to spoil their party, but it was already clear that the final Test was going to be a financial success for everyone.

15

WEDNESDAY 13 AUGUST:
2.15 P.M. TO 3.03 P.M.

JESSOP AND JACKSON KEEP ENGLAND IN THE HUNT

JESSOP AND JACKSON came out different men after the lunch interval. Jessop now had his eye in, and shaped up with the confidence of someone who knew it. He did not rush at the bowling as he had before the break, but took a view about each ball as to whether it could be hit or should be defended. There would come a time when he could cut loose, but for the moment he was going to approach the situation with care, or at least with as much care as his predatory instincts would allow. He had clearly resolved on a plan and was going to stick to it.

'The interval seemed to do Jessop good, and on starting afresh he played with extreme confidence,' the *Daily Telegraph* commented the next morning. '[He] was playing with great discretion, not hitting indiscriminately, but picking out the ball he thought he could safely punish.' C. B. Fry agreed: '[He] picked his balls with finest judgment. On such a wicket the sureness of the drives was astonishing.'

Jackson, by contrast, was barely recognisable from the batsman of the morning, when he had shown impeccable judgement and demonstrated to his team-mates – above all, Jessop – that the bowling was not unplayable and could be handled with the right approach. In that hour or so that he batted, he proved again what a great player he was on a tricky pitch. He may have calculated during the lunch break, or shortly afterwards, that with Jessop going well his principal duty was to stay in and keep his partner company; provided they both remained, they could yet drag England back into a winning position. But it did not prove so straightforward. The more Jackson retreated into himself, the less reliably he played. 'Jackson's display was full of faults, that even his closest friend could not overlook,' stated the London *Echo*. 'Many times during his stay he deserved to be out, for the bowling completely beat him.' Interestingly, Robert Lyttelton, in his unsigned match report for *The Times*, ignored the blemishes of Jackson's innings and heaped as much praise on his performance as that of Jessop, but then Lyttelton, like Jackson, belonged to political nobility, his younger brother Alfred being an MP closely involved in post-Boer War reconstruction planning. He stayed loyal to his class.

No one, though, could quibble with Lyttelton's verdict on Jackson that 'There is no batsman in the world whose nerve is so surely to be relied on.' There was never any question that Jackson's temperament was equal to the magnitude of the situation. Jessop enjoyed the same immunity from pressure, once saying: 'Nerve strain when actively engaged [in a match] never particularly troubled me.' What was clear to everyone, though, was that, had Jackson not stayed at the crease as long as he did, Jessop could never have played his great innings.

How Jackson felt about being obliged to play second fiddle to Jessop, a cricketer whose methods he was known to distrust, and whose status as a 'limited-income amateur' he frowned upon, can only be imagined. He had been party to Jessop's omission in earlier Tests, and seen Jessop bowl only six overs in the match after his credentials as an all-rounder were made a condition of his selection. Now Jackson was standing 20 yards away as Jessop played the innings of his life, and an innings that many – including Jackson and the 11 Australians on the field – thought was beyond him. But equally, watching Jessop at work, Jackson might have thought that the reason he was playing so well was because he was finally bringing a little of Jackson's own methods to his game. Jessop once said that Jackson's great strength was knowing which balls to play and which to leave, and he himself was showing that kind of judiciousness now.

Would the two of them have spoken tactics during the lunch break? This must be considered unlikely. As a rule, amateur cricketers of this era, and even later ones, did not think it appropriate to tell each other what to do; a professional might be told – indeed an amateur captain was obliged to tell the professionals beneath him what to do – but a gentleman's independence was to be respected, even if he was educated at a grammar school.

At least Jackson did not need to worry about Jessop's running between the wickets as he had when Jessop played his first game for England in 1899 – the only other time apart from this that they would ever bat together in a Test match. Jessop may have run out MacLaren in Australia but that was a rare error for someone who, despite his eagerness to make runs quickly by whatever means, had himself not been run out in first-class cricket for five years. His running in this innings was described by the *Field* as 'brisk and enterprising, and overall admirable'.

*

Jessop's quiet start after lunch was partly down to him seeing much less of the strike than Jackson. But he nonetheless seemed content to get a measure of things for a while, because even when he was on strike he did not attempt anything extravagant. Four of his first five scoring shots were singles, the first two sharply taken off Saunders, to whom Darling again turned along with Trumble. Both bowlers had caused problems before lunch, and were rested and ready to go again. Jessop's first real shot of note was a late cut against Trumble down to the Vauxhall End for which he and Jackson were able to run four. Then, just after four byes brought up England's 100, he came close to hitting a rare boundary off Trumble but Darling's athletic dive restricted a powerful off-drive to one run.

The threat from Saunders was subsiding but then, suddenly, Jackson made a bad mistake. Advancing down the pitch, he was beaten by the turn and the resultant outside edge presented a chance to slip, where Trumble could not hold onto a low, difficult catch, the ball running away for two. Jackson clipped the next delivery off his legs for another two, taking his score to 45, but from now on would be virtually an onlooker to what happened at the other end.

Trumble was posing a relentless challenge; for Jessop in particular, after all his past struggles against him, he was the problem that needed solving. They were engaged in a fascinating duel, Trumble trying to entice him into hitting at the wrong ball, Jessop being wary and bold in turns. Jessop took an early decision that was to stand him in good stead: he was not going to attempt to hit Trumble to leg at any point. He had gauged that playing across the line to a bowler so skilled at varying his pace and bounce, especially on a pitch on which the ball had been kicking, and against someone bowling out of the gloomy backdrop of the pavilion, was simply too dangerous an option. He therefore decided to keep his favourite sweeps and pulls under lock and key. Jessop said that this act of self-restraint was the thing that pleased him most about his innings:

> I had previously fallen a victim on too many occasions to Australian bowlers owing to my propensity for the 'cow shot', but I had it firmly fixed in my mind before I went in to bat that whatever stupid shot I might be tempted to perform, it would not be that cross-bat lunge to the on side against a right-handed bowler breaking into one. I kept to that resolve throughout, even carrying it to excess, for against Trumble when I received one or two balls on the leg stump simply 'asking for it', I smothered my greed and contented myself with a single. I had neither a three nor a boundary against that bowler [Trumble] on the leg side.

The former Australia player Jack Worrall, writing of Jessop during the Test series the previous winter, said that he took too many risks with his 'sweeping shot' on Australia's faster pitches to be successful. Australia's best hitters, he pointed out, 'hit straight'.

Another part of Jessop's post-lunch plan was to not hit aerially down the ground to the Vauxhall End, as he had done against Saunders in the morning when he gave the chance to Trumper at long-off. The boundaries at that end were simply too long to attempt to clear safely. It was a different matter when facing Trumble from the Pavilion End, where the straight boundaries were shorter. This was why he had been prepared to chance hitting Trumble onto the awning of the pavilion before lunch – and why he would take this option again towards the end of his innings. As he began to open up in the afternoon, Jessop took advantage of the larger areas at the Vauxhall End against both bowlers, driving along the ground and pulling Saunders for threes and late cutting Trumble again, this time with the ball running away for an all-run five to huge cheers from the crowd. Trumble's recollection of events in later life were not always accurate, but he remembered this stroke as 'a ferocious cut through the slips to the distant corner of the Vauxhall End'. Trumble was being made to pay for cautiously keeping his bowling a little short of a length out of fear of being driven.

That late cut took Jessop to 49 and past Jackson's score for the first time, Jackson having added only 14 to the 31 he had made when Jessop walked out to join him. A single off the first ball of the next over from Saunders brought up Jessop's fifty after about 45 minutes of batting, prompting further cheers from spectators as they contemplated a scoreboard now reading: England 118 for five. But any mounting optimism at the sense that Jessop was starting to open up was tempered by Jackson being given an increasingly torrid time by Trumble. First he was beaten and nearly bowled, then dropped at wide slip on 48 as he rashly aimed a cut that flew hard into Armstrong's chest before bouncing away.

Australia were fielding outstandingly in the deep, but their close-catching was beginning to let them down. The pressure was starting to tell.

The *Field*'s correspondent marked the start of Jessop's acceleration from the point of his cut for five; it was with this 'clean chop cut' that his hitting 'became indescribable'. Saunders was now Jessop's principal target. Off the final ball of the over in which he brought up his fifty, Jessop savagely square-drove him over backward point for four and in his next over sent the crowd into a frenzy of excitement by hitting each of the first four balls for four, followed by a single. All four boundaries were scored on the leg side with the kind of strokes Jessop had set himself not to play against the metronomic Trumble, and had hardly played against Saunders either until he was into the forties. The *Sporting Life* described the over thus:

> He hit the first ball to the square-leg boundary, going down on his knee, got the second round to leg for four, the third – a full toss – was pulled to square-leg for four, the fourth – a half-volley – was similarly treated, and the fifth was played to the off for a single.

Jessop was taking spin out of the equation by getting right to the pitch of the ball (though of course it helped when Saunders began to overpitch as he wilted under the barrage), but he took care not to step out of his crease and risk being stumped, but rather, in Stainton's words, 'stretched forward in that unique crouching manner'. One account stressed how

Gilbert Jessop, photographed by R. W. Thomas of Hudson & Kearns in front of the Lord's pavilion in 1895. Jessop was aged twenty and in his first full season of first-class cricket.

The bat used by Jessop at the Oval in 1902 has survived and carries a silver plaque (right) commemorating his achievement. It simply states how many runs he scored and that England won, not how many minutes he batted or how many balls he faced.

Jessop's bat (far right) was a Crawford Exceller, which was used by many leading batsmen of the day, but his were made with unusually long handles and shorter blades. The handle is 4cm longer than is common today.

THIS BAT WAS USED BY
G. L. JESSOP
IN TEST MATCH
ENGLAND V AUSTRALIA
PLAYED AT THE OVAL
AUG 13 1902
SCORING 104 RUNS
ENGLAND WINNING

ONE OF THE BIGGEST HITTERS EVER SEEN IN THE CRICKET FIELD: MR. G. L. JESSOP.

Mr. G. L. Jessop, the famous Gloucestershire batsman, who has been described as "one of the biggest hitters ever seen in the cricket field," was born at Cheltenham in 1874. He got his blue at Cambridge in 1896, and later became captain. On going down he assumed the captaincy of Gloucestershire. In batting he has attitudes and strokes entirely his own, but marvellously effective. Numerous centuries stand to his credit: three times he has made two in one match, and five times he has exceeded 200, his highest score being 286 against Sussex at Brighton in 1903. The great innings of his life, however, was his 104 in a Test Match at the Oval in 1902, which turned defeat into victory for England. This year, so far, he has not done much in the Test Matches. Against South Africa in June he only made 3, and last week 16 and 1. He did not play against Australia in June.

DRAWN BY FRANK REYNOLDS.

Jessop's athletic fielding and dynamic batting made him a natural subject for cartoonists and illustrators, including Frank Reynolds in *The Sketch* in July 1912. The caption reads: "In batting he has attitudes and strokes entirely his own."

Three amateurs – Stanley Jackson (left), Jessop (centre) and captain Archie MacLaren (right) – lead the England XI onto the field at Bramall Lane, Sheffield, for the third Test match.

Stanley Jackson's coolness under pressure made him the ideal partner for Jessop during his great innings, but their personalities were like 'chalk and cheese' and they rarely saw eye-to-eye.

The fourteen-man Australian team of 1902 was feted as one of the best to have toured England. Joe Darling, the captain, sits in the centre of the middle row; Hugh Trumble, their star bowler, is third from the left at the back, next to the bowler-hatted manager, Ben Wardill.

Charles Fry: extraordinary sportsman, extraordinary man. He played in three of the five Test matches in the series and wrote authoritative daily reports for the *Daily Express* on all of them. He was one of Jessop's biggest fans.

The Oval's main scoreboard shows England at around their lowest point of the Test, 89 for six in their first innings and well adrift of Australia's score of 324. Jessop has just been dismissed for 13.

A photographer working for *Country Life* captures an image of George Hirst (left) and Len Braund leaving the pavilion to resume England's battered first innings after lunch on the second day.

The only known photograph of Jessop batting during his sensational innings on the final afternoon. As happens several times, he is hitting left-armer Jack Saunders into the leg side.

England have won the game and the players hurry for the pavilion as spectators begin to swarm over the field. 'You simply had to rush with the crowd or you would have been jumped on,' said one spectator. 'The torrent of cheering surged like a great wave.'

The Oval pavilion around the time of the 1902 Test: 'the best of its kind in England'.

Jonny Bairstow celebrates reaching his century against New Zealand at Trent Bridge in 2022. It took him 77 balls, the second fastest hundred for England after Jessop.

Harry Brook, seen here batting in Pakistan in 2022, scored 87 off 65 balls during the Rawalpindi Test, having struck an 80-ball century earlier in the game. No England batsman has scored more than 1,000 Test runs for England at a faster rate than Brook.

Head coach Brendon McCullum, seen here taking part in a six-hitting competition during team training, and Ben Stokes, looking on, urged England's Test batsmen to play with a ceaseless aggression not seen since Jessop.

low he got to the second ball, describing it as a remarkable shot, 'down on his knee'.

Nor was he always able to keep his balance. 'Stalwart' in the *Scottish Referee* said that having hit the last of the four successive boundaries, Jessop ended up 'down on his knees as if to supplicate the gods in favour of the Old Country'.

This burst of 17 runs in one over created a hubbub throughout the entire ground. Anyone charged with keeping abreast of the score was having their work cut out, and one spectator noted that 'the scoreboard boy had a lively time'. At about this point, someone spotted the Australian manager, Major Wardill, standing close to the Colonial enclosure, still smiling cheerily, seemingly unaware that the game had shifted on its axis. All around, the crowd was in tumult, as the *Edinburgh Evening News* graphically described:

> The crowd could scarcely contain itself, and when he [Jessop] outdid all his previous efforts by hitting four consecutive fours off the irresistible Saunders to the square-leg boundary the crowd looked like a white poplar tree in a storm. Everyone stood up and waved something, a hat or a handkerchief or a hand, and the buses passing down the flanking [Harleyford] road pulled up to see the cause of the excitement.

One of these four pulls or sweeps against Saunders may have been the shot captured by George Beldam in the only known surviving photograph of Jessop's innings. The whole of the field is not in shot but from what is visible it is clear there must be several men in the deep; Darling is known to have put two extra men onto the leg-side boundary after the first two hits.

Unnoticed, Jessop's first four of the over took him to his best Test score of 58, passing the 55 he had made at Sheffield. He was doing enough to justify his selection.

Darling had no choice but to pull Saunders out of the attack. His two principal men had got through 39 overs unchanged but had not managed a wicket since the 19th. At 145 for five – Jessop 72, Jackson 48 – Australia's captain turned to Armstrong's wrist-spin in an effort to stifle Jessop. Armstrong did not spin his leg-breaks extravagantly, but they turned enough to make a batsman watchful and, bowling wide of leg stump to a packed leg-side field of five men on the boundary and a short leg, he offered few safe means of picking up runs. For a while the move worked well: Jessop was not comfortable with this line of attack and in Armstrong's first over he managed only a single off the final ball. 'Mr Jessop must have longed for Mr Saunders again,' Lyttelton wrote in *The Times*. 'He could not hit Mr Armstrong's leg balls ... in his usual style.'

Trumble backed up Armstrong's good start with a tight over of his own from which Jessop managed only one scoring shot – one that brought up the century partnership, of which Jessop had contributed 75 and Jackson 18. By Armstrong's second over, Jessop had decided the best way to counter his spoiling tactics was to step back to leg and target the vacant off side, and the first time he tried this it brought four. 'Jessop cut him [Armstrong] by jumping well to the leg side of the wicket,' the *Daily Mail* stated. 'Thus he avoided the fieldsmen clumped down on the on side.' Later in the same over Jessop managed to find a way through the leg side anyway, but there were still balls he was having to leave alone. Armstrong was having some success in keeping the scoring in check.

Increasingly, the game became one of cat and mouse between Jessop and Darling, as the Australian captain grappled to contain him. Jessop, though, was seemingly always one step ahead. One of the best features of his innings was his placement and manipulation of the fields set by Darling. George Hirst, who batted with Jessop towards the end of his innings but would have watched the earlier stages from the pavilion, would recall: 'It was a great treat to me watching their bowlers' faces change with wonder and consternation in their efforts to try and block his shots by changing the field.' The *Illustrated Sporting and Dramatic News* enjoyed watching the struggle just as much:

No matter how Darling placed his men, the ball generally went where there was nobody to stop it. When Jessop hit into the air, the ball fell well short of the fieldsman, went high over his head, or dropped among the spectators. In fact, it was quite a masterpiece of accurate as well as 'hard and often' hitting. It was quite funny, when Darling placed his men fairly deep, to see Jessop urge the ball away for a single; and, when the Australian captain brought some of his men closer in, to watch Jessop clout the ball over their heads. He seemed to have a particular liking for Saunders' deliveries, which, rising comparatively slowly from the pitch, he was able to time carefully, and smack away to leg. Little wonder that the fielders scarcely knew which way to turn, but this was all part of Jessop's way of disrupting even the best-organised teams.

Even as Jessop ran amok, the lot of the spectator remained an anxious one. Things were going well, but could it last? A Mr Wheeler of West Worthing remembered the tales with which his father had regaled him as a small boy of watching Jessop bat that day: 'The part that always remained in my memory was my father stating that everybody nearly had heart failure when Jessop hit out. The man sitting next to my father said, "I cannot look any more. Tell me when he is out," and covered his face with his hands. There was another roar as Jessop hit again. "Is he out?" "No," my father replied, "another four".'

The more England's score mounted, the more people realised they still had a chance. But then, just after Armstrong's second over to Jessop, disaster struck. Trumble was once again bowling to Jackson, who had not scored a run against him for an age. Trumble kept pitching slightly shorter and shorter, and Jackson kept pushing the ball back, thinking he was smothering the danger. But finally one bounced a little more, and Jackson could not keep down his defensive prod. The ball flew back low and Trumble stuck out a long, lean right arm to pouch it.

Scarcely able to believe what he had done, Jackson banged his bat into his pad and swished the air in fury as he walked back past Trumble and Jessop to the pavilion. 'Though he was savage with himself for his failure,' Stainton wrote, 'he had played a rare part.' In the previous 11 overs, Jackson had scored 4 to Jessop's 43, but overall had stayed with him in a partnership worth 109. England were now 157 for six, still needing 106. Australia were back on top.

16

WEDNESDAY 13 AUGUST: 3.03 P.M. TO 3.17 P.M.

JESSOP BLAZES TO HIS CENTURY

THE LOSS OF Jackson might have made Jessop hesitate about how he should approach things. As long as he stayed there, England were in the game. Should he rein himself in? Caution never crossed his mind, it seems. He decided to embrace the danger and go even harder. As George Hirst came out to take Jackson's place, and passed Jessop on his way to the far wicket to face the final ball of Trumble's over, Jessop was seen to speak a few words to him. We do not know what was said, but the gist of it was soon apparent: the Australians are on the ropes, we keep going at them. Jessop certainly did not suggest that Hirst should drop anchor and leave the scoring to him, because in the early stages of Hirst's innings he played as though intent on making himself a second Jessop. Darling seemed to be expecting as much because from the outset he kept men on the boundary whoever was on strike. It is possible that both batsmen also had one eye on the skies, because in the previous few overs clouds had built up and rain once again looked possible. If it was going to rain, the faster England scored the 106 runs they needed the better.

That said, Hirst's innings almost did not get off the ground. On his very first ball he was struck on the pad and it looked to many as though umpire Richardson might give him out. Jessop, standing at the other end of the pitch, had feared an early lbw shout. 'Knowing Hirst's propensity for getting in front of the wicket, I dreaded an appeal against him coming at any moment for lbw,' he recalled. 'And it came sure enough, for Hughie Trumble bowling round the wicket pitched a ball which seemed to me to favour middle and off stump, which turning quickly struck George on the pads ankle high … I thought he must be out, but I was mistaken.' Edward Dowson, a Surrey player watching from the pavilion, thought it 'the plumbest of plumb lbws'. But Richardson's finger stayed down and Trumble picked up the ball without evident discontent. Kelly's indignation was plain.

It was the nearest the Australians would come to dismissing Hirst, a man whose iron temperament was perfectly fitted to situations such as these. Soon he and Jessop were flying along in a short but explosive stand that brought 30 runs in the next three overs. According to Stainton, little thought was given to Jessop closing in on his century because the match hung so finely in the balance:

> Though Jessop was not out, what had to come was, on paper, none too good, though we knew what sort of batsman Hirst was. 'Let Jessop fall, and the end is at hand,' the quidnuncs said. But Jessop did not fall. He seemed the more nerved by the downfall of his partner; he seemed

to feel that, so far as the crowd was concerned, the issue rested very largely with him. His cricket to the end of the innings was of a remarkable character ... the nearness to his hundred seemed to strike no one for the moment. I have never known a crowd in which individualism was so sunk in the desire for a team's success. It mattered not who got runs so long as they were got, and as, with Hirst as his partner, Jessop went on his scoring spree the uproar grew into one long and tremendous cheer. The discomfiture of the Colonials obviously grew; even the smile of the Major [Wardill] became a trifle strained.

Off Armstrong's next over, Jessop worked a single first ball and Hirst then enterprisingly managed to get two balls through the thickly set leg-side field behind square for fours despite two of Australia's best fielders, Darling and Hill, patrolling that part of the rope.

Then Jessop launched his most spectacular assault yet on Trumble, hitting him for 12 with a straight four high into the pavilion, two drives for two, one of which was prevented from being a boundary only by a great stop from Hill, and then another four, also hit high to the pavilion, this time off what one observer described as a half-volley – a rarity for Trumble and another indicator of the pressure Jessop was applying. 'The crowd, now fairly let loose on the chance of an English victory, cheered again and again,' the *Sheffield Daily Telegraph* noted. 'Its roar might have been heard in the provinces almost, for its continuous outbreak was akin to the rattle of cannon as Jessop went on thumping.' Another newspaper report estimated that the cheering lasted 'a full minute'.

That Jessop should mete out such treatment to Australia's best bowler was in itself sensational, but to add to the sense of wonder and awe among onlookers was the size of the two straight hits into the pavilion, particularly the second. Most accounts seemed to accept that the first hit landed on the large awning that covered the outdoor seats in front of the pavilion – onto which Jessop had already hit one ball from Trumble before lunch.

There was some confusion as to actually how far, or high, the second hit went, probably due to the fact that anyone sitting in the press box would have been unable to tell precisely where it landed, beyond it being somewhere high up to their left. From their vantage point, they would simply have known that it had gone very high, but they would have needed witnesses better placed than themselves to clarify precisely where it had pitched. The evening papers, who were under the heaviest time constraints, tended to confine themselves to saying simply that Jessop had made two hits on top of the pavilion, meaning somewhere into the area of the pavilion, but publications with more time to gather information were more explicit in their details over the hours (and days) that followed.

Several made reference to the ball clearing or going over the 'pavilion' or 'players' pavilion', by which they meant simply the middle tier of the building which contained the dressing-rooms and balconies from which the players could watch the game. C. B. Fry in his report for the *Daily Express* the next morning stated that the second hit had landed 'high up above the balcony'. Stainton in his evening paper piece said Jessop had twice in the over made hits 'on the pavilion' but in his morning paper piece the following day provided the most explicit claim yet, stating that Jessop had 'landed the ball by a tremendous soaring drive on to the very top of the building itself'. The *St James's Gazette* similarly stated that he put the ball 'onto the pavilion roof itself'.

No newspaper reporter suggested that the ball carried right over the roof of the uppermost tier. Had this happened it would, apart from anything else, have necessitated a search for the ball, and if one could not be found, a call for a replacement – and probably the awarding of six runs. However, a piece that appeared in the *Dover Express* nine days after the game by 'A Dover Visitor', who seemingly watched the game from the far end of the ground, claimed that 'twice in an over the ball landed at the top of the balcony of the pavilion, and once had a journey clean over the building'. Another eyewitness, Canon Maurice Fitzgerald, writing in the *Cricketer* in 1943, suggested that both hits landed onto the building rather than the awning, stating that 'these drives – to on and off respectively – pitch on the roofs of the covered stands'.

Interestingly, at the time of Jessop's death in 1955, *Wisden*'s obituary stated that one hit was actually caught on the players' balcony by H. K. Foster, the Worcestershire captain, who was able to watch the game because his county's match against Yorkshire in Harrogate had finished a day early. It is surprising that, had Jessop hit the ball directly to the players' balcony and it had then been caught by Foster, this claim did not receive wider attention. It is also conceivable, of course, that the ball landed on the roof tiles above before dropping onto the balcony where Foster was sitting, and he threw it back onto the field, or onto the awning and thence down onto the concrete steps below.

A Dr L. Gill, of Bicester, whose father had overheard Jessop's exchange with MacLaren as he left the pavilion to start his innings, wrote in 1974 that he had witnessed the final day of the Test as a ten-year-old boy and recalled, imprecisely but nonetheless interestingly: 'When Jessop was approaching his century he hit an almighty swipe ... onto the pavilion steps, so making his century with a six. Unfortunately the ball rolled back onto the ground [playing area] and according to the rules at that time, he only scored four. The protests of the crowd were very insistent, but to no avail.' This suggests that the idea that each ground had its own 'local rules' about what constituted a six still held sway with the public, who may well have been unaware that in Test matches it had been agreed that sixes would only be given for out-of-the-ground hits. Some members of the crowd, it seems, were urging the umpires to award Jessop a 'six'.

Ben Travers, another youthful spectator of the game, says he remembers that both these big hits off Trumble resulted in the ball ending up on the canvas awning, but his account is also imprecise in some respects, hardly surprisingly as he was writing almost 80 years after the event.

The 12 runs Jessop scored off Trumble took his score to 96, so even if he had been awarded an additional two runs for the second 'six' – as Dr Gill's letter suggested was urged upon the umpires by sections of the crowd – his score would only have been 98, but there does seem to have been some confusion as to exactly which scoring shot brought up Jessop's hundred. It is possible that the operators of the main scoreboard were unsure whether Jessop had just hit a six, or indeed had even just hit two sixes, or possibly they had just lost count, and as a consequence Jessop's score was briefly posted incorrectly. One report said that when he got to his hundred his score went to 102 rather than 100.

Had over-the-boundary hits been awarded six runs as a matter of course at this time, this third hit by Jessop off Trumble into the pavilion (the first having come before lunch) would have taken his score to 102, and he would have reached his hundred off one fewer balls than was actually the case.

Armstrong bowled again. Hirst took a single off the first ball to put Jessop back on strike, needing four for his hundred, and leave England needing 84 for victory. Jessop again stepped away to leg to access the off side, and with a hard late cut similar to the one he had played earlier against Armstrong the ball sped away to the third-man boundary. Pandemonium immediately broke out. Jessop had his century. People were shouting and screaming, and straw boaters were being thrown into the air. Everyone went mad with excitement.

Modern matches are often brought to a halt for individuals to celebrate personal milestones; it is expected that they will acknowledge the applause and savour the moment. But in earlier, less self-indulgent, less demonstrative times, it was much rarer for such things to happen. But on this occasion the game did stop, such was the reception for Jessop's landmark. 'Round the terraces, in the stands, and in the pavilion the spectators rose to their feet, cheering enthusiastically, men waving their hats, and ladies their handkerchiefs,' the *Daily Mail* reported. 'The demonstration continued for some minutes.' Others also noted the hold-up. The *Dover Express* correspondent said 'the vast assemblage made such a demonstration that for a couple of minutes the game was stopped'. The *Nottingham*

Evening Post said 'the scene lasted some minutes'. Only in the Australian stand was the reaction muted; in fact one eyewitness said: 'There was not a movement. The touch of partiality was never more strongly shown.'

How Jessop himself reacted is not known. Might he perhaps have raised his bat in recognition of the applause? What, if anything, did Hirst or the Australians say? Some commentators did not fail to note that Jessop's moment of triumph was also a bitter pill to swallow for those detractors who thought him not good enough to play Test cricket.

As has already been mentioned, the exact timings of events were hard to pin down because contemporary estimates tended to be just that, estimates, but most of the early reports stated that Jessop batted 75 minutes for his hundred. It was common for timings to be given to the nearest five minutes, although the *Yorkshire Post* stated that Jessop reached his hundred 'after a stay of less than 80 minutes', which perhaps suggests the 75-minute estimates were on the low side. Anyone doing a broad calculation probably reckoned that Jessop batted 20 minutes before lunch and 55 minutes afterwards, but the evidence relating to the timings of Jessop's – and England's – innings, and how many balls he faced, will be looked at fully in Chapters 20–22.

Of more immediate concern was what Jessop did next. Moments later he swung Armstrong into the leg side off a rather uppish hit that fell close to Hopkins at deep square leg before bouncing away for four. The narrowness of this escape may have slightly thrown Jessop, because when he got a similar delivery later in the over he reached forward again but did not commit as he had before. 'Hesitating to make the full square-leg drive, [he] cocked the ball round with a quarter-stroke to Noble at short leg,' Fry wrote. Stainton called it his one weak stroke of the innings. The Australians who a few minutes earlier had been downcast were now jubilant again. Noble threw the ball up with glee, while the Australian troopers in the crowd filled the air with a cascade of khaki hats. As Jessop turned to go back to the pavilion, Kelly patted him on the back and the Australian players applauded him heartily, admiration mingled with relief.

In a spine-tingling moment, everyone rose again and continued cheering until Jessop disappeared from view, and if ever Jessop felt emotionally overwrought at what he had done it was surely now. 'As the man of the moment walked up the pavilion steps through a long line of admirers every fibre of his body must have thrilled at the magnificent reception which he had so richly earned,' the *Morning Leader* stated.

Jessop had scored 104 of the 139 runs added since he came to the wicket, with the other runs made up of 27 off the bat (Jackson 18, Hirst 9) and eight extras. Such was the drama at the end of the game that the evening newspapers did not have as much space as they might have done for a rounded appraisal of Jessop's innings that night, but Stainton offered this assessment for his morning paper:

It was not mere hitting; I should like to make that clear. It was a combination of coolness and resolution, a combination of well-judged and powerful hitting with excellent defence when the bowling was too good to be hit. But it was in the complete and utter audacity of his hitting of balls that most men would have been content to play that the innings stood out most prominently, and in this respect there could have been nothing so fine from anyone else. Only a Jessop could have played the innings that Jessop played yesterday, and his return to the pavilion was one which a returning hero from South Africa might have envied.

As Jessop walked back, doubtless fearing he had not done enough to help England win, the responsibility for seeing them home now shifted firmly to Hirst. England were 187 for seven, still needing another 76. There was much work still to be done. The previous day there had been a break of around 20 minutes from 3.25 p.m. for the change between innings. There would be no such interruption in play this time and there would be no tea interval. The players were to keep going. There was no respite for anyone until the game was done, for good or ill.

17

WEDNESDAY 13 AUGUST: 3.17 P.M. TO 4.24 P.M.

HOW THE MATCH WAS WON

JESSOP MAY HAVE got out with work still to be done, but he had brought the target of 263 within range, and done so with such speed and violence that he had given the England innings a momentum it would never lose. What still needed to be done was within the scope of the players left. Hirst was the best bowling all-rounder in the country, was having an excellent game and had scored 9 off the six balls he had faced since narrowly surviving his lbw call. The three who would help him – Bill Lockwood, Dick Lilley and Wilfred Rhodes – were all capable batsmen. Lockwood had 15 first-class centuries to his name, Lilley had ten and Rhodes had scored his maiden hundred the previous season. Rhodes over time in fact would develop into a highly accomplished batsman, opening the batting in Test matches and sharing a then record opening partnership of 323 with Jack Hobbs in Australia in 1912. He would amass more than 40,000 first-class runs.

They would all play their parts in seeing their team across the line in partnerships worth 27, 34 and 15 unbroken.

A square mass of uncompromising muscle, Hirst effortlessly took upon himself the role of senior man. A number of reports refer to him smiling as he went about the tricky business of winning the match – 'a broad happy smile', Stainton wrote, 'which showed that, as far as he was concerned, there was no fear, no want of heart or pluck'. One of Roland Hill's four cartoons for the *Evening News* next morning was of Hirst's smiling face.

Nor was Hirst going to be hurried either; between every ball he took a breathing space and twirled his bat in preparation. R. L. Hodgson described how he shaped over these closing stages:

> Hirst had a habit of settling his pads between each ball; he would draw his hand up one leg, then up the other; he never failed to carry out that little ritual. He would also pat the ground and remove tiny obstacles. Hirst was taking no chances … But the terrible length of time it occupied! Those long drawn-out, nerve-racking minutes, whilst the result hung in the balance!

Each of his partners showed immense character, too. Lockwood played only one scoring shot, very early on, but hung in grimly thereafter; Lilley went for his shots, alarming the crowd with some uppish hits, but added vital runs; and Rhodes was utterly imperturbable at the end even though Darling's fielders crept up close whenever he was on strike. When the ninth wicket fell he strolled out, fastening the elastic fixings of his gloves, chatted to Hirst and patted the pitch.

While this was going on, Stainton, the Sheffield reporter, was asked by an anxious London journalist sitting next to him in the press box whether Rhodes had any pluck; in other words, could he be relied on in this gravest of crises. Stainton said: 'He has no fear.' When Hirst went up to Rhodes and exchanged a word with him, the crowd yelled with joy, the *Daily Mail* noted. 'Hirst, they said, was imparting a word of instruction.'

Whatever was said when Hirst and Rhodes first met in the middle is unknown. The claim that Hirst advised his young partner, 'We'll get 'em in singles', was propagated by Neville Cardus many years later and would be dismissed as fabrication by Rhodes. Nor is that how they scored all the runs, although Hirst mainly dealt in singles because Darling set his fields so deep to him. Rhodes said that he could not recall what words were passed between the co-villagers. For two Yorkshiremen with a match on the line, not much needed to be said, though it seems that Hirst was taking no chances. In his report of the last-wicket stand, Pullin in the *Yorkshire Post* commented of Hirst: 'His game, and one that he evidently impressed upon his partner, was to get the runs by singles, and to take absolutely no risk. Up and down went his arm like a semaphore warning his partner when not to run, though, truth to tell, Rhodes was every whit as cool and self-controlled as himself.'

*

It was a close thing, though. The pitch was not as difficult as it had been in the morning, but it was still a bowler's wicket. With Jessop gone, Darling immediately withdrew Armstrong from the attack, as he had served his purpose, and brought back Saunders in tandem with the tireless Trumble. This move would not work and arguably Darling would have been better off turning straightaway to Noble, rather than later, because Noble kept a tighter check on the scoring. As it was, Hirst pulled Saunders' first ball through square leg for four before driving his second to the boundary through the off side. Not long after, Hirst off-drove him for another four before almost coming unstuck attempting something similar again, nearly hitting a catch to Armstrong at deep mid-off. Lockwood, meanwhile, was enduring a torrid time as Trumble worked away at trying to trap him lbw, but somehow survived seven overs in which time he and Hirst raised the score from 187 to 214, Hirst's share 24, Lockwood's 2. Finally, Trumble went round the wicket and got his man.

Trumble's change of tactics was prompted by a realisation that by bowling over the wicket he was making the ball break too much; he needed to make the batsman play more. So he went round the wicket with two short legs standing close in. By these tactics he gained an excellent chance of a catch, but having secured Lockwood's wicket with an lbw he found it hard to achieve another one because he was bowling from the extreme right-hand end of the crease but still needing to pitch the ball in line with the stumps. The angles were against him and the Australians. 'The Colonials [were] appealing for everything hereabouts,' the *Nottingham Evening Post* stated.

Lilley stalked out moodily with England eight wickets down, still needing 49. He consulted with Hirst and it soon became clear that they had agreed that Lilley would be the aggressor while Hirst played things safe. Lilley's start was hardly serene as he nearly gave a catch and then almost played on against Saunders. He was also nearly caught and bowled by Trumble, but the ball travelled just out of the bowler's reach. At the end of the over the target had come down to exactly 40, and both batsmen then struck off-side boundaries against Saunders in an over that yielded 11, bringing the runs needed down to just 29. Darling had seen enough of Saunders and pulled him out of the attack for the last time in favour of Noble. By now, a light drizzle was falling. It was not enough to halt play, but the players requested more sawdust.

Things were getting desperate. The Australian fielders made a number of fine stops but despite Noble starting with two tight overs the pressure was released by Lilley bravely opening his shoulders against Trumble and getting four through the off side. But when the indefatigable Trumble had Lilley on strike again shortly after, he signalled to his captain at mid-off to drop several yards deeper, and sure enough a few balls later Lilley lashed out again and Darling intercepted a hard, skimming drive with both hands above his head. It was a fine catch and Darling was quickly surrounded by grateful team-mates. Lilley had scored 16 valuable runs and with Hirst's help had briefly made England favourites. Everything was now back in the balance.

England were 248 for nine, still needing 15. It was just after 4 p.m. and it had been a long, emotional day already, but the most painful moments were now upon everyone. 'How the crowd surged and swayed!' the visitor from Dover wrote of the moments after Lilley was out. 'Men were continually removing and wiping their pince-nez, and nobody could sit still.' The *Daily Express* detected similar erratic behaviour: 'England's backers were tipsy with excitement ... some laughed, some could not sit still, others dug their nails in their hands, while one man was seen folding up his gloves quite methodically, and making a parcel of them in a score-card, quite beside himself.' Every house overlooking the ground, every tram car and omnibus now reined up on Harleyford Road had occupants shouting encouragement to the two Yorkshiremen.

Across the Thames in the West End gentlemen's clubs, members were in suspended animation, waiting for the latest updates from the telegraph. 'In the clubs, men lived over the news machines,' the *Sheffield Evening Telegraph* reported. 'Every whirr, every click of the instrument, sent a thrill through those followers of a game perhaps three miles distant. When it came to the partnership between Rhodes and Hirst a sudden wave of pessimism passed over many. "Here's the end now," was the common remark every time the machine ticked out its time, before it gave the score.' At Kempton Park there was supposedly a race meeting going on, but the horses were forgotten in favour of waiting for telegrams from The Oval. 'The interest, the pent-up feelings, reminded me of the grim days when the war was at its height,' Stainton wrote.

Darling consulted with Trumble again. There was one ball left in the over and Rhodes, the new batsman, was facing. By an extraordinary coincidence, Rhodes found himself going out to the middle with the number of runs needed precisely the same as it was in the previous Test at Old Trafford, only then he was batting at No 10 rather than No 11, and there were two wickets remaining, rather than one. In the last match he had seen Dick Lilley and Fred Tate get out, and was stranded on 4 not out. Could he do more this time to ensure the game was won, and not lost?

From this point until the game was done, the bowlers would approach the wicket amid a deathly silence before a terrific cheer rent the air every time a run was scored, every time the ball was defended, every time it was left alone. The first ball rapped Rhodes on the hand before falling safe, Rhodes tapping down the offending piece of turf from which it had leapt. Some of the Australian troopers were seen moving down to the rails in front of the pavilion, in readiness to celebrate should the last wicket fall.

Hirst cut Noble coolly for a single to bring up his own fifty but was hit on the shoulder by Hill's throw to the non-striker's end, making him wince. This left Rhodes to deal with some wide tempters from Noble, inviting him to give a catch to an array of close fielders. He resisted most of them but did play at one and was fortunate to get four runs off the edge.

This brought the target down to 10 and it moved into single figures when Hirst took a quick single off the first ball of Trumble's next over. Moments later there were gasps around the ground as Rhodes was almost caught by a diving Trumper at short leg. With Hirst happy to keep taking the singles Darling was offering him, Rhodes was back on strike early in Trumble's next over and this time an edge did carry to a fieldsman, but only to the outstretched fingers of Armstrong at slip, and he had no real chance to get his hand under the ball. The crowd let out a groan of anguish. One eyewitness described it as 'a difficult chance off a slow dropping ball which came to him very low down'. At around this point the drizzle became heavier which, Lilley said in an interview with a Birmingham paper the following morning, made batting somewhat easier: 'up to that time the bowlers could always get a good deal of work on the ball'. One way or another, the game would be done in a few minutes and play continued. Apart from Rhodes' escape, this was a good over for England because he and Hirst stole three singles to bring the runs required down to five.

These near misses for England's No 11 and the agonisingly small reductions in the runs needed raised the pressure to fresh heights. A number of middle-aged spectators found the strain too much and left the ground, their nerves so shattered that they would not buy a paper giving the result in case it was a defeat. 'During the last hour, the tension was so great that the vast crowd became almost hysterical ... trembling and over-wrought,' the *Daily Mail* said. Hirst and Rhodes were being offered no end of advice from the crowd: 'Lay back in your ground', 'run another', 'run a three'. A burry man up from the country shouted: 'For Heaven's sake, Hirst, put us out of our agony!' Jessop and the other England players, their parts in the match over, sat huddled on the dressing-room balcony, helpless to influence events. 'The closing minutes of the game were positively painful,' Jessop wrote later. 'We experienced thrills of anxiety sufficient to last a lifetime.'

Noble bowled again. Hirst tapped the ball into the leg side and he and Rhodes scampered through for a single which was suddenly turned into two when Hopkins sent in a wild throw. 'The Oval seemed to rock with the shouts,' said one witness. Hirst was laughing, even Rhodes was smiling, and Noble gave a rueful grin. Hirst then pushed the ball gently up towards mid-on for one. Two needed.

There was not a sound as Trumble began what transpired to be the final over, the Australian fielders crouched in the attitude of wicketkeepers. Hirst waited until the third ball for his chance, stepping out and driving coolly up to long-on for the one run that, amid tremendous cheering, brought the scores level. Some observers thought that there was the possibility of two runs, which would have won the game, but Hirst was content to play safe. But there was also a suggestion that the main scoreboard had lost track, one account stating that Hirst, after going through for the first run, 'turned expectantly to the scoring board, but only a tie was chronicled'.

If that was the case, he was not the only one unsure as to the state of the game. A clergyman thought Hirst's run had secured England's win and began running across the ground at full pace towards the pavilion. He was so excited he did not realise his mistake until he was well out in the field with a policeman in pursuit. The cleric might have been relieved to know that others were also struggling to cope. The *Nottingham Evening Post* reported:

> The crowd went dangerously near to losing its head, never to recover it again. Everybody howling and screaming, and shouting, and singing, and generally seeing how much noise each and everyone could make ... I saw staid old gentlemen howling like wild Dervishes, and doing and saying all sorts of ridiculous things. As far as the eye could see, this sort of thing was going on to a perfect babel of sound.

Everybody rose from their seats in anticipation of the winning hit. Trumble shifted his field a little, and Gregory came up almost to Rhodes's bat. Trumble's next ball was too good for Rhodes to score off, but the one after that was overpitched, Rhodes leaned into it, and it raced away along the carpet through the gap between bowler and mid-on, into the long field.

Whether it was one run or four runs, no one waited to see. Rhodes simply hurtled up the pitch and kept on running all the way to the pavilion. England had won.

ENGLAND: SECOND INNINGS

Archie MacLaren	b Saunders	2
Lionel Palairet	b Saunders	6
Johnny Tyldesley	b Saunders	0
Tom Hayward	c Kelly b Saunders	7
Stanley Jackson	c and b Trumble	49
Len Braund	c Kelly b Trumble	2
Gilbert Jessop	c Noble b Armstrong	104
George Hirst	not out	58
Bill Lockwood	lbw b Trumble	2
Dick Lilley	c Darling b Trumble	16
Wilfred Rhodes	not out	6
Extras (byes 5, leg-byes 6)		11
Total (9 wickets, 66.5 overs)		**263**

Fall of wickets: 5-1 (MacLaren), 5-2 (Tyldesley), 10-3 (Palairet), 31-4 (Hayward), 48-5 (Braund), 157-6 (Jackson), 187-7 (Jessop), 214-8 (Lockwood), 248-9 (Lilley)

Bowling: Trumble 33.5-4-108-4, Saunders 24-3-105-4, Armstrong 4-0-28-1, Noble 5-0-11-0

18

WEDNESDAY 13 AUGUST:
4.24 P.M. TO 10 P.M.

THE RACE TO GET THE NEWS INTO PRINT

PANDEMONIUM ENSUED. As the ball sped past the last fielder, a wild yell went up around the ring and thousands of men leapt over the ropes and made tolerable attempts to fly to the pavilion and salute their heroes. 'You simply had to rush with the crowd or you would have been jumped on,' said one, caught up in the melee. 'The torrent of cheering surged like a great wave – everyone seemed [to be] taxing their vocal powers to the very utmost capacity – [and] hats and articles quite unused to aerial passages were rising and falling in all directions.' Having run to the Vauxhall End of the pitch, Hirst had the farthest to go to escape the pursuers. He ran hard but was caught just short of the pavilion gate by a spectator who dragged him back, and he was hoisted shoulder-high and carried into the pavilion precincts where, eventually, he was rescued by six policemen.

George Beldam captured the invasion in his final image from the upper echelons of the pavilion. It showed umpires

Richardson and White gathering stumps and bails, while 11 of the 13 players on the field can be seen running or jogging for safety, three of them not yet off the square, while in the distance hundreds of spectators are charging across the field. Taking in the scene from the press box, Fry wrote: 'The Australians, with the batsmen, dash for the pavilion, with thousands pouring into the field from each wing; rushing for the pavilion, they manage to carry Hirst the last half dozen yards, then settle down to yell.'

A large crowd quickly built up in front of the pavilion, where they remained for half an hour despite the rain gradually falling more heavily, and destined not to relent for two hours. 'They cheered and cheered, and cheered again,' Jimmy Catton wrote. 'They were drunk with delight and they compelled the players to bow on the verandah.' Jessop and Hirst were the players most in demand, and such were the demands from the spectators that they and other England players had to return again and again to the windows of the pavilion to wave to them. 'Outside the pavilion the crowd long remained, calling for the principal actors in the great performance to show themselves, and when they did do so the hurricane of cheers broke out with renewed vehemence,' Pullin wrote in the *Yorkshire Post*. Fry also noted how gratified the public were by the sight of Jessop and Hirst. 'They scream, they shake hands with perfect strangers, sing about persons being jolly good fellows, shriek their delight at an English triumph for half an hour, then rain sends them home – England has won in time!'

It was clear that had not Jessop scored his runs so phenomenally fast, England would not have got to their target before the weather denied them again.

No one present could remember scenes such as these before, and it only cemented in the minds of everyone that they had witnessed something completely out of the ordinary. The *Daily Mail* the next morning called it: 'The greatest cricketing drama of modern times.' V. A. S. Beanland in the *Leeds Mercury* acclaimed it as 'perhaps the finest sporting finish that has ever been seen in a Test match'. The wild celebrations were a direct consequence of the pent-up feelings of earlier: there had to be a release. Even those in the Colonial stand offered up 'Three cheers' to the England team.

*

Things were no less chaotic in the press box. Not only were the reporters as frazzled as everyone else, but those working for evening newspapers had deadlines upon them. A finish to the game at almost half past four left most with little or no time to play with, and they were grappling with pieces that needed to do justice both to Jessop's sensational innings and a pulsating finish. Some admitted they struggled to maintain their usual calm, independent demeanour in such a frenzied atmosphere.

The first rule of press boxes down the ages is: do not cheer, do not clap. It is important to appear neutral, even when you are not. All these things were and are easy to say, but on certain occasions quite hard to do. This was one such time.

Alfred Pullin inserted into a lengthy report for the *Yorkshire Evening Post* a confessional aside: 'At 3.50pm, 29 runs are wanted. What an exciting time! How can one write?' And once the match was done, he drew his readers into another secret: 'Even some of the prosaic occupants of the press box discarded their natural and phlegmatic decorum.'

He may have had in mind Catton, who admitted during a lengthy analysis for the *Athletic News* several days later that when Rhodes hit the winning run he had breached the usual etiquette: 'I plead guilty to standing on a chair and forgetting my profession as I cheered ... I hope I may be pardoned. In spirit I was with the thousands upon thousands who swarmed on to the playing piece in the endeavour to see the players as they sprinted for the pavilion.' He further explained: 'I live these joyous seconds again as I write, for a chronicler though I be, I am an Englishman first.' He also broke a favourite pipe in his excitement. Glancing around the press box at the end of the game, V. A. S. Beanland spotted, in the corner near the door, 'a veteran of the field with tears running unashamedly down his cheeks'.

Stainton confessed to his readers in his evening paper piece the next day that the excitement may have adversely affected the quality of everyone's copy. 'In the press box, yesterday, the tension was tremendous, and in the last hour, as each run was made, seasoned journalists had to own a strain which told badly against good work. I am afraid that whatever may have been written about the finish, and indeed about the last innings, as a whole, must fall sadly short of what the play deserved.'

Shortly after the finish, several journalists went into the pavilion to seek out the players. Who they spoke to may have depended on their social class and that of the player; whether the Honourable Stanley Jackson would have deigned to speak to the Fourth Estate's lower ranks must be doubted. To their relief, they got something out of Hirst, the man who had exhibited such nerve under pressure and finished the game with 101 runs and six wickets to his credit. 'He [Hirst] was as cool after the game was over as the proverbial cucumber,' the *Sportsman* related. '"Are you excited?" he was asked directly after the big finish. "Take my hand," he replied, and a grasp of that far from tiny member was firm as a rock. Not the slightest sign of quivering, which, under the circumstances, would have been excusable.'

As this was the last day of the last Test of their tour of England, the Australian cricketers sent up an autograph book for press representatives to sign, a rare case of the supplicated becoming supplicants. Nearly every live paper had a signatory.

Reporters who did not have deadlines to meet that evening slipped away from the ground first. These included 'Stalwart' of the *Scottish Referee*, who headed back towards the City and the newspaper offices there. 'An hour later [after the finish],' he recounted in a reflective piece the following week, 'I look in at a barber's shop in Fleet Street, and found a wreck of a colleague, who had been watching the game over the tape, having a shampoo ... [and] sorting out his grey hairs.' Frank Thorogood of the *Daily News* recalled: 'A few hours later I seek relief for shattered nerves in a London theatre, and my distinguished companion, still in a high fever, is James Catton.'

Once he had filed his piece for the morning editions, Stainton also headed to the environs of Fleet Street where he saw people catching up with the London evening papers. 'I heard one man indulge in sadly profane language last night,' he recalled the next day, 'as he opened his paper, saw the result, and turned to his friend. "Why, they've won," he exclaimed, "and I left the Oval at lunch." Then came the language. There were hundreds in that position – hundreds who had given the game up and gone back to town rather than watch England's downfall. Theirs was a sad fate!'

*

Most evening newspapers found it a challenge to get details of the result into their final editions. Many did not manage it. Those that did were mainly the bigger publications in the bigger cities, those equipped with the better telegraph services and the better lines of communication, and in the regions where cricket news was a priority – Lancashire, Yorkshire, the Midlands and to a lesser extent the West Country, as well as the bustling metropolis of London with its many news outlets. These were the places where the five Tests of the 1902 series were staged, and where the England players involved in the match came from.

The way newspapers presented their stories in 1902 was very different from today. Not only were there no photographs but there was no means of running headlines across more than one column. Instead, multi-layered headlines were the fashion, so that for instance the *Gloucestershire Echo*, which naturally had a particular interest in Jessop, led off its account of the last-day drama as follows:

TODAY'S CRICKET ENGLAND v AUSTRALIA
THE FIFTH TEST MATCH

DULL WEATHER AT THE OVAL
COLONIALS ALL OUT FOR 121
ENGLAND SET 263 TO GET TO WIN
HOMESTERS' DISASTROUS START

BRILLIANT STAND BY JACKSON AND JESSOP
109 ADDED FOR THE SIXTH WICKET
THE CHELTONIAN TOPS THE CENTURY
HIRST AND LILLEY MAKE ANOTHER STAND
A MAGNIFICENT STRUGGLE
FIFTEEN RUNS TO GET WITH THE LAST MAN IN
ENGLISH TEAM VICTORIOUS BY ONE WICKET

Although the final headline revealed that England won, the *Gloucestershire Echo* had time to include in its report only one sentence on the last-wicket partnership that sealed victory. A number of other papers faced similar difficulties. The match ran too late for them to process much, if any, copy coming in from the agencies or their own correspondents at The Oval, so they fed into their pieces whatever snippets of material they had and attached headlines with as much up-to-date news as they could.

The late edition of the London *Evening News*, which ran to four pages, gave over most of two columns on page three to the Test match under the headings:

THE FIFTH TEST

The Old Country Starts Badly, but Retrieves Itself

JESSOP HITS OUT

He Scores 104 Runs in Seventy-five Minutes

The lengthy report that followed was a long account of play from the start of the day through to Jessop's dismissal at around 3.15 p.m. The scorecard that followed actually went up to the dismissal of Lockwood at around 3.40 p.m., at which point England were 214 for eight. To discover the thrilling coda, readers needed to look to the Stop Press section on the same page:

LATEST NEWS

In the event of any important news arriving when the paper is going to press it will be found in this space

TEST MATCH RESULT
ENGLAND WON BY ONE WICKET

For the newspapers in Yorkshire, the story was a particularly big one because the county had three representatives in the England team in Jackson, Hirst and Rhodes, all of whom played prominent parts on the final afternoon. The *Halifax Evening Courier* extended to a six o'clock edition in which it provided run of play through to shortly before 4 p.m., at which point England needed 25 more. Its scorecard showed England 251 for nine – still 12 runs short – but the headlines contained the important news:

TO-DAY'S CRICKET
FINAL TEST MATCH
SENSATIONAL FINISH

ENGLAND WIN BY ONE WICKET

YORKSHIREMEN TO THE RESCUE
JESSOP PASSES THE CENTURY
OLD TRAFFORD DEFEAT AVENGED

The 'Late News' section on another page provided another nugget for local audiences: 'Rhodes made the winning hit.'

What was also striking was that the vast majority of reports, and certainly those under the tightest time constraints, made little or no attempt to come up with an arresting first paragraph. The idea that a cracking opening sentence might better draw in the reader barely existed, and perhaps printing logistics made it difficult to shuffle around whole paragraphs at short notice. Broadly speaking, those with more time to produce considered articles for the following morning's papers provided better analysis, but there were some fine reports even among those facing significant deadline pressure on this madcap afternoon.

The London *Echo* had a 7 p.m. edition with an account 'By Our Special Representative' that ran to two full columns, owed nothing to the agency updates that many others leaned on heavily, and willingly passed judgement on players in a way that was then quite uncommon. Of Jessop, it said: 'To score 104 in barely 75 minutes is a task few men are equal to, and [it] needed a man of Jessop's pluck and skill to place England in such a good position.' There was even a newsy first paragraph: 'At the Oval this afternoon England gained a brilliant victory over Australia by one wicket, amidst a scene of indescribable excitement.' It also gave four sentences on the last-wicket stand between Hirst and Rhodes, which was more than most.

The most complete account of the closing stages came from Pullin in the *Yorkshire Evening Post*:

NOTES BY 'OLD EBOR'

ENGLAND'S REMARKABLE VICTORY
GRAPHIC DESCRIPTION OF THE CLOSING STAGES

Despite his tension-soaked aside some 30 minutes from the end, 'How can one write?', Pullin managed to take his readers through the seven overs that Hirst and Rhodes were together without missing any of the salient details, and mentioning Yorkshire almost as many times as he did England. The paper also got the Australian bowling figures into its scorecard, which not many of the evening papers did. The 'Last Edition Extra' of the *Manchester Evening News* also described the last-wicket partnership at length but drew heavily on agency updates, and the *Birmingham Daily Mail* provided something similar, while highlighting the plucky efforts of local boy Lilley.

Stainton's piece for the *Sheffield Evening Telegraph*, under its customary banner of 'Notes on the Game by Looker-On', did not go beyond Lockwood's wicket, some 45 minutes before the match finished and less than 30 minutes after Jessop was out, but as a description of Jessop's astonishing performance and England's fightback, it was not bettered by anyone on the day. He concluded his piece with a flourish, too, by having a dig at his rival V. A. S. Beanland, a long-time Jessop sceptic, and listing all of Jessop's scoring shots in order, presumably compiled from his own notes. It was the first time they had been published, although in fact the list as it appeared in the paper was missing two singles (ascertained from subsequent reports and marked in square brackets below). Whether the error belonged to Stainton or his printers is unclear. Stainton wrote:

His innings was more than that of a hitter, though it contained more hits than anything else, and he included a five, 17 fours, two threes, and four twos in his great-hearted display, which had lasted no more than 75 minutes.

What will Jessop's critics say now forsooth, especially that particular one who comes from Leeds?

Here are his hits in sequence:

1 2 4 1 1 4 4 1 4 1 4 1 1 1 1 4 1 [1] 3 1
3 5 1 4 4 4 4 4 1 1 1 2 4 4 [1] 4 2 2 4 4 4

They make two pretty rows.

Although there was not time for the paper to take words from Stainton on the finish, a bulletin on another page carried the following:

STOP PRESS NEWS

Hirst made the match a tie with a single from Trumble, and Rhodes won the match with a single off the same bowler

There was also a noteworthy report in an Extra Special Edition of the *Westminster Gazette*, in which it was stated that 'Jessop had received just 75 balls' for his 104. This was the first source to mention how many balls Jessop had faced for his entire stay, and it was not the figure that has come to be associated with this great innings, but even fewer.

19

THE AFTERMATH

THE MANIA did not subside. There was not much time for the players to remain at the ground because all of them had matches to play the next morning. Extraordinarily to modern eyes, the players of this era routinely got through two three-day matches per week – Sunday always being a day off – so, as in this case, they were required to travel on the evening of a match finishing on a Wednesday evening in order to be ready for a Thursday morning start. In this respect, Test matches were treated no differently from county games. England's players, moreover, owed their first loyalty to their counties.

Fortunately, some of these games were taking place in London so the players could simply return to their hotels. The Australians were due at Lord's to play the MCC, while four of the England team were to return to The Oval for a championship game between Surrey and Lancashire. Those who needed to rush off to get trains for fixtures further afield included Dick Lilley, who had to get himself to Derby, and the Somerset pair Len Braund and Lionel Palairet, who headed for Taunton. Jessop and the Yorkshire trio of Hirst, Jackson and Rhodes were all destined for Cheltenham, where Gloucestershire and Yorkshire were playing.

Bizarrely, therefore, the three team-mates who had done most to ensure Jessop's incredible innings resulted in an England victory were in opposition to him only a few hours later. Moreover, for the only time in their lives, Jessop and Jackson, the chalk-and-cheese pair who had just shared a match-shaping partnership, now faced off as rival captains, Jackson deputising for Lord Hawke who was still unavailable for Yorkshire because of his injured hand. Hawke had attended the second day of the Oval Test but missed the finale.

Trumble recalled his surprise at the strange spectacle of Hirst hurriedly changing into his clothes and leaving, 'while 20,000 people in front of the pavilion were roaring in one continuous, monotonous chant, "We want Hirst, we want Hirst."' Hirst was no doubt uncomfortable at being fêted in this way but he also had a long train journey ahead of him. The four players did not reach Cheltenham until very late.

Jessop was to spend the first week of his new life as a national hero back in and around his home town as Gloucestershire's match against Yorkshire was followed by a three-day game against the Australians as part of the Cheltenham Week, the first day of which attracted a crowd of 5,000. Like Hirst, Jessop found all the attention that came his way discomfiting.

All the participants were trying to process the amazing game that had just finished. What was striking was that, despite the series having already been settled, the match was fought from start to finish as if everything depended on it. Given that they had had the worst of conditions, the England players felt the win was no more than they deserved, and Lilley in his autobiography wrote that the Australians were magnanimous in defeat: 'I think on the play of the game we quite deserved to [win]. The Australians congratulated us – Mr Jessop most warmly of all – and I think they thought so too.'

That the Australians had so vocally questioned Jessop's abilities in the past made his success now somewhat awkward, and this point was not lost on the England players. 'The Gloucestershire captain performed little less than a miracle of batsmanship,' Lilley added, '[and] I was particularly delighted as the Australian players had repeatedly declared that Mr Jessop would never score a hundred against them.' Their principal point was that he did not have the method to do well in Australia, where the greater bounce made hitting across the line all the harder. Hill would say: 'Jessop was a great hitter. He was not a success in Australia, his highest score in Tests being only 35, but in England, where the wickets are slower, he would jump out and hit the ball very hard.' The technical nuances of the argument were lost on most people; they simply knew that the Australians maintained they knew how to get him out, anywhere, any time.

A couple of hours after the Test finished, an enterprising reporter from the *Sportsman* went to the Australians' hotel in High Holborn and managed to secure an interview with Darling and Trumble. The team were just finishing dinner in a private room when he arrived but the pair agreed to speak. One of the first questions Darling was asked was,

'What do you think of Jessop now?' Perhaps rather like Tim Paine, who, after Ben Stokes had won the Headingley Test of 2019 for England in the face of similarly long odds, played down the magnitude of his own failure by insisting 'a guy had a day out', Darling was not inclined to heap too much praise on Jessop:

> It was of course far and away the best innings he has ever played against us, either here or in Australia. He certainly hit splendidly, though he offered a couple of chances of earlier dismissal, which were not accepted … It was just as well for England that Tate had not to come in as last man, or I think we should have again just managed to pull through. As it was, Rhodes offered a difficult chance after his arrival.

The reporter noted that not only had the Australians retained the Ashes but 'their exchequer has received a big inflow from the [Oval] game', which he said probably explained the big smile on the face of Major Wardill, their manager, even in defeat. The *Morning Leader* the next day would put Australia's share of the proceeds at 'considerably over £1,000'. Trumble was not asked about Jessop directly but he did later concede that he could not remember any batsman 'making me scratch my head so much'.

Trumble was also interviewed by the *Australasian* on his return to Melbourne three months later when he was fulsome in his praise of Jessop's performance. The newspaper paraphrased him as saying:

> Saunders would be a great bowler if he were a little less variable and erratic … the change from absolutely first-class

to mediocrity was sudden and inexplicable. At the Oval he beat the first two [actually four] men completely, but as soon as Jessop started to hit lost all his sting … The Australians should have won, for the wicket was helping them. The only man living who could have beat them did beat them – and that was Jessop. Though he had a lot of luck at the outset, his hitting was splendid.

The *Sportsman* sent another reporter to interview Bobby Abel, the England batsman dropped after the fourth Test, who lived in a neighbouring road to Lockwood just round the corner from The Oval. Abel had watched the game and declared of Jessop, 'he had never seen anything so remarkable on a wicket of the kind'.

Both camps came to the conclusion that Darling had got his tactics wrong. Lilley thought that he should have made more use of Noble, who was not brought on until late in the innings after Jessop was out, rather than persisting so much with Saunders: 'Although Saunders bowled well, I should have preferred the former with the state of the game as it was, for Noble's experience and head-work are simply invaluable.' Noble had dismissed Jessop three times in recent Tests. Clem Hill, speaking in the 1930s, maintained that Darling's mistake was not bowling Trumble from the Vauxhall End, with its longer straight boundaries, and suggested this was a view shared by others.

Darling was a great captain, but we thought he was in error in this match. The only way Jessop could play Trumble was by jumping out and hitting him. One end of the Kennington Oval is longer than the other. Trumble was bowling from the short end, known as the Pavilion End, with the result that Jessop was hitting him into the grandstand. If he had been on at the long end, and Jessop had continued making the same lusty hits, he would have been caught in the outfield.

The counter-argument to this is that Jessop would surely not have continued hitting straight down the ground had Trumble changed ends. As we know, Jessop was well aware of the risks of hitting straight when facing Saunders from the Vauxhall End, and stopped trying to do so after nearly being caught by Trumper. Hill's comments really cannot be taken at face value. He appeared keen to put the blame for the result on Darling for his flawed tactics, and on Kelly for missing a clear-cut stumping chance when – according to Hill but no other witnesses – Jessop was yards out of his ground. But no one was actually more to blame for Australia's defeat than Hill himself for failing to catch Lockwood in the first innings; had that catch been taken, England would almost certainly not have saved the follow-on, and they would have ended up being well beaten.

Given the time difference, the cables relaying news of the final result did not reach Australia until early on Thursday, and it was not until the morning papers there on Friday that people began to absorb what had happened. Darling came in for a fair deal of criticism for not changing his bowlers more, but Australia's defeat at the hands of a player so often denigrated did not escape notice. 'Hitherto Australians have not had much respect for the crouching Jessop and his sloping bat,' the *Daily Telegraph* in Sydney stated. 'This attitude was justified by his showing on the fast wickets out here a few months ago. But he has now chosen a subtle and effective method of revenge.'

*

Those who had reported on the Test match also had to pick themselves up. C. B. Fry had to put down his pen and get himself to Hove where on Thursday morning he opened the batting for Sussex against Middlesex and was leg-before first ball. Pelham Warner set off for Trent Bridge where, after fielding for most of the day while Nottinghamshire scored 198, he was required to open the batting and was also lbw without scoring. Writing about such an eventful Test match may not have been easy, but it was easier than playing.

Such experienced full-time reporters as Pullin and Stainton were also suffering post-traumatic stress. As correspondents of Yorkshire newspapers, both had to make the early morning run down to Cheltenham. Pullin told his evening paper readers:

> 'Tis a pleasant and peaceful scene that awaits one here after the storm and stress of the wonderful international match at the Oval yesterday. One needs something easy, too, after the reaction of the never-to-be-forgotten encounter. If we had many such matches to describe I think I should throw over the duties of a cricket annotator for those of the less exciting post of war correspondent.

Stainton, as an avowed admirer of Jessop, had plenty he wished to reflect on in his piece from the Cheltenham College ground for the *Sheffield Evening Telegraph*:

Nothing is talked about here but the wonderful victory gained by England at the Oval, and the great part four of the men who are taking part in this match played in that triumph ... Jackson, Hirst, Rhodes and Jessop, who were yesterday's heroes of the cricket world ...

After the long drawn out and tense excitement of the Oval, the calm of Cheltenham is delightful, though the stress of such a Test match finish resulted in getting up horribly early this morning to catch fearsome trains West for a three hours' journey from Paddington.

It was very funny to watch people on the train as we came along. Your real Londoner is a zealous student of newspapers, and each man, having lighted up, sat back and read all about the Test match. Nothing else in the papers was of any account to him ... Over all there rose triumphant Jessop and Hirst, who had been left out of the Manchester match.

We should have won the rubber had they played there, and I am unblushingly ready to congratulate myself on having so sedulously advocated the smiter's claims.

The newspapers that Stainton's companions were reading on the train, and that were being read all over the country, battled to make sense of the incredible drama that had unfolded. Whereas the previous evening, when the late editions of the papers were being put together, there was a natural emphasis on the parts played by Hirst, Lilley and Rhodes in securing England their win under enormous pressure, the morning papers took a broader view, and a greater emphasis was placed on Jessop's part. This had certainly not been ignored the previous day, but it was now possible to pay more fulsome tribute to a great innings. Many of the headlines, for instance, gave Jessop pride of place ahead of his team-mates. The *Birmingham Daily Mail*'s coverage was typical:

ENGLAND'S GREAT TRIUMPH
JESSOP'S MATCH
MEMORABLE SCENE AT THE OVAL

The *Morning Post* echoed the sentiment that the match would be forever associated with just one player: 'The game will be known always as "Jessop's game", but for whose hurricane hitting it would have been impossible to have made the runs required before the heavy rain which came on soon after the winning hit had been scored.' To the *Sporting Life*, too, the credit lay in one place: 'The feat that they [England] accomplished was one of the most astonishing ever achieved in the history of the game ... The hero of the day was unquestionably Gilbert Jessop, who played the innings of his life. It was well known that the Australians had a poor opinion of Jessop as a hitter ... To Jessop belonged the great glory of the triumph.'

The most authoritative tribute once again came from Fry, and the prominent positioning it was given – middle column on the *Daily Express*'s front page – may have brought him some comfort as he tried to get over his embarrassingly swift dismissal at Hove:

It is no exaggeration to say that a finer batting performance has never been achieved ... It was not an absolutely sticky wicket, but it was beyond doubt a difficult one. A score of 150 would not have been a bad one under the conditions;

200 a very good; 263 was a triumph, against such bowling as
the Australians possess … Not only did the ball break, but it
came along at different paces and heights, and several times
kicked up nastily, chest-high … It is impossible to do justice
in prose to this superb innings [from Jessop], which put
victory within the sphere of the possible. He made all the
bowling, except Trumble's, appear trash, which it was not.

One can imagine Jessop's sister Winnie having a busy few
days filling scrapbooks with all the cuttings generated by
Gilbert's most astonishing performance yet.

Readers across the country were captivated. One man, a
Gilbert Ball, walked with a friend to Bath, stopped for a
drink at the Rising Sun at Bitton, and was so preoccupied
by a newspaper account of Jessop's century that he forgot
to ask for his change. When he returned to the pub later to
demand his money the landlord gave him short shrift. In late
September, Ball took his grievance to the Bristol County
Court, but the judge found in favour of the landlord.

Having beaten Jackson at the toss, Jessop did not have to wait
long to bat at Cheltenham after Hirst and Rhodes combined
to take three quick wickets. As he walked to the middle, the
crowd gave him a rapturous reception, the cheering lasting
long after he had taken up his place at the wicket. In fact, he
had to wait until the applause died down before facing his
first ball. If he found the welcome disconcerting, it did not
affect his cricket as he gave a typically belligerent display,
hitting 42 out of the next 46 runs scored in 40 minutes
before being caught at slip off Rhodes.

This proved to be comfortably Gloucestershire's top score of the match as they were skittled by Yorkshire's powerful bowling for 104 and 55, the game being finished in two days. Jessop had the satisfaction of dismissing Jackson, caught at slip for 41, but was stumped for one off the only ball he faced from Rhodes in the second innings. Rhodes was no doubt well satisfied with twice claiming the wicket of the man of the moment, but he was probably at least as occupied with awaiting news from home of the birth of his baby daughter, which eventually came several days after this via a telegram to Catford, where Yorkshire were playing Kent.

Interestingly, on the evening that Gloucestershire's match with Yorkshire ended, and therefore barely 48 hours after the conclusion of the Test match, Jessop wrote a letter to the *Sportsman*, which promoted a Cricketers' National War Fund to support the families of soldiers who had served in South Africa, effectively complaining at being inundated with requests for autographs.

> To the Editor of the Sportsman
>
> Sir, Since the Test match the autograph fiend has been greatly *en evidence*, so much so that if one were to grant everybody's request one's spare time would be seriously encroached upon. As a means of protection, would you mind inserting a paragraph in your paper to the effect that for the future autograph hunters can have an autograph provided they enclose a P.O. [postal order] for five shillings, made payable to your Fund.
>
> Yours etc, Gilbert L Jessop
>
> Belle Vue Hotel, Malvern. August 15

That Jessop should have sought to kill off autograph requests so quickly was a reflection of the public's great interest in their hero, or his own intense desire for privacy, or both.

Soon enough, too, he would give away the bat he had used at The Oval. He presented it to a friend and signed it accordingly: 'Chris Lewis from Jessopus.' The bat now resides in the museum at Lord's, although when I saw it and handled it, it was on temporary loan to Gloucestershire County Cricket Club's museum in Bristol. The inscription is still legible, as are the initials GLJ at the top of the blade, and the front of the darkened wood still bears clear indentations from its contact with the ball as well as a number of imprints of the ball's stitching. A small silver plaque is attached to the back:

This bat was used

By
G. L. Jessop
In Test Match

England v Australia
Played at the Oval
Aug 13 1902

Scoring 104 runs

Inevitably, some who had written off Jessop as too unreliable found it hard to credit his genius now that it had manifested itself on the biggest stage. V. A. S. Beanland had hailed England's victory as one for the ages, but in the *Leeds Mercury* he doubled down on his original position. 'Despite Jessop's great batting, I do not go back from my original view that choosing [him] was a great risk,' he wrote. 'He went for the bowling before he got his eye in.' But his was a largely isolated voice of dissent.

In the days immediately following the Test, there were other manifestations of Jessop's new fame. Ben Travers recalled that 'two or three nights' after witnessing the end of the match he was taken to Daly's Theatre in the West End to see *A Country Girl*, a musical comedy. The shows at Daly's would typically include a topical song, with suitable lyrics, delivered by a popular vocalist called Rutland Barrington. On this occasion his character was called the Rajah of Bhong and he produced the following final encore:

> There's a game that we play on a bright summer's day
> With a bat and a ball and a wicket,
> And we always had thought that when we joined in
>   the sport
> That we really were playing at cricket;
> But Australians came just to give us a game
> And, although it is painful to say it,
> They were teaching us fast we were things of the past
> And we really don't know how to play it.
> Peace – two innings apiece
> And none of them last very long:
> Only Jackson and Mac could withstand the attack
> Of our friends from the Valley of Bhong.
> Peace – two innings apiece
> And none of them last very long,
> Until Jessop and Hirst brought old England in first –

Travers' recollection was that if Barrington sang a last line, no one heard it: 'The whole audience burst into a roar. Many of the male customers rose spontaneously to their feet. It was just one illustration of the almost hysterical general jubilation at the result of Jessop's match.'

＊

Eight weeks after the Test match, Jessop and Millicent Osborne were married at Christ Church in Lancaster Gate. It was stated that the wedding was kept as quiet as possible on account of so many of the bride's family and friends being in Australia, but it was also described as a large gathering at the church, with a crowd outside eager to spot celebrities. The guests included W. G. Grace and Archie MacLaren, as well as Jack Mason, the Kent all-rounder who had vied with Jessop for a place in the England team at the start of the summer. Charles Townsend, the Gloucestershire player, was Jessop's best man, and Winnie Jessop was one of the bridesmaids. Among the wedding presents was a cheque from the Gloucestershire club and a large clock from Jessop's county team-mates. Millicent was given away by a Dr Jenkins, an Australian cousin of the bride.

The newspaper coverage was predictable. One headline said simply, 'Jessop Caught', while the *Daily Express* went with, 'The Idol's Wedding', before explaining, 'The cricket spectators' "idol" was married yesterday ... The bridegroom looked as radiant as if he had just made a century in a Test match, and as unperturbed.'

PART THREE

THE LEGACY

20

THE *MORNING LEADER* REPORT

THE FIRST BALL-BY-BALL LIST EMERGES

OF ALL the material published about the match in the days after the finish of the Oval Test, the most eye-catching to the modern reader was a small table that appeared near the top of the third column of page 6 of the *Morning Leader* on Thursday 14 August, the day after the game ended. It was presented with little fanfare: there was no headline or words of interpretation as to what followed; there was no indication as to who compiled it. But what followed was both striking in its forensic detail, groundbreaking in the depth of the information it provided, and also of huge historical value. It tells us a lot that we would not otherwise know.

It consisted of what it said was every ball that Jessop had faced the previous afternoon, given in chronological order with the number of runs scored off each ball alongside the name of the bowler. What is more, not only did the list include the balls from which Jessop did not score – what we would now call 'dot' balls – but it categorised these dot balls into two types: the balls that Jessop failed to hit (denoted by a cross +) and the balls that he hit but did not score off (indicated by an asterisk *). The former would be balls that Jessop either played at and missed, or ones that he chose to leave alone, although there were probably few of those. The latter were balls where Jessop's hits were stopped by fielders.

As was discussed in Chapter 7, the concept of keeping 'batsmen versus bowler' records was little heard of in English cricket at this time, and was only just developing in Australia. Moreover, the notion of maintaining notes about whether a batsman played at a ball, or missed it, was rarer still; John Atkinson Pendlington may have done something like this some years earlier; Johann Gottlieb Jackschon was not known to have done so in Australia before 1906. Such details were not features of either official scoring, or of newspaper coverage, in England, and there is no published record of anything similar from the period. Clearly it was done here by someone who thought a Jessop innings was worth such analysis. If it was a one-off act, it was an inspired punt, but perhaps notes like this were being kept in relation to Jessop, but had not previously been worth committing to print because Jessop had not come off in such spectacular fashion.

Fascinating though the *Leader*'s list is as a breakdown of one of the greatest Test innings ever played, one readily ascertained conclusion from it stands out above all others: it suggests that, 4 deliveries before he was finally out, Jessop reached his century off just 71 balls. This is five fewer than what is now viewed as the generally accepted figure of 76 balls.

The *Leader* makes one allusion to its ball-by-ball list when, in a report of the final day of the Test on the previous page, 'Astral', the correspondent, said of Jessop: 'Statisticians elsewhere will tell you that he scored a five and 17 fours and that he only had 75 balls served up to him.' This, therefore, repeated the claim made in the *Westminster Gazette* the previous afternoon, that Jessop's innings of 104 had spanned 75 deliveries.

Here is the *Leader*'s breakdown of Jessop's innings as it appeared in the edition of 14 August. Above the table was an explanation that a cross represented a ball that he failed to play, but the obvious corollary that an asterisk denoted a ball he had played but did not score from was left unsaid. Below the table was a summary of the number of runs Jessop scored off each of the three bowlers he faced.

THE *Morning Leader* ANALYSIS OF JESSOP'S INNINGS

Here is the record of his innings, ball for ball. The cross indicates that he failed to play the ball.

1 Trumble	1 Saunders	4 Saunders	+ Trumble
2 Saunders	* Trumble *(Note 1)*	4 "	+ Armstrong
4 "	1 Saunders	4 "	4 "
1 "	4 Trumble	1 "	+ Armstrong
1 Trumble	1 "	* Trumble	+ "
+ "	* "	* "	4 "
+ Saunders	* "	+ "	1 "
4 Trumble	* "	1 "	* Trumble
4 "	1 "	+ Armstrong	4 "
1 "	* Saunders	+ "	2 "
4 Saunders	3 "	* "	* "
+ "	+ Trumble	+ "	2 "

+	"	I	"	*	"	4	"
*	"	*	Saunders	I	"	4	Armstrong
*	"	3	"	2	Trumble	4	"
I	Trumble	5	Trumble	*	"	*	"
4	Saunders	I	Saunders	+	"	*	"
I	"	4	"	*	"	out	
I	Trumble	4	"	+	"		

Total: Trumble, 40; Saunders, 46; Armstrong, 18 – 104

Note 1 (above): as will be explained in the next chapter, this ball was probably bowled by Saunders rather than Trumble.

*

The *Morning Leader* was a London daily paper. It had been set up in 1892, priced a halfpenny, and was owned by Colman's, the mustard family. It was liberal in outlook and was one of the newspapers that incurred the government's displeasure by opposing the South Africa war. Like a number of papers, it struggled to hold its share of the market amid the rise of popular papers such as the *Daily Mail* and the *Daily Express*, and eventually merged with the *Daily News*, a paper of similar political persuasion founded by Charles Dickens, in May 1912. Subjected to several subsequent mergers, the resulting newspaper survived until 1960.

In the early years of the twentieth century, the *Leader* typically ran to eight pages and sport featured prominently, often extending beyond one page. Its cricket coverage was lively and informed. Unlike some of its rivals, it did not rely on agency copy, preferring to air its own thoughts on the action and it presented its articles in a lively way, with lots of cross-heads and statistical tables, albeit most of them conventional. In its issue of 14 August, it devoted two columns on page five to its match report by 'Astral', whose true identity is unknown, although he would continue to write for the paper on various sports, principally cricket and rugby, until the late 1930s.

'Astral's' reports bore comparison with some of the best on the 1902 series; he had an eye for interesting detail that others missed, and was willing to pass judgement when necessary. On the following page was an unsigned secondary piece made up of a series of short items relating to features of the previous day's play. It was into this piece that Jessop's ball-by-ball analysis was cut. This page also contained a piece by F. S. Ashley-Cooper, a young but already noted cricket historian and statistician, under the headline 'Jessop v Time', which went through Jessop's major centuries in detail. It had first appeared in *Cricket* the previous year but the *Leader* rightly calculated that it was a good time to reproduce it.

One of the paper's leading sports writers was Alfred Gibson, who was a noted author on football but also well established in cricket circles. For many years he edited a cricket annual backed by the paper and during the Ashes Tests of 1902 and 1903-04 wrote a number of informed pieces about the teams and players. His pieces sometimes appeared under his own name but he also wrote as 'Rover'. He was close to Ranjitsinhji, for whose book on the 1897-98 tour of Australia he had written an introductory chapter, and he may have played his part in some players being recruited as columnists such as Albert Knight and Percy Fender. When the *Leader* and *Daily News* merged, Gibson became sports editor, with 'Astral' remaining the voice on cricket. Gibson wrote in 1904 of the *Leader*'s cricket coverage: 'We have always given the necessary detail, together with a story of the game, in which the human and dramatic elements mingle to complete a finished picture. In this manner the *Leader* descriptions have always differed from the reports in other papers.'

A Scot who moved south in 1889, Alfred Gibson lived in Dulwich, less than three miles from The Oval, and although it was not known that he was in attendance for Jessop's innings, it is quite likely he would have been. It is conceivable he was the compiler of the ball-by-ball list.

Among the plethora of London and regional publications of the time, the *Morning Leader* was forgotten faster than it deserved to be as a sports paper, in part because of its merger with the *Daily News*. Had it not been added to the digital British Newspaper Archive in June 2023, its coverage of Jessop's match would have probably lain undiscovered.

*

The ball-by-ball breakdown allows us to draw a number of conclusions about Jessop's innings. In some cases it merely serves to confirm impressions gained from the many eyewitness accounts, but some details become clearer with the benefit of this additional information.

First of all, Jessop's duel with Trumble, who bowled unchanged throughout the innings from the Pavilion End and was a constant threat, went through three phases. Jessop began strongly against him when he started batting before lunch, scoring 11 off his first six balls. He also finished strongly, with the big over that saw him make two hits into the pavilion and brought Jessop 12 runs in five balls. That second flurry raises the interesting question as to what Darling would have done had Jessop not got out to Armstrong in the following over. If Jessop was still in, and still on strike for the start of the over after that, would the Australia captain have risked keeping faith with Trumble, who had just gone for his most expensive over of the match, or would he have turned to Noble (as he would do later in the innings)? Between these two salvos, Trumble kept Jessop pretty quiet, only two of his deliveries going for more than one run – one of which was a late cut down to the long boundary at the Vauxhall End which resulted in an all-run five.

What is also plain is how well Armstrong managed to stifle Jessop when he first came into the attack after Saunders had gone for 17 in an over. Armstrong bowled a whole over to him which yielded only one single off the final delivery and crosses against the first, third and fourth balls show that Jessop was unable to even make contact with three balls; this supports some newspaper reports that Jessop struggled to find a way to counter Armstrong's wide leg-breaks. Jessop got to grips with him in the end, but the *Leader* list shows that Jessop did not make contact with six of the first ten balls he received from Armstrong.

Between them, Armstrong and Trumble kept Jessop quiet for quite a long period while he was raising his score from 71 (which was what he was on at the end of the Saunders over that went for 17) to above 75. Jessop actually spent six balls on 75, his longest barren period of the innings, before moving to 79 not out with a late cut off Armstrong for four. Starting with that stroke, he plundered 29 in the space of 13 deliveries up to just before the point at which he was out.

Just how much punishment he meted out to Saunders is also clear. One brief period before lunch aside, when he came close to having Jessop stumped and then caught, Saunders struggled to assert any sort of control over him.

The list provides a useful check as to whom he made his main hits off; although the vast majority of his 17 fours and one five are described in detail by eyewitnesses, evidence of some of these strokes was hard to come by. The London *Evening News*, for instance, was one of the very few newspapers to make clear that Jessop's final boundary of the morning session came over cover point off Saunders. When Charles Davis drew on contemporary reports to produce his own over-by-over reconstruction of Jessop's innings in the 2010s, he put this four against Trumble. Another boundary that was barely described by reporters (though there was no question it came off Armstrong's bowling) was Jessop's last boundary before he was out; it came moments after he had reached his century and such was the pandemonium that it is a fair guess that many chroniclers failed to properly take note. A wagon wheel of Jessop's one five, seventeen fours, two threes and four twos (which made up 87 of his 104 runs) confirms Jessop's claim that he had neither a three nor a boundary against Trumble on the leg side – and that in fact all four of his hits to the boundary against Trumble were in the safety of the 'V' between mid-on and mid-off. As Jessop knew to his previous cost, Trumble's bounce and accuracy made hitting him across the line a dangerous business.

The *Leader*'s analysis also tallies with a number of other assertions made in eyewitness accounts. In terms of the evolution of Jessop's innings, and the progress of his score, as we know it from these accounts, it does not throw up any obvious contradictions. For instance, we know he got off the mark with a single first ball – the ball from Trumble that nearly bowled him off an inside edge – and the *Leader*'s list confirms he began with a run off his first ball. Most reports also suggested that he gave a stumping chance on 22 and was dropped in the deep on 27 and there were indeed times when he was facing Saunders with those scores to his name.

We also know his cut for five off Trumble took his score to 49 before a single brought up his fifty. Again, this breakdown confirms that was the case. It shows him scoring 17 in the space of five balls from Saunders and taking 12 off a Trumble over to move to 96, before reaching his hundred with a four off Armstrong. The *Westminster Gazette* the previous day had said of the start of Jessop's innings that 'for more than four overs he scored from every ball he received except two, and those two added leg-byes to the score', and in the first five overs we can see here that he did score off every ball except two. (We also know independently that two leg-byes were scored during the Jessop–Jackson stand before lunch.)

The sequence of scoring shots given here also tallies precisely with the list produced in the *Sheffield Evening Telegraph* the previous day – except for the two singles the *Evening Telegraph* omitted in error.

However, as we shall see, the *Morning Leader* ball-by-ball list, although more thorough than anything else produced around this time for a Test innings played in England, was not alone. Others were also taking a close interest in Jessop's batting and accordingly keeping careful notes. This interest may well have been stimulated by Jessop's explosive innings during the Test match in Sheffield almost six weeks earlier, when he struck 55 off 49 balls. This attracted some detailed analysis including in the following week's issue of *Cricket: A Weekly Record of the Game*. F. S. Ashley-Cooper published an item in his regular column 'At the Sign of the Wicket' in which he thanked a correspondent, a Mr Hamish Stuart, for sending him a ball-by-ball list of the deliveries faced by Jessop, specifying from which bowler he received them and how many he scored. Ashley-Cooper then listed each of Jessop's three innings in the Test series to that point – one at Edgbaston and two at Bramall Lane – with total runs scored (73) and balls faced (61), and concluded: 'This must be considered a wonderful feat for such important cricket.'

Ashley-Cooper was a Surrey man. He frequented The Oval and had contributed to a major history of Surrey cricket in 1901. It was highly likely he would have attended Jessop's match, and in the light of Jessop's fast scoring in the Test matches he may have been among a small number of people recording every delivery Jessop faced in the final Test match, just in case he did something else extraordinary.

WAGON WHEEL OF JESSOP'S MAIN SCORING SHOTS

PAVILION END

VAUXHALL END

Scoring Outcome

● 5 ● 4 ● 3 ● 2

21

THE *ATHLETIC NEWS* REPORT

FIVE DAYS AFTER the Test finished, and four days after the appearance of the *Morning Leader* ball-by-ball list, the *Athletic News* produced its first coverage of the match. The *Athletic News and Cyclists' Journal*, to give it its full title, was a weekly sports paper based in Manchester and published every Monday, covering the weekend's sport extensively, particularly cricket and football, along with a number of other sports except horse racing, which was dealt with by its sister paper, the *Sporting Chronicle*. It had been founded by Edward Hulton in 1875 and was highly regarded, at least in the north of the country which was home to most of its readership.

It was edited by Jimmy Catton, a small, lively and excitable journalist who had made his name as a prolific and industrious writer on football and cricket. He was now in his early forties and had spent years in the hard-drinking culture of Manchester journalism. Neville Cardus, who came across Catton in the 1920s in his early years as a cricket writer for the *Manchester Guardian*, recounted how Catton had told a story of him being so drunk that he had slept through an English Cup final on the floor at the back of the press box, 'dead drunk'. Cardus described him as 'incredibly small in height, red in the face, round as a ball, gold spectacles, white moustache, bald head at the front, twinkling eyes', adding that 'a wild youth' was now behind him. Catton would stay in temperance hotels as a means of keeping out of trouble.

Both Cardus and Catton may have embellished their stories, but it would surely have been based in some degree of fact. Whether or not Catton was a reformed character by 1902 is unclear, but it is unlikely that he would have been appointed editor of the *Athletic News* two years before this if there was a question of his reliability. As we have already seen from Catton's own admission about how he reacted to England's nerve-jangling victory, he remained a passionate character, jumping up on his press seat to celebrate, and later going to the theatre with Frank Thorogood, 'still in a high fever'.

Catton was a highly capable reporter. His report of the Oval Test, using the pseudonym of 'Tityrus' and spanning four columns on page 5 of the issue of 18 August, is thorough and authoritative. He had been attending Test matches in England almost from the time that the Australians first toured, and at his death in 1936 his knowledge of footballers and cricketers was praised as second to none. He reputedly kept files on all the leading players.

In these still relatively early days, he felt acutely his lack of sporting credentials. He was not a sportsman himself and was intimidated by his first meeting with the athletically imposing C. B. Fry, who was one of his contributors when he first took over the editorship. Catton would describe how Fry looked down at him with an expression of incredulity, as though to say: 'What, *you* appointed editor of the *Athletic News*? You are an undersized rat of a fellow that I could put in my pocket.' If this was chiefly an expression of Catton's own insecurities, Fry did actually call Catton in his autobiography, 'the smallest man who ever edited a newspaper'. Soon, though, Fry was parting ways with Catton and the *Athletic News* after making an outlandish expenses claim for telegraphing a long piece from the Outer Hebrides while on a fishing trip. Fry moved onto writing for monthly magazines before the *Daily Express* signed him up.

Catton may have been overawed by the presence of an all-round sports star such as Fry – cricketer, footballer, track and field athlete – but his regular beat covering Lancashire matches home and away had brought him close to MacLaren and Tyldesley. He even shared a hotel room in London with Tyldesley during the Lord's Test of June 1902. As a non-drinker and non-smoker, Tyldesley would have been safe company.

Catton's overview piece of the Oval Test did not contain any great revelations; by this stage, almost everything had been said. He did, though, reiterate how remarkable England's run-chase was, saying that 'on a wicket which had lost its surface and never recovered from the rain, it was a stupendous feat'. He also spared a thought for Lord Hawke's panel in the wake of what Hirst and Jessop had done at The Oval after their inexplicable omissions from the previous, narrowly lost match at Old Trafford: 'The selection committee must feel their position so acutely that hard words would only harrow their anguish.'

However, among two and a half columns of unsigned reflections on the Oval Test on the *Athletic News*'s front page, there appeared the following item:

To show exactly what Jessop did, we have prepared a little plan of his innings, the dots representing the balls that he either played or allowed to pass his wicket, while the hits will speak for themselves. Perpend:

12411..441.4....141.11

1.41...1.3.1.3514..4444

1....1.....12......4..41.

42.244.4. c Noble b Armstrong 104

In other words, Gilbert Jessop received 79 balls, 41 of which he hit for 104, and 38 of which escaped punishment. He made his runs in rather less than an hour and a quarter.

Here, then, was a second published ball-by-ball list. Who compiled it is unknown. It is not attributed, but the *Athletic News* had many contributors. It may have been gleaned from a statistician such as Ashley-Cooper who kept the necessary notes, although at this time Ashley-Cooper was not yet one of Catton's contributors, although he would later become one. As we have suggested, a number of people may have been keeping close tabs on the balls Jessop faced. Catton would not have been one of them, although he did have an opportunity to consult with Fred Boyington, the Surrey scorer, over the next few days, because Catton stayed on at

The Oval to report on Lancashire's county championship match with Surrey (his piece appeared on page 4 of this same issue of 18 August). Whether Catton would have thought to check with Boyington, or considered that Boyington could have helped provide ball-by-ball details for Jessop's innings, given that he was an old-school scorer using an old-school scorebook, may be doubted.

The *Athletic News* list was not as detailed as the one in the *Morning Leader*. It did not attempt to put each ball against a bowler's name, or differentiate among the 'dot balls' as to which ones Jessop had hit or missed (or, as the *News* preferred, 'allowed to pass'). As we shall discuss shortly, this list – which actually amounted to 80 balls in total including the ball Jessop was out to – differs from the *Morning Leader* one in a number of small respects, beyond it containing five additional 'dot balls'. What is actually most striking, though, is how similar the two lists are to each other, and to the list of scoring strokes first published in the *Sheffield Evening Telegraph* (albeit with its two missing singles). All the scoring strokes are the same and appear in precisely the same order. Overall, they do a great deal to support each other.

However, there were now two alternative versions: one had Jessop reaching his century off 71 balls, the other off 76 balls.

*

Before we look further into that, it is first worth highlighting other reports that helped establish how Jessop's innings unfolded. The *Daily Express* on the morning of Thursday 14 August, the day after the game, offered some crucial statistical details. First, Fry's match report, which vividly captured the drama of the run-chase, spelt out thoroughly how the closing stages of the game unfolded. He wrote:

> The great possibility of an English win was realised with electrical suddenness, and a gasp of surcharged feeling was distinctly heard. 'How many do we want?' was asked on all sides. 'Oh, 50 to tie, and 51 to win!' And, 'We are now 212!' 'Hurrah, another two; now we only want 49!'

Then, Lockwood was out; England's eighth wicket had fallen. But the runs required continued to come down, as Fry further explained:

> We had gone by steps. We wanted 47, 45, 44, 42, 41, 40, 36, 35, 33, 29, 26, 25, 24, 23, 19, 18, 17, 16, 15. We shall win, then another gasp of despair – Lilley has gone! Last man, and still 14 to tie and 15 to win! Captain Darling consults with his first mate, Trumble; no use, our Yorkshiremen hadn't a tremble in them. Ten to win – 9, 8, 7, 6, 5, 3, 2, 1. We have tied!

And so on, until the winning hit is made. This account is important because it explains precisely the sequence of scoring shots made by the England batsmen over a lengthy period of the innings. It helps establish, for instance, that 13 of Hirst's last 14 scoring shots were singles (rather than 13 of his last 15), which was something that reports did not agree on. Moreover, on the back page of the same issue of the *Daily Express*, in a regular column called All Sorts of Sports, containing all manner of interesting titbits from the match, it was stated: 'There was method in Jessop's big hitting. Twenty-two overs were sent down between his first and second roof drives.'

This was an important detail because contemporary reports hardly ever referred to the number of overs that had been bowled in a team's innings or during a phase of the game – and why would they, when there was no second new ball in Test cricket in England until 1909? Scoreboards did not carry a running total of the number of overs bowled in an innings at this time.

As it was relatively easy to confirm that Jessop's first hit onto the pavilion 'roof' occurred in the fifth over of his innings, and his second hit in the over before he was out, it becomes possible to frame Jessop's innings within the compass of 28 overs from start to finish. Through detailed analysis of the newspaper reports of the early stages of the England innings, and the *Daily Express* countdown of the runs needed towards the end of the innings, it can be calculated, with some degree of certainty, that Jessop began his innings towards the end of the 19th over, and was dismissed at the end of the 46th over. (See Appendix for full breakdown of the England innings during Jessop's stay at the crease.)

*

In reviewing all of this evidence, much of it previously undiscovered or ignored, I would conclude that there were essentially two ball-by-ball lists compiled in the press box and drawn on by those reporters in the vicinity who considered them of interest.

One list supplied figures used by the *Westminster Gazette*, the *Birmingham Post*, the *Leeds Mercury* and the *Athletic*

News to state that Jessop scored 29 off 21 balls before lunch, took 38 balls to reach his half-century and 76 balls for his hundred, and faced 80 balls overall. Interestingly, the first paper known to indicate that Jessop received 79 balls (plus the ball that got him out) was not the *Athletic News* but the *Edinburgh Evening News* the day after the game. The other list provided the *Westminster Gazette*, the *Morning Leader* and the *Pall Mall Gazette* with the claim that Jessop faced 75 balls overall for his 104, something repeated by some West Country local papers in the days following the match. Note that the *Westminster Gazette* – possibly through the figure of Warner – appeared to take claims of a 38-ball fifty from one list and a 75-ball 104 from the other. None of these other papers published either of the full ball-by-ball lists, but simply picked out what they considered the most striking details.

No contemporary account has been found which stated explicitly how many balls it believed Jessop took to reach his hundred; reports only ever talked about how many balls he faced for his entire innings. As previously stated, minutes batted was considered the key metric in terms of reaching a hundred.

We now need to examine these two versions more closely to determine how they differ, and if it is possible to ascertain which is the more likely to be accurate, and in what regard. This should enable us to conclude more precisely how many balls Jessop actually faced. I have described them below as the *Morning Leader* and *Athletic News* versions, but they may well not have originated with them, merely been published by them.

JESSOP 18 NOT OUT
(*ATHLETIC NEWS* HAS AN EXTRA DOT BALL COMPARED TO THE *MORNING LEADER*)

Jessop moves his score to 18 with successive hits for four, four and one at the start of an over from Trumble, at which point the strike passed to Jackson, who is known to be on 36. As Jackson's only remaining scoring shot before lunch is a three in Trumble's next over, and the only extras before lunch (two single leg-byes) have already been taken, Jackson must play out the over without scoring and Jessop must start the next over from Saunders on strike. The *Morning Leader* has Jessop facing five balls (40000) but he must face all six, and the missing dot ball must be at the start of the over while his score is still 18. **Extra dot ball confirmed.**

JESSOP 28 NOT OUT
(*ATHLETIC NEWS* HAS AN EXTRA DOT BALL)

The *Morning Leader* has Jessop facing only one ball in what is the final over before lunch from Trumble, and scoring a single to move to 29, leaving Jackson on strike. We know Jackson faced most of the over and was in difficulties (although confusingly one report suggests Saunders was bowling, but we know Saunders started the afternoon session). It is possible Jessop faced a dot ball before the single, but there is no firm evidence either way. **Extra dot ball unproven.**

START OF AFTERNOON SESSION

The *Morning Leader* list suggests that Jessop faced only one ball in each of three overs after lunch (single off Saunders, dot ball against Trumble, single off Saunders). This does not tally with several reports which indicate that three runs came off the first over of the afternoon, two of them singles to Jessop, who had resumed on 29 not out. The *Daily Express*'s calculation that there were 22 overs between Jessop's 'roof hits' supports this correction, because the *Morning Leader* list implies 24 overs. Also, after Jessop is back on strike again in this over, the *Morning Leader* says he went dot ball and single, while the *Athletic News* says he scored a single straightaway, followed by a dot ball, which can only have come at the start of the next over against Trumble. Both are possible scenarios but make no difference to Jessop's overall tally of balls.

JESSOP 54 NOT OUT
(*ATHLETIC NEWS* HAS TWO EXTRA DOT BALLS)

The *Athletic News* list claims Jessop faced two dot balls between the four he hit off the last ball of an over against Saunders to move to 54 and the four successive fours, followed by a single, that he hit at the start of Saunders' next over. Catton's report in the *Athletic News* spells out clearly that these five fours came in five balls from Saunders ('Jessop made five consecutive fours from Saunders') so there could not have been any dots off Saunders between. We also know that Jackson faced Trumble in the intervening over because he was dropped at slip and it is clear from other details that Jessop cannot have faced any balls in that over. **Claim of two extra dot balls incorrect.**

JESSOP 71 NOT OUT
(*ATHLETIC NEWS* HAS AN EXTRA DOT BALL)

Directly after the over in which Jessop hits 17 off Saunders he faced Trumble in an over which saw the score raised by three, one run by Jessop and two single leg-byes. We know this from a score update published in the *Australasian*. The *Morning Leader* list suggests that Jessop faced four balls in this over but he could have faced five. There is no firm evidence either way. **Extra dot ball unproven.**

JESSOP'S FINAL OVER

Both sources agree that Jessop faced four balls in Armstrong's over after reaching his hundred. The *Morning Leader* says he hit his very next ball for four, followed by two dot balls before he was out; the *Athletic News* says there was a dot ball before the boundary, then another dot ball and the dismissal. Probably because of the celebrations following the hundred, the reports of what happened next are a little imprecise. No account specifies off which ball Jessop's final four came. Both scenarios are possible but make no difference to Jessop's overall tally of balls.

CONCLUSION

On the best available evidence, it must be concluded that neither the *Morning Leader* nor the *Athletic News* list is wholly accurate in terms of the number of balls Jessop faced. The *Morning Leader* has probably missed at least one ball and the *Athletic News* probably overcounted by two. With two other dot balls listed by the *Athletic News* uncertain, the best we can do is offer a range for the number of balls faced by Jessop: the fewest he can have faced to reach his hundred is 72 (one more than the *Morning Leader* originally suggested) and the most he can have faced is 74 (two fewer than the *Athletic News* claimed). **Jessop reached his century off 72–74 balls. His overall innings of 104 occupied 76–78 balls.**

22

HOW LONG DID JESSOP BAT?

CLAIM OF 75-MINUTE CENTURY IS SUSPECT

ANOTHER MAJOR question about Jessop's innings was how long he batted. As has already been mentioned, time rather than balls faced was for many years the standard means of measuring the length of a batsman's innings, and the time commonly given for Jessop's hundred – one hour and a quarter, or 75 minutes – was fêted for its speed. This was only to be expected because the tempo was remarkable. It was hailed as a 'hurricane' of hitting. Although the number of deliveries a player receives is today the primary measure of how fast someone scores (with a strike-rate of runs per 100 balls the standard unit of batting speed), record books such as *Wisden* still provide tables of the fastest Test match hundreds in terms of minutes.

In *Wisden's* 2025 edition, Jessop was still recognised as third on the all-time list. Although no known contemporary reports compared it to other Test centuries in terms of time spent at the crease, Jessop's century was the fastest on record at that time, beating Darling's 91-minute hundred at Sydney in 1898 and Jack Brown's hundred for England at Melbourne three years before that, which spanned 95 minutes. So there was no doubt that Jessop's was a whirlwind performance. And nobody *did* doubt it. Indeed, everyone seemed only too eager to celebrate its electrifying pace.

This brings us back to the original point raised in the introduction to this book, that society in 1902 was in thrall to the breaking of barriers. People were growing accustomed to the idea that man was capable of pushing back the boundaries of human endeavour, including touching ever greater heights of athletic excellence. Arthur Duffey, an American sprinter who ran at a meeting at Stamford Bridge in July 1902, was celebrated as the world's fastest man over 100 yards. C. B. Fry equalled what was then the world long-jump record while at Oxford in 1893, and in 1901 scored six successive first-class centuries, an unprecedented feat not matched until Don Bradman in the 1930s. In 1895, Archie MacLaren had posted a world-record individual score of 424 for Lancashire against Somerset at Taunton. When Jessop made his Test century on the afternoon of 13 August 1902, it astonished those present not only because it gave England hope that they might yet win a game that appeared lost, but because he scored it so fast. And people wanted to *know* that it was fast; they wanted to *read* that it was fast. There was an incentive, if not a temptation, to every reporter present, to portray what had happened in the most exciting, and flattering, light.

Judging by how variable was the reporting of times during the England innings – such as when it began (anything from 11.30 a.m. to 11.40 a.m.) to when it finished (4.20 p.m. to 4.30 p.m.) – there was no communal agreement in the press box as to what the clock said at any given point. But it was noticeable how unified reporters were behind the notion that Jessop took 75 minutes to get to his hundred. There were a few exceptions; a small number suggested he got there in 70 minutes, others thought it took him just shy of 80 minutes, but in this pre-digital age the hour and a quarter mark had a nice ring to it.

It is not necessary to read many reports of Jessop's match – although I scrutinised dozens – to realise that, when it came to timings, journalists instinctively rounded things up or down to the nearest five minutes. When timepieces themselves were so variable, running a little fast here or a little slow there, few people seemed interested in calibrating things beyond that. Even on the athletics track the convention was for timings to be rounded up or down to the nearest one-fifth of a second; Duffey's best time, for instance, was 9.6 seconds. Timekeeping in everyday life was still a relatively imprecise art, and although cricket was a game played in sessions measured by the clock, there is an abundance of evidence that these session times were adhered to quite loosely. And with an ordinary watch, how could anyone be sure that their timepiece was really more accurate than the next man's? That said, a very occasional report from the Oval Test would offer a precise timing, and these may provide important clues about when a particular event actually occurred.

Even within themselves, some reports could be inconsistent. The *Sheffield Daily Telegraph* stated that Jessop's partnerships with Jackson and Hirst – the only ones he had during his innings – occupied 68 minutes and 12 minutes, but Jessop himself batted 'no more than 70 minutes'. There were numerous anomalies of this sort. This is where the absence of official scorebooks could be acutely felt because these might have contained some specific timings, even if only as to the start and end of a team innings.

However, I would argue that there is a relatively simple way to come close to establishing how long Jessop batted, and how long it took him to reach the various landmarks of his innings. One clear fact underpinned the events of England's innings on 13 August and it was that, if one discounts two short hold-ups in play (for the injury to James Kelly and the celebrations following Jessop's hundred), Australia maintained an average of just short of 20 overs per hour, or one over almost every three minutes (to be precise, they bowled 66.5 overs at a rate of 19.65 per hour excluding the two hold-ups). This was slower than the rate England's bowlers managed on the first day of the game of 21.5 overs per hour, but that was to be expected as play that day was relatively uneventful, and about the same as on the second day when 18 wickets fell. This, too, was to be expected as there was a lot of incident on both days; on the final day nine wickets fell and a lot of boundaries were hit.

By modern standards, though, all these over-rates are high, which reflects just how briskly overs can be got through when there are no interruptions for drinks breaks, umpire reviews, 12th men running on with towels and changes of gloves for batsmen, and the like. Importantly for our purposes here, play appears to have proceeded at a steady, unrelenting and largely predictable tempo. Once start and finish times for the team innings, and the lunch interval, are established, it is possible to provide approximate (but reasonably accurate) time slots for each over. A few overs might have been shorter than three minutes because they were uneventful, or longer than three minutes because a lot happened, but not many. And thanks to the granular detail provided by the *Morning Leader* and the *Daily Express* reports, I believe it is possible to establish in which overs many key events took place. With the main events in place, a timeline can be plotted, as follows.

These estimated timings are the basis for the timings given in the headings to Chapters 11 to 18, and within the text of those chapters.

11.38 A.M.: ENGLAND, NEEDING 263 TO WIN, START THEIR SECOND INNINGS

Most reports suggested that Australia, resuming on 114 for eight overnight, batted another 20 minutes before being all out for 121, and that MacLaren had then asked for almost ten minutes of the heavy roller on the pitch between innings. Various times were given for the start of England's second innings with many opting for 11.35 a.m. or 11.40 a.m., but the *Birmingham Evening Despatch* offered the slightly more specific 'rather before 20 minutes to 12'. I have therefore gone for 11.38 a.m. as the time MacLaren and Palairet walked out to bat.

12.17 P.M.: RAIN STOPS PLAY; ENGLAND 28-3 OFF 12 OVERS AFTER 39 MINUTES, JACKSON 14, HAYWARD 6

To the first ball of the sixth over, at around 11.53 a.m., there was a delay when Kelly was hit in the eye by a bail when Palairet was bowled by Saunders. Estimates as to how long the stoppage lasted varied but Kelly received medical attention. I have allowed four minutes. Jackson was the new batsman and faced his first ball at about 11.58 a.m. But rain took the players off after 12 overs. Some reports timed this at 12.15 p.m., others at 12.20 p.m., but the *Derby Daily Telegraph*, possibly using agency copy, stated, 'at 12.17 there was a postponement through rain'.

12.48 P.M.: PLAY RESUMES

Reports typically put the length of the delay at 30 minutes, but some suggested longer. I have gone with a slightly longer stoppage of 31 minutes, but no more than that because of the overs that need fitting in before lunch.

1.08 P.M.: ENGLAND 48-5 OFF 18.5 OVERS AFTER 59 MINUTES, JACKSON 31, BRAUND OUT

Braund is out, which brings in Jessop. Jessop is commonly said to have batted 20 minutes before lunch but some Yorkshire papers, possibly again based on agency reports, were more specific. The *Leeds Mercury* said 22 minutes and the *Halifax Evening Courier* went with 23 minutes. However, it is unclear if these times were calculated working back from the official break for lunch at 1.30 p.m. or the actual time Jessop spent at the crease. I have assumed they were calculated back from 1.30 p.m. Jessop himself remembered many years later that 'there was some 20 minutes to get through before the luncheon interval'. In a quiet period since the restart following rain, England had faced 6.5 overs in 20 minutes before this.

LUNCH BREAK 1.31 P.M.: ENGLAND 87-5 OFF 27 OVERS AFTER 82 MINUTES, JACKSON 39, JESSOP 29

Between the start of Jessop's innings and lunch, there was a lot of action: England add 39 in 8.1 overs, with Jessop striking five fours, including a hit onto the pavilion awning, and Jackson two threes; there was also a dropped catch and a missed stumping. It seems likely therefore that the final over, which was uneventful, began just before 1.30 p.m. and went on just past that point. I am assuming Jessop had been batting 23 minutes by lunch.

2.15 P.M.: AFTERNOON SESSION

The afternoon session started promptly at 2.15 p.m.

2.40 P.M.: ENGLAND 118-5 OFF 35.1 OVERS AFTER 107 MINUTES, JACKSON 45, JESSOP 50

Twenty-five minutes after lunch, Jessop brings up his fifty with a single. Since the session began, England have added 31 in 8.1 overs, Jessop's scoring shots including an all-run five, an all-run four and two threes. There have also been four byes and Jackson has hit two twos. Almost all reports state that Jessop reached his half-century in 45 minutes, or 'about 45 minutes'; they are probably working on the simple calculation of him being at the crease 20 minutes before lunch and 25 minutes afterwards. More likely he had been batting around 48 minutes. England have faced 16.2 overs since he came in, or an average of just under three minutes per over.

3.03 P.M.: ENGLAND 157-6 OFF 42.5 OVERS IN 130 MINUTES, JESSOP 83, JACKSON OUT

Jackson is out. England have added 39 in 7.4 overs in 23 minutes since Jessop reached his fifty: Jessop adding 33 runs (with seven fours), Jackson 4. Jackson's innings was typically said to have lasted one hour 45 minutes, but he probably batted just over one hour 50 minutes. His partnership of 109 with Jessop, often put at 65–67 minutes, was more likely just over 70 minutes.

3.12 P.M.: ENGLAND 183-6 OFF 45.2 OVERS IN 139 MINUTES, JESSOP 100, HIRST 9

Jessop reaches his hundred. The *Yorkshire Evening Post* said he had been batting 70 minutes but its sister paper, the *Yorkshire Post*, the following morning stated he reached his hundred 'after a stay of less than 80 minutes'. As we saw in the previous chapter, the *Athletic News* said he batted 'rather less than an hour and a quarter'. Most reports went for 75 minutes. However, weighing all the evidence, 80 minutes appears most likely: 23 minutes before lunch and 57 minutes afterwards. There had been a flurry of activity since Jackson was dismissed: Hirst surviving a first-ball lbw appeal, then hitting two boundaries off Armstrong; Jessop taking 12 off an over from Trumble including two hits high into the pavilion; then Jessop's four off Armstrong to bring up his century. England had added 26 in the last 2.3 overs, and in nine minutes, since Jackson was out.

3.17 P.M.: ENGLAND 187-7 OFF 46 OVERS IN 144 MINUTES, HIRST 9, JESSOP OUT

When Jessop reached his hundred it led to a hold-up in play as the crowd celebrated. The *Dover Express* said 'for a couple of minutes the game was stopped'. The *Daily Mail* and *Nottingham Evening Post* put the demonstration of delight at 'some minutes'. Jessop faced three more balls, one of which he hit for four, and was then out. Some reports stated that his innings lasted only another two minutes after he got to his century, which suggests they were overlooking the stoppage in play, but other reports reckoned for another five minutes, putting his total time at the crease at 80 minutes. I reckon he batted 85 minutes in all. His stand with Hirst added 30 runs in 14 minutes.

4.24 P.M.: ENGLAND 263-9 OFF 66.5 OVERS IN 211 MINUTES, HIRST 58, RHODES 6; ENGLAND WIN BY ONE WICKET

After Jessop was out, England made the remaining 76 runs they needed in 20.5 overs and 67 minutes, the slower over-rate reflecting the tension in the closing stages and the Australians regularly adjusting their fields. Lockwood stayed with Hirst for just over 20 minutes and Lilley stayed for just over 25 minutes. The final partnership between Hirst and Rhodes spanned 20 minutes. Hirst batted just over 80 minutes. Reports as to when the match ended varied by several minutes either way but the *Birmingham Post*'s on-the-whistle report timed the winning hit at 4.25 p.m.

CONCLUSION

In summary, I would maintain that based on the number of overs bowled and the time England batted, it is reasonable to argue that Jessop batted several minutes longer to reach the principal landmarks in his innings than commonly believed through claims based on loose timekeeping and a lack of attention to detail. He batted about 48 minutes for his fifty (not 45) and 80 minutes for his hundred (not 75). This would mean him dropping from third to equal fifth in the all-time list of fastest Test hundreds in terms of time. He was at the crease 85 minutes for his entire innings of 104. It is worth noting that, based on the rule-of-thumb rate of three minutes per over, the 27.1 overs Jessop spent batting would equate to 82 minutes, without taking account of the hold-up in play when he got to his hundred.

Add in that stoppage, and an overall time of 85 minutes for his innings sounds entirely reasonable.

Jessop reached his century in 80 minutes. His overall innings of 104 occupied 85 minutes.

23

THE SPLIT WITH JACKSON

JESSOP ALMOST BREAKS HIS OWN RECORD

JESSOP HAD PLAYED a never-to-be-forgotten innings, but it did not guarantee him selection for England. In fact, although he was only twenty-eight years old at the end of 1902, he featured in just eight more Tests, only three of them against Australia. There was much less Test cricket going on than in later times, but even so he missed more home matches than he played for England during the remainder of his career, and never toured abroad again. Various selectors still needed convincing that he was worth the gamble, and he again came up against opposition from Stanley Jackson, who appeared unmoved by what he had seen of Jessop's genius from 20 yards away at The Oval. To him, it was as though that performance had never happened.

Jessop's form with the bat was more uneven than it had been – he went more than two years without a century between June 1905 and July 1907 – but his highs were as astonishing as ever, and if anything he seemed more capable of sustaining his destructive moods than in earlier years.

Of his next nine first-class hundreds, four were double-centuries and another three topped 150. His fielding remained as exceptional as ever.

He still struggled to make things work financially while playing so much cricket. He was invited to join an England tour of Australia in the winter of 1903-04, organised by the MCC, whose secretary Francis Lacey assured him without going into details that all amateur expenses would be met, but as a newly married man it was not as easy as it had been for him to tour for several months, even if his wife was Australian and would have liked to see New South Wales again had she been able to accompany him. Her parents were no longer alive, but she still had relatives there.

Jessop had also received a more attractive counter-offer to write comment pieces from home on the Tests for the *Daily Mail*, based on cabled reports, as Alfred Harmsworth sought to outdo his rivals by signing up the star of the 1902 series. C. B. Fry also did not join the tour and continued writing for the *Daily Express*, and neither did Archie MacLaren, who secured work as a columnist for the *Daily Chronicle*. Jessop in his articles was able to draw on his knowledge of Australian conditions from his visit under MacLaren's captaincy in 1901-02 and his pieces generated a reasonable amount of interest. He was not afraid to criticise the Australian authorities over the crowd disturbances witnessed at some matches and the way local umpires were selected in the face of protests from the English team. By 1904, Jessop and his wife were living at Kensington Square Mansions, where they stayed until 1907 before leaving London following the birth of their son Gilbert Laird Osborne Jessop the previous September.

Jessop also appeared to negotiate more favourable terms under which he could continue captaining Gloucestershire in 1904, after reports emerged that he might be forced to quit playing unless the club could provide him with more 'support', which can have only meant more generous expenses.

For the 1903-04 tour, the England captaincy had gone to Pelham Warner rather than MacLaren, whose shamateur theatrics particularly irked the MCC. It was a decision that caused fierce press debate – Warner had not previously featured even as a rank-and-file player in matches against Australia – but was vindicated by results. Thus, when Australia next toured England in 1905, the selectors had few qualms about passing over MacLaren a second time and this time going for Jackson, who like Jessop had declined to go to Australia. Jackson had a brilliant all-round series – 492 runs, 13 wickets – and led England to a comprehensive 2-0 win, but for Jessop his appointment was not good news. England won the first Test at Trent Bridge but Jessop contributed little and was promptly dropped, not to return.

Jessop admitted that he did not help himself in his one appearance, but then Jackson hardly helped him either, batting him at No 8 behind Bernard Bosanquet and John Gunn, who respectively averaged 13 and 10 in Test cricket. Going in with his side in difficulties at 119 for six, Jessop was bowled attempting to flick his first ball from Frank Laver to leg in what he conceded was 'an uncouth manoeuvre'. It was the first ball he had faced in Test cricket since The Oval almost three years earlier.

Jessop was probably thinking of this innings when, as part of a series of anonymous letters written under the pseudonym 'Incognitus' to famous cricketers and published in the *Athletic News* the following year, he chided himself for 'your grotesque, frog-like contortions at the wicket' and over-eagerness to score fast:

> You seem to me to pander too much to what has been to you on not a few occasions a somewhat unfortunate proclivity. Time after time I have seen you sacrifice your wicket to this craze when there was no earthly object in your obtaining runs quickly ... What is it which makes you want to hit every ball to the boundary?

Nor did Jackson call on Jessop to bat in the second innings when England were looking for quick runs ahead of a declaration. It was a situation tailor-made for a Jessop onslaught. Jackson instead promoted Rhodes to No 7 and the two of them added 108 in 75 minutes on the final morning before Australia were left four and a half hours to get 401. They were bowled out by Bosanquet in the first instance of a wrist-spinner winning a Test match for England on home soil.

Jessop's omission for the later Tests was not a great surprise as he was showing little form in county cricket, but it was a moot point as to whether Jackson would have backed his inclusion had he been playing better and others on Lord Hawke's committee had pushed for his selection. And he did show good form, spectacularly, a week ahead of the third Test with a blazing double-century against Somerset, but he was still overlooked. 'Jackson always shook his head over Jessop: he always expected our "Croucher" to try to hit the first ball bowled to him to long leg, no matter if it were a fast straight good-length ball on his middle stump,' C. B. Fry wrote. Brodribb stated: 'Jessop's one irresponsible stroke made it certain that he would not be chosen again for the series under Jackson's captaincy.'

Jessop largely kept his thoughts to himself on Jackson, but could not resist addressing one of his anonymous 'Incognitus' letters to Jackson in July 1906. In it, he had a dig at him for his privileged upbringing and what Jessop clearly felt was an unnecessarily disparaging view of cricketers (such as himself) who tried to support themselves through journalism.

Jessop may have been emboldened to write this piece when he did because it was becoming clear by this stage that Jackson had all but quit first-class cricket for politics, and they were unlikely to often cross paths again. He began his letter, 'Dear Jacker, If ever there was a cricketer born with a golden spoon in his mouth truly you are the man. You have had everything that money could buy to make your path smooth ...' He then sweetened the pill – 'there are few cricketers less devoid of side than yourself' – before arriving at his main point:

As a director of an influential newspaper you have some connection with journalism, which makes me wonder why you are unsympathetic with him who wields the willow while wielding the pen. The limited income amateur, my dear Jacker, is just as enthusiastic on the game as he who is more fortunately placed. In order to still continue his favourite pastime he has three courses open to him. Firstly, if he is good enough, he may induce the authorities to appoint him to an assistant secretaryship; secondly, if he has any ability whatever in the direction of putting his thoughts on paper he can accept the opportunity of doing so; and lastly, he may become a professional ...

What Jackson thought of this attack, and whether he knew who the real author was, is unknown, but their relationship never improved. In fact, on the contrary. When Charles Britton sought to collate reminiscences from contemporaries for his book *G.L.: a Complete Record of his Performances in First-Class Cricket*, published in 1935, he was rebuffed by Jackson when he wrote asking for memories of Jessop's Test century. To his credit, Britton did not shy away from expressing astonishment at Jackson's supposed amnesia:

> Sir Stanley Jackson could not be drawn into writing about this innings, but he did write that, 'It [the match] took place rather too long ago for me to remember accurately what took place on that occasion, beyond a very wonderful innings by Jessop'.
>
> What a pity! Partner with Jessop during half of the greatest innings in the history of cricket, what a tale he could have told! How almost breathless should we have read every word he wrote! But there it is ...

*

Jessop did play one more spectacular innings in Test cricket, so spectacular in fact that he came close to breaking his own record for England's fastest century in terms of balls faced. It may not have been quite as big a contest as a game against Australia, but in its own way it was a significant occasion – the first day of the first Test ever played between England and South Africa in England. It took place at Lord's on 1 July 1907 and drew a crowd of more than 20,000, and Jessop – back in favour under a new captain, R. E. Foster, despite his shortage of runs – lit up the day with one of his most explosive performances. He struck 93 from what was probably 64 balls, although some reports, probably discounting the delivery to which he was out, stated that he faced only 63. No scorebook appears to survive for this match either. It was a sensational display, one that the *Daily Telegraph* thought worthy of comparison with his heroic hundred five years earlier. 'The London evening paper placards last evening held one great name, "Jessop",' said the *Sheffield Daily Telegraph* the next day.

There was certainly nothing easy about the South African bowling. J. J. Kotze was possibly the fastest bowler in the world at the time, while Bert Vogler and Aubrey Faulkner were both leg-break bowlers who had turned themselves into early masters of the googly, a delivery created by Bosanquet and passed to them through Reggie Schwarz, another member of the attack, who had played alongside Bosanquet at Middlesex. Jessop had not faced Kotze, Vogler or Faulkner before, nor Gordon White, another wrist-spinner, but he seemed unfazed by the problems they posed. His assault was completely at odds with the more sedate tempo of the rest of the day: when he went in, England were labouring at 158 for five, but in a little over 75 minutes, he and Len Braund then raised the score by 145. Jessop's share was 93, Braund's 47.

Jessop's innings took place later in the day than the one at The Oval in 1902 – he went in at around 3.10 p.m. and was out at approaching 4.30 p.m. – but the evening newspapers just about had time to get in most of the salient details. The *Daily Express* the next day produced another of its wagon-wheel scoring charts, which showed the extent to which Jessop swept or pulled the spinners, but also hit them straight. His driving was described as terrific and there was one particularly notable hit high into the pavilion off Vogler. Quite how high this hit went is unclear but it may have reached the top tier. One account said that he sent a ball from Vogler 'among the members on the top of the pavilion ... a magnificent hit'; another that he planted the ball 'amongst the frock-coated gentlemen in the pavilion enclosure'. The *Daily Express* also gave a breakdown of how many runs Jessop took off each bowler: Vogler 30, Kotze 25, Faulkner 18, White 15, Jimmy Sinclair 3 and Schwarz 2.

Jessop's attack on Vogler was telling because before he went in the England batsmen were having difficulty dealing with him; Vogler had taken the first five wickets to fall. But Jessop struck him for two fours before depositing him into the pavilion – a hit still worth only four runs – and much later in his innings took nine off him in the space of three balls. He did have one near miss when he hit Vogler just over the head of White at extra cover when he had scored five, but otherwise made few mistakes. He also tore into Kotze's bowling, inflicting most of the damage during a three-over spell that cost 28 before Kotze withdrew in a huff, pulling his cap back onto his head in dudgeon at being shown so little respect. Kotze did not feature in the remaining two

Tests of the series, perhaps because the pitches did not really suit his pace, but he may have been licking his wounds, too. Nor was Vogler as dangerous again.

Jessop was eventually out to a fine running catch by Faulkner in front of the sightscreen at the Nursery End off Vogler's bowling, when he was only a couple more big hits away from a century in under 70 balls. Jessop rarely seemed concerned about personal landmarks, but he may have been on this occasion, the *Birmingham Post* noting that, once his score was in the eighties, 'for a time he played very carefully, being anxious to secure his century'. One of the reasons his rate of scoring was so fast was that when he was not hitting boundaries he kept ticking over with twos and ones. In all, he hit 14 fours, one three, ten twos and 14 singles.

C. B. Fry, who was playing in the game and posted a 54-run opening partnership with Hayward before being bowled by Vogler for 33, wrote a glowing tribute of Jessop's innings in the *London Daily Chronicle*:

Jessop hit beautifully, and his summary success against the bowling is no discredit to the bowlers. I have seen him play many fine innings, but never a finer than this. He timed the ball perfectly, showed perfect judgment in picking the ball to hit, and in spite of the rapidity of his scoring displayed no trace of wildness. He was, as usual, most severe upon the fast bowler, in this case JJ Kotze, but his treatment of AE Vogler's excellent mixture of leg-breaks and off-breaks was even more meritorious, for Vogler's bowling is not easy to hit ... He is much to be congratulated on one of the very best innings ever played in big cricket.

This was the last great day of Test cricket Jessop enjoyed. He played in the rest of the South Africa series but in two relatively low-scoring games made few runs and did not bowl. He was selected for the first Test against Australia at Edgbaston in 1909, struck a quick 22 in an England win, but was then surprisingly left out of the second game at Lord's in a chaotic reshuffle of the team caused in part by Lord Hawke's absence through ill-health. Even the support of MacLaren, returned to the captaincy in part because of a lack of alternatives, could not save him. Barely a newspaper in the country spared the selectors their ire and Jessop's omission was a particular focal point. England lost and, as he did when he was left out at Old Trafford in 1902, Jessop went away and wreaked havoc on county bowling, in this instance scoring 161 and 129 against Hampshire at Bristol in a match that began the day after England's defeat. He was swiftly reinstated for the third Test, but more misfortune was around the corner.

Just over an hour into the match at Headingley, Jessop badly strained his back firing in a sharp return from cover in an attempt to thwart a quick single. He was not only unable to take any further part in the game, but did not play again that summer.

By this point, he had been appointed Gloucestershire secretary, a move which necessitated he and his family living in Bristol, but brought him some financial stability. In 1911, he had one of his best seasons with the bat, scoring more than 1,900 runs with seven centuries, prompting an invitation to join the winter tour of Australia but he again declined. He played two more Test matches, both against South Africa, in 1912 in a series that formed part of a three-way triangular tournament involving England, South Africa and Australia. Again, he did little with the bat and did not bowl. He was also 12th man for one of the Australia Tests. He continued to play for Gloucestershire until 1914 when war broke out, but had stepped down as county captain at the end of 1912, and it was clear that his playing days were approaching an end.

24

WHAT THE PLAYERS DID NEXT

JESSOP'S TRAGIC ACCIDENT

THE THEORY that luck dealt harshly with England during the summer of 1902, and that there was actually little to choose between the teams despite Australia winning the series – a theory given many an airing in leader columns the day after the Oval Test – was further bolstered by Pelham Warner taking a team Down Under in the winter of 1903-04 and winning handsomely. The final score looked close at 3-2 but Warner's team won the series with a match to spare and showed themselves clearly the better side. It ended a run of four series defeats to Australia and was greeted with a mixture of delight and relief. The tour having been organised by the MCC, it cemented the club's future ownership of England affairs for a generation, and beyond.

What was striking was that none of the amateurs who represented England at The Oval – MacLaren, Jackson, Jessop and Palairet – went on the tour, but six of the seven professionals did. They contributed much to the triumph, too: Hayward and Tyldesley played crucial innings at the top of the order and Braund scored a century during a match-winning stand with R. E. Foster in the first Test. Rhodes took 31 wickets and Hirst 15 as well as scoring 217 runs, while Lilley completed eight catches and seven stumpings. The only professional absentee was Lockwood, who was 35 and fast approaching the end of a long, back-breaking career.

There were a few ructions in advance of the tour, with the Victorian Cricket Association objecting to a proposal from the MCC that Jim Phillips accompany the England team as travelling umpire, quite a common practice at this time, though it had not happened on the last tour of Australia. The VCA's objection was that Phillips, who stood in the third Test at Sheffield in 1902, had written to them questioning the fairness of Saunders' action. Phillips was one of the leading voices in a recent purge of 'suspect' bowlers, so his view carried weight, and there were concerns in Australia that if he came and stood in the Tests he would 'call' Saunders for throwing. As a result, Major Wardill made it clear that Australia's cricket associations did not favour any visiting umpires travelling with the English team, and as a result none was sent.

Saunders took six wickets in the first two Tests, both won by England, and did not appear again. Saunders was not picked to go to England in 1905 for fear of being called by Phillips (who stood in four of the five Tests), but took a full part in the series in Australia in 1907-08, finishing as the leading bowler on either side with 31 wickets. There were fleeting discussions in the English press about Saunders' action towards the end of the 1902 series, in which the main concerns seemed to be that he might have thrown the occasional ball when trying to bowl a faster ball, or one with extra nip.

With half the players involved in the Oval Test of 1902 under the age of 30 at the time, it was unsurprising that many remained involved in Test cricket for several years. Across the course of the 1903-04 and 1905 series, at least 13 of the 22, and sometimes as many as 16 of them, took part in any one match, and as late as the 1909 series there were often ten involved. Darling missed the 1903-04 series but returned as captain in England in 1905, but with Trumble retired and Saunders not around, he was in charge of an attack that was incapable of dismissing England twice on any occasion. He faced criticism for being too defensive.

The youngest players on either side in 1902 – Rhodes for England, Armstrong for Australia – both played for their countries beyond the First World War. Rhodes had reinvented himself as a successful opening batsman before the war, but subsequently was picked again as a left-arm spinner. This included being called up for a deciding Test against Australia at The Oval in 1926, Rhodes by now aged 48, and he duly helped England regain the Ashes with six wickets. Armstrong, himself now in his forties, was Australia's first post-war captain, and oversaw eight straight victories over England (five at home and three in England) in as many months in 1920-21 and 1921. It set a benchmark for Australian dominance and instilled in English hearts a desire for vengeance which led directly to the Bodyline tactics deployed by Douglas Jardine, who as a young batsman at Oxford had been coached by Hayward. It was December 1924 before England and Australia met without any survivors from Jessop's match taking part.

*

The class of 1902 on both sides were in the main fortunate to be young enough to carry on playing cricket for many years, but old enough that by the outbreak of the First World War in 1914 most were into their forties and not immediately required, if ever at all, for military service.

This was a conflict on an altogether different scale from the Boer War that dominated people's lives in 1902. Men still in their thirties who had played Test cricket such as Colin Blythe, Major Booth, Kenneth Hutchings and Leonard Moon, all of England, Tibby Cotter of Australia, and Schwarz and White of the 1907 South Africa team, all died while on military service (Schwarz succumbed to Spanish flu). Rhodes, who was 37 when hostilities began, was sent to work in a munitions factory in Huddersfield and spent the war there.

Not that our two groups of players did not experience tragedies of other sorts. Australia's young opening batsmen from Sydney, Reggie Duff and Victor Trumper, both died young. Duff toured England again in 1905, and scored 146 in the final Test at The Oval, but it was his one real highlight of the trip. Returning home, he descended into alcoholism, and died broke and broken in 1911, aged 33. Trumper toured England twice more and would have done so again but for a dispute between players and board which resulted in him and five others not coming in 1912. Trumper's reputation as the world's purest and most dazzling batsman had only grown, but in 1914 his health declined rapidly and in 1915 he died of kidney disease, aged 37. Duff's funeral was paid for by sympathetic team-mates; Trumper's was attended by 250,000, with Armstrong, Gregory and Noble among the pallbearers.

Jessop, aged forty, volunteered for service at the outbreak of war and within months was commissioned as captain in the 14th Manchester Regiment. In 1915 he and MacLaren took part in a recruitment campaign. In 1916 he was transferred to the Lincolnshire Regiment and, suffering from severe lumbago, was sent for steam treatment to Bath, a process that involved total immersion in a heated, upright container for 30 minutes. In a tragic accident, Jessop was left unattended and the catch on the container fell, preventing him from releasing himself. According to Brodribb's account, when Jessop was rescued it was found that his heart had been seriously damaged. He was invalided out of the army in November 1917 and the following year suffered a serious heart attack. It was nearly two years before he could walk any kind of distance. He never played any sort of cricket again and his days as a serious golfer were also over. He recovered enough to write his autobiography and resume his journalism, contributing pieces to the *Daily Mail* on the 1926 Ashes and writing a number of boys' adventure novels. He and his wife spent much of their later lives living with their son G. L. O. Jessop, who took the holy orders that his father had once contemplated.

Despite these serious health setbacks, Jessop outlived all but two of the other participants of the Oval Test. He died in May 1955, a week short of his 81st birthday and two years after his beloved wife of more than 50 years passed away. He was buried alongside her in a cemetery in Dorchester. Braund died later the same year, while Rhodes survived until his 96th year in 1973. Jessop left an estate worth £2,044, eight years after Jackson died leaving £85,620. Like Jessop, Jackson survived a near-death experience, being the target of an assassination attempt while serving as Governor of Bengal in 1932.

25

HOW JESSOP'S RECORD LIVED ON

BAZBALLERS HUNT THE ENGLAND RECORD

JESSOP'S LEGEND burned as brightly as anyone's from his generation. It helped that no one remotely like him came along for many years. As an entertainer, he remained out on his own. No one else hit with his consistent ferocity. Also, times changed. By the 1920s, the freewheeling amateur cricketer was entering his long decline, and as the county and Test game became dominated by professionals whose outlook was more utilitarian, so the enterprise went out of English batsmanship. This needed to happen if England were to compete with the hard-headed Australians and it was notable that when they did manage to secure rare series victories in Australia it was done through the grim accumulation of runs, or under disciplinarian captains such as Douglas Jardine and Len Hutton for whom risk-taking was anathema. Even a batsman with the attacking capabilities of Denis Compton came under pressure to rein in his enthusiasm. All this only served to encourage those who could remember the long, golden Edwardian summers to think of them with even greater fondness. No one pointed out that 1902 had been largely grey, and wet.

As the number of Test-playing countries expanded, so the game became ever more nationalistic, and ever more defensive; the urge to avoid defeat trumped the desire to win. The 1950s, the decade of Jessop's death, saw Test matches played in an unprecedentedly attritional manner. The rate of scoring – 2.30 runs per over – had never been as slow; nor would it be as slow again. Some 18 months after Jessop died, Peter Richardson, an opening batsman from Worcestershire, scored the slowest century ever made for England, in a Test match in Johannesburg; it took him more than eight hours. You could have fitted six Jessop centuries into that time. But the fallow years went well beyond the fifties: in no calendar year between 1922 and 1974 was the rate of scoring in Test cricket as fast as it was in 1902. It took the rise of West Indian cricket, and the introduction of the one-day format into county cricket in the 1960s, to bring the first stirrings of a renaissance.

Jessop was cherished as a symbol of a vanished era and a lost spirit of adventure. Neville Cardus, who was too young to have attended Jessop's match but not too old to absorb some of the glamour of the man, wrote a heartfelt essay in the late 1940s entitled, 'A Cry for a Jessop', which in part served as a rebuke to the stonewalling batsmen of the new age, and there were plenty of other nostalgics like him. When Jessop died, Jack Hobbs, who in August 1902 had yet to escape Cambridge for Surrey and begin his rise to cricketing greatness, but would eventually play against him many times, said that Jessop drew crowds in a way that not even Don Bradman matched.

There was a more specific point in respect of English cricket as to why so few batsmen dared to even think of playing as Jessop did. Englishmen may have been cautious by instinct in any case, but the English climate, and as a consequence English pitches, tended to be more helpful to bowlers than many other places. While it is true that the lack of bounce assisted Jessop's cross-batted strokes, often the ball simply nipped around too much on the uncovered pitches to encourage someone to play in his vein. Safety first was everyone's first instinct. England produced many great Test-match opening batsmen, who knew how to scrap and survive against the moving ball, but not so many aggressors of Jessop's sort. Look at a list of the fastest Test match centuries, and it is dominated by players from other nations, playing in other climes, where it was possible to hit through the line of the ball without fear of the consequences.

Things really began to change in the 1970s. An influx of overseas stars into the county game, and the explosion of one-day cricket, led to batsmen from all regions embracing new ideas. Growing up at Somerset alongside Viv Richards, an Antiguan and a brutal destroyer of bowling, Ian Botham developed into the most destructive England batsman since Jessop. In the Ashes series of 1981, Botham struck a century at Headingley off 87 balls and another at Old Trafford off 86 balls against an Australian team led by a captain, Kim Hughes, who faced similar criticism to Darling in 1902 about over-using his frontline bowlers and generally losing the plot. That it was known that Botham had taken this many deliveries to reach his hundreds was due to what was by then the accepted practice of using the linear scoring system that had been developed by a few pioneers before the First World War without becoming commonplace. Bill Ferguson remained one of its few advocates through to the 1950s. In the end, it was popularised as much as anything by the scorers employed by radio and television commentary teams who needed a ready supply of statistical information; Bill Frindall, who supported BBC radio's *Test Match Special* commentators from 1966 until his death in 2009, even published a series of his linear scorebooks from the mid-1970s. County scorers began using the linear method from the early 1970s. The various forms of one-day cricket, operating on the principle that both teams received the same number of overs, affirmed the idea that balls faced was more important than minutes or hours batted.

Botham's Ashes' hundreds, and a 71-ball century by West Indies opener Roy Fredericks in a Test in Australia in 1975, galvanised interest in measuring and comparing the speed of hundreds in terms of balls received. In 1986, the debate gained fresh impetus when Richards flayed a hundred off just 56 balls against England in a Test in his native Antigua.

Researchers went back to Ferguson's linear scorebooks to establish that Jack Gregory of Australia had struck a 67-ball century in South Africa in 1921, and Gerald Brodribb's biography of Jessop, published in 1974 to coincide with the centenary of Jessop's birth, brought to notice an unidentified newspaper cutting (though actually from the *Athletic News*) that suggested his Oval hundred had taken 76 balls. Brodribb introduced more readers to this claim when he contributed an article about fast Test hundreds to the 1983 *Wisden*.

Interestingly, though, not everyone went with the claim of 76 balls. When James Gibb, a schoolmaster from the North-East, published his *Test Cricket Records* in 1979, he stated that Jessop's hundred came off 75 balls, possibly derived from one of the various sources that stated Jessop faced 75 balls for his entire innings of 104. Then, when Frindall took over *Wisden*'s records section and introduced a table listing the fastest Test hundreds in terms of balls received, Jessop's hundred was given as coming off 75 balls in both the 1987 and 1988 editions, before it was changed to 76 balls in 1989.

Jessop's innings was also subjected in the 2010s to a reconstruction by Charles Davis, the Australian statistician. Using scorebooks, where available, and newspaper reports, Davis attempted to reconstruct a number of celebrated Test matches or individual Test innings. Regarding Jessop's hundred, he described it to me in an email in 2023 as 'a rough analysis a few years ago that would not stand up to close scrutiny', adding: 'What I did was take Brodribb's ball-by-ball [list] and fitted the rest of the innings around it as best I could … I used a variety of newspaper reports wherever they reported individual shots and scores at particular stages of the innings.' Davis's sequencing of Jessop's 80 balls could not quite match the Brodribb original in respect of the placement of two dot balls, which perhaps reinforces how difficult it is to create a precise reconstruction, especially without the assistance of any kind of scorebook. In terms of his broad project, Davis described his reconstructions as 'a best rendering of important innings that in turn allow estimates of balls faced and other important statistics'. Davis accepted they were 'not exact'.

With the additional information acquired from the *Morning Leader* breakdown, plus other details gleaned from newspapers not used by Davis, my reconstruction is radically different from his. With respect to Davis's prodigious efforts, I am confident my version is wholly more accurate.

*

The first time Jessop's record came under serious threat was after England radically altered their approach to Test cricket in 2022, when Ben Stokes and Brendon 'Baz' McCullum took over as captain and head coach. The team had previously spent long periods in bio-secure bubbles during the Covid-19 pandemic, and endured a lengthy run of poor results, and the new management was eager to liberate players who had mislaid their sense of enjoyment. McCullum himself had been a highly aggressive batsman in his playing days with New Zealand and in his final Test appearance in 2016 had lowered the world record held by Viv Richards by two balls. The batsmen were told to stop worrying about getting out, to always take the aggressive option, and 'run towards the danger', in a style of play that became known as 'Bazball'. They were essentially told to play like Jessop. In the space of the next two years, five of the batsmen scored hundreds off 90 balls or fewer, and by the end of 2024 they owned as a group seven of the 11 fastest Test centuries ever made for England.

The transformation was astonishing. In the second match under the new regime, Jonny Bairstow, who was always ultra-attacking in outlook when playing at his best, struck a blistering 136 not out off 92 balls to win a game against New Zealand at Trent Bridge, a venue with the shortest boundaries of any Test ground in England following its redevelopment. As in Jessop's match, England's run-chase did not get off to the best start, as they lost three wickets for 56 and a fourth at 93 in pursuit of 299, but Bairstow was urged by Stokes, his partner, to remain positive. By taking 16 off an over from Trent Boult, Bairstow moved to 88 from 68 balls, and two fours off his next three balls from Matt Henry took him to 96 off 71. However, his next 5 deliveries yielded 0, 2, 1, 0 and 0 before a drive through the covers for three took him to a hundred off 77 balls. Bairstow's two dot balls on 99 were both checked shots into the off side: his desire to make sure he got to his hundred, or perhaps a wish to not get out through an over-eagerness to get there and jeopardise his team's chances, made him take a little more care and cost him the chance to beat or equal what was then accepted to be Jessop's record of 76 balls.

The following year, during the home Ashes series of 2023, Bairstow came close to another very fast century when he ran out of partners at Old Trafford having hit 99 not out off 81 balls during a mammoth England score of 592 off only 107.4 overs. However, Bairstow accelerated strongly towards the end, hitting 44 off his last 26 deliveries, so he was never really in with a chance of rivalling Jessop.

Remarkably, Harry Brook, who first came into the team following an injury to Bairstow, nearly beat the 76-ball mark twice in one game. On the first day of a series in Pakistan in December 2022, on a flat pitch in Rawalpindi that suited England's aggressive intentions to perfection, four of their top six plundered swift centuries as they racked up a record first-day score of 506 for four: Zak Crawley reached his hundred off 88 balls (the fastest ever by an England opener), Ben Duckett off 105 balls, Ollie Pope off 90 balls and Brook in just 80. Brook was going well, but not spectacularly so, at a run per ball when Pakistan brought on part-time spinner Saud Shakeel. Brook plundered 24 off his first over to move to 84 off 64 balls, which soon became 89 off 66 balls. But then, inexplicably, he lost momentum and managed only 8 from his next 13 balls before a cover drive off Naseem Shah brought him his hundred. Three days later, with England seeking quick second-innings runs ahead of a declaration, Brook raced to 84 off 60 balls – so, even faster than he had got to that score in the first innings – but after stalling a little was bowled by Naseem for 87 off 65 aiming a big hit through midwicket.

Asked around this time if he knew who Gilbert Jessop was, Brook replied: 'I do now.' And it felt like only a matter of time before Jessop's record – whether it came off 72, 73 or 74 balls – finally fell.

Appendix

JESSOP'S INNINGS: OVER BY OVER

In order to build up the best picture of what happened while Jessop was at the crease during his great innings, I made a careful study of the many contemporary reports of England's entire second innings at The Oval on 13 August 1902. Through these, it was possible to plot a course of events, both known and surmised; even if not every scoring shot was described somewhere, the many references to the 'live' England score and the respective scores of the batsmen at the crease at the time helped draw conclusions about shots that had been missed. Naturally, some passages of play were less well reported than others; for instance, more details about the stands between Jackson and Braund, and Hirst and Lockwood, would have been useful.

Importantly, it was possible to ascertain at what points the 11 extras (five byes, six leg-byes) were scored; a single run from a bye or leg-bye leads to the strike passing between batsmen without any change in their individual scores, so it is essential to know when byes and leg-byes happened, and when such switches may have taken place.

A fundamental problem was that almost no mention was made to the number of overs that had passed in the innings. The *Daily Express*'s allusion to there being 22 overs from Jessop's first 'roof' hit to his second was an isolated, and invaluable, exception.

However, I am reasonably confident that by the time Jessop went out to bat with England 48 for five, 18.5 overs had been bowled by Australia in what I have calculated as about 58 minutes, and that after he was out another 20.5 overs were bowled in what I have put at 67 minutes. Between times, Jessop was at the crease for 27.1 overs and 85 minutes, during which time he faced just under half the 163 deliveries that were bowled. By my estimation he faced 76–78 balls in his entire innings, while his partners received 85–87 balls (Jackson 78–80, Hirst 7).

To summarise the three phases of the innings:

Phase	England score	Main run-scorers	Extras	Overs bowled	Time batted
Before Jessop went in	48 for five	Jackson 31	0	18.5 overs	58 minutes
While Jessop was batting	139 for two	Jessop 104 Jackson 18 Hirst 9	8	27.1 overs	85 minutes
After Jessop was out	76 for two	Hirst 49 Lilley 16	3	20.5 overs	67 minutes

Here is my recreation of the second of these phases, during which Jessop batted. While not every scoring shot and dot ball can be placed exactly within each over, especially when Jackson was the one on strike, the ball-by-ball lists published by the *Morning Leader* and the *Athletic News*, in conjunction with other evidence, allow us to assemble a more detailed picture than ever before. It is, in essence, an attempt to construct the kind of 'linear score' that is standard in modern cricket, and summarises the evidence outlined in Chapters 20 and 21.

Time	Pavilion End bowler	Vauxhall End bowler	Jessop	Runs (balls faced)	Jackson	Runs	England score at end of over	Over no.
1.08	Trumble (to finish) 10		1	1 (1)	-	31	49-5	19
1.08		Saunders 10	2 4 1 - - -	8 (4)	- - 0 0 0	31	56-5	20
1.11	Trumble 11		1 - - 0 (lb1) - -	9 (6)	- 0 3 - 0 1	35	62-5	21
1.14		Saunders 11	- - - - - 0 (lb1)	9 (7)	0 0 0 0 1 -	36	64-5	22
1.17	Trumble 12		4 4 1 - - -	18 (10)	- - 0 0 0	36	73-5	23
1.20		Saunders 12	0 4 0 0 0 0 (Note 1)	22 (16)	- - - - -	36	77-5	24
1.23	Trumble 13		- - - - 1	23 (17)	0 0 0 0 3 -	39	81-5	25
1.26		Saunders 13	4 1 - - - -	28 (19)	- 0 0 0 0	39	86-5	26
1.29	Trumble 14		1 - - - - (Note 2)	29 (20+1)	- 0 0 0 0 0	39	87-5	27
							LUNCH	
2.15		Saunders 14	1 - - 0 1	31 (23+1)	- 0 0 1 - -	40	90-5	28
2.18	Trumble 15		4 1 - - 0 0	36 (27+1)	- 0 1 - -	41	96-5	29
2.21		Saunders 15	- - - - - -	36 (27+1)	0 0 0 0 (b4) 0 0	41	100-5	30
2.24	Trumble 16		0 1 - - - -	37 (29+1)	- 0 0 0 0	41	101-5	31
2.27		Saunders 16	0 3 - - - -	40 (31+1)	- 0 2 2 0	45	108-5	32
2.30	Trumble 17		0 1 - - - -	41 (33+1)	- - 0 0 0 0	45	109-5	33

Time	Pavilion End bowler	Vauxhall End bowler	Jessop	Runs (balls faced)	Jackson	Runs	England score at end of over	Over no.
2.33		Saunders 17	0 3 - - - -	44 (35+1)	- - 0 0 0 0	45	112-5	34
2.36	Trumble 18		5 - - - - -	49 (36+1)	- 0 0 0 0 0	45	117-5	35
2.39	Trumble 19		1 - - - - 4	54 (38+1)	- 0 0 2 1 -	48	125-5	36
2.42		Saunders 18	- - - - - - (Note 3)	54 (38+1)	0 0 0 0 0 0	48	125-5	37
2.45		Saunders 19	4 4 4 4 1 -	71 (43+1)	- - - - - 0	48	142-5	38
2.49	Trumble 20		0 (lb1) - - 0 0 1 (Note 4)	72 (47+2)	- 0 0 (lb1) - - -	48	145-5	39
2.52		Armstrong 1	0 0 0 0 0 1	73 (53+2)	- - - - - -	48	146-5	40
2.55	Trumble 21		2 0 0 0 0 0	75 (59+2)	- - - - - -	48	148-5	41
2.58		Armstrong 2	- 0 4 0 0 4	83 (64+2)	1 - - - - -	49	157-5	42
3.01	Trumble 22		- - - - - -	83 (64+2)	0 0 0 0 W Hirst 0	49	157-6	43
3.04		Armstrong 3	1 - - - - -	84 (65+2)	- 0 4 0 4 0	8	166-6	44
3.07	Trumble 23		0 4 2 0 2 4	96 (71+2)	- - - - - -	8	178-6	45
3.11		Armstrong 4	- 4 4 0 0 W (Note 5)	104 (76+2)	1 - - - - -	9	187-7	46

Note 1: the list published in the *Morning Leader* suggested Jessop did not face the first ball of this over, but circumstantial evidence – as well as the list in the *Athletic News* – indicates that he must have done; a dot ball has therefore been debited to him.

Note 2: the *Morning Leader* list suggests Jessop took a single off the first ball of this over, the *Athletic News* implies that he did so off the second after playing a dot ball; there is no way of being sure, so a possible additional ball has been debited against Jessop.

Note 3: the *Athletic News* list suggests Jessop faced two dot balls in this over, but weighing all the evidence this is not possible.

Note 4: the *Morning Leader* list indicates that Jessop faced four balls in this over, the *Athletic News* list that he faced five; there is no way of being sure, so a possible additional ball has been debited against Jessop. That there were two single leg-byes in this over may have led to some confusion as to which batsman was on strike for which balls.

Note 5: the *Morning Leader* list indicates that the three balls before Jessop was out went 4, 0, 0 while the Athletic News lists states 0, 4, 0. I have gone with the *Leader* here.

APPENDIX

FASTEST TEST CENTURIES FOR ENGLAND:
BY BALLS FACED

72–74	**Gilbert Jessop**	**v Australia, The Oval 1902**
77	Jonny Bairstow	v New Zealand, Trent Bridge 2022
80	Harry Brook	v Pakistan, Rawalpindi 2022 (1st inns)
85	Ben Stokes	v New Zealand, Lord's 2015
86	Ian Botham	v Australia, Old Trafford 1981
86	Zak Crawley	v Pakistan, Rawalpindi 2022
87	Ian Botham	v Australia, Headingley 1981
88	Kevin Pietersen	v West Indies, Trinidad 2009
88	Ben Duckett	v India, Rajkot 2024
90	Ollie Pope	v Pakistan, Rawalpindi 2022
91	Harry Brook	v New Zealand, Wellington 2024

(Up to 21 May 2025)

THE FOLLOWING CAME CLOSE TO SCORING
FAST HUNDREDS FOR ENGLAND:

93 off 64 balls	Gilbert Jessop	v South Africa, Lord's 1907
87 off 65 balls	Harry Brook	v Pakistan, Rawalpindi 2022 (second innings)
84 off 68 balls	Ben Duckett	v New Zealand, Mount Maunganui 2023
99* off 81 balls	Jonny Bairstow	v Australia, Old Trafford 2023
84 off 75 balls	Ben Duckett	v Pakistan, Multan 2024
89 off 81 balls	Harry Brook	v New Zealand, Mount Maunganui 2023
86 off 79 balls	Ben Duckett	v Sri Lanka, The Oval 2024

(Up to 21 May 2025)

FASTEST TEST CENTURIES: BY BALLS FACED

A recalculation of Jessop's balls faced for his hundred from 76 balls to 72–74 balls moved him up from 15th to 11th place in the all-time list of fastest Test centuries. Jessop is the only player on this list who was playing in a match in England, or batting in the fourth innings of the match. He was also one of only three players, along with Gilchrist and de Grandhomme, to have been batting as low as No 7.

54	Brendon McCullum	New Zealand v Australia, Christchurch 2016
56	Viv Richards	West Indies v England, Antigua 1985
56	Misbah-ul-Haq	Pakistan v Australia, Abu Dhabi 2014
57	Adam Gilchrist	Australia v England, Perth 2006
67	Jack Gregory	Australia v South Africa, Johannesburg, 1921
69	Shiv Chanderpaul	West Indies v Australia, Georgetown 2003
69	David Warner	Australia v India, Perth 2012
70	Chris Gayle	West Indies v Australia, Perth 2009
71	Roy Fredericks	West Indies v Australia, Perth 1975
71	Colin de Grandhomme	New Zealand v West Indies, Wellington 2017
72–74	**Gilbert Jessop**	**England v Australia, The Oval 1902**
74	Majid Khan	Pakistan v New Zealand, Karachi 1976
74	Mohammad Azharuddin	India v South Africa, Calcutta 1996
74	Brendon McCullum	New Zealand v Sri Lanka, Christchurch 2014
75	A. B. de Villiers	South Africa v India, Centurion 2010

(Up to 21 May 2025)

FASTEST TEST CENTURIES: BY MINUTES BATTED

A recalculation of the time Jessop batted to reach his hundred from 75 to 80 minutes dropped him down from third to joint fifth in the all-time list of fastest Test centuries in terms of time.

70	Jack Gregory	Australia v South Africa, Johannesburg 1921
74	Misbah-ul-Haq	Pakistan v Australia, Abu Dhabi 2014
78	Richie Benaud	Australia v West Indies, Kingston 1955
78	Brendon McCullum	New Zealand v Australia, Christchurch 2016
80	**Gilbert Jessop**	**England v Australia, The Oval 1902**
80	Jimmy Sinclair	South Africa v Australia, Johannesburg 1902
81	Viv Richards	West Indies v England, Antigua 1985
86	Bruce Taylor	New Zealand v West Indies, Auckland 1969
90	George Bonnor	Australia v England, Sydney 1885
90	Les Ames	England v West Indies, Kingston 1930
91	Joe Darling	Australia v England, Sydney 1898
91	Stan McCabe	Australia v South Africa, Johannesburg 1935
92	Percy Sherwell	South Africa v England, Lord's 1907
94	Victor Trumper	Australia v England, Sydney 1903
95	Jack Brown	England v Australia, Melbourne 1895

(Up to 21 May 2025)

BEST STRIKE-RATES IN ASHES SERIES

Such was the interest in how fast Jessop batted that the number of balls he faced was referred to in respect of a number of his innings in the 1902 series. It was reported that he scored 6 off six balls in the first Test, and 12 off nine balls and 55 off 49 balls in the third Test. His two innings at The Oval are known within narrow limits, with the evidence pointing to his first innings of 13 lasting nine or ten balls, and his 104 spanning 76–78 balls. It is therefore possible to calculate that his strike-rate for the series was higher than for anyone else playing in an England–Australia series based on a minimum of 175 runs.

Strike-rate	Runs	Balls	Batsman	Series
125.0-127.5	190	149–152	Gilbert Jessop (England)	1902
102.5	333	325	Adam Gilchrist (Australia)	2002-03
101.8	229	225	Adam Gilchrist (Australia)	2006-07
93.2	399	428	Ian Botham (England)	1981
90.7	340	375	Adam Gilchrist (Australia)	2001

(Minimum 175 runs; strike-rate = runs per 100 balls)

ENGLAND v AUSTRALIA (Fifth Test)

The Oval, London, 11, 12, 13 August 1902
Toss: Australia. Result: England won by 1 wicket

AUSTRALIA

Victor Trumper	b Hirst	42	run out		2
Reggie Duff	c †Lilley b Hirst	23	b Lockwood		6
Clem Hill	b Hirst	11	c MacLaren b Hirst		34
*Joe Darling	c †Lilley b Hirst	3	c MacLaren b Lockwood		15
Monty Noble	c & b Jackson	52	b Braund		13
Syd Gregory	b Hirst	23	b Braund		9
Warwick Armstrong	b Jackson	17	b Lockwood		21
Bert Hopkins	c MacLaren b Lockwood	40	c †Lilley b Lockwood		3
Hugh Trumble	not out	64	c Tyldesley b Rhodes		2
†James Kelly	c Rhodes b Braund	39	not out		7
Jack Saunders	lbw b Braund	0	lbw b Lockwood		0
Extras	(B 5, LB 3, NB 2)	10	(B 7, LB 2)		9
Total	**(123.5 overs)**	**324**	**(60 overs)**		**121**

ENGLAND

*Archie MacLaren	c Armstrong b Trumble	10	b Saunders		2
Lionel Palairet	b Trumble	20	b Saunders		6
Johnny Tyldesley	b Trumble	33	b Saunders		0
Tom Hayward	b Trumble	0	c †Kelly b Saunders		7
Stanley Jackson	c Armstrong b Saunders	2	c & b Trumble		49
Len Braund	c Hill b Trumble	22	c †Kelly b Trumble		2
Gilbert Jessop	b Trumble	13	c Noble b Armstrong		104
George Hirst	c & b Trumble	43	not out		58
Bill Lockwood	c Noble b Saunders	25	lbw b Trumble		2
†Dick Lilley	c Trumper b Trumble	0	c Darling b Trumble		16
Wilfred Rhodes	not out	0	not out		6
Extras	(B 13, LB 2)	15	(B 5, LB 6)		11
Total	**(61 overs)**	**183**	**(9 wkts; 66.5 overs)**		**263**

ENGLAND	O	M	R	W		O	M	R	W
Bill Lockwood	24	2	85	1		20	6	45	5
Wilfred Rhodes	28	9	46	0		22	7	38	1
George Hirst	29	5	77	5		5	1	7	1
Len Braund	16.5	5	29	2		9	1	15	2
Stanley Jackson	20	4	66	2		4	3	7	0
Gilbert Jessop	6	2	11	0					

AUSTRALIA	O	M	R	W		O	M	R	W
Hugh Trumble	31	13	65	8		33.5	4	108	4
Jack Saunders	23	7	79	2		24	3	105	4
Monty Noble	7	3	24	0	(4)	5	0	11	0
Warwick Armstrong					(3)	4	0	28	1

FALL OF WICKETS

	A	E	A	E
Wkt	*1st*	*1st*	*2nd*	*2nd*
1st	47	31	6	5
2nd	63	36	9	5
3rd	69	62	31	10
4th	82	67	71	31
5th	126	67	75	48
6th	174	83	91	157
7th	175	137	99	187
8th	256	179	114	214
9th	324	183	115	248
10th	324	183	121	

Umpires: Archibald White and Charles Richardson

Close of Play – Day 1: A(1) 324; Day 2: A(2) 114-8; Day 3: E(2) 263-9

Sources

The best available source for revisiting the events of 1902 was contemporaneous newspapers and periodicals. On the day of Jessop's innings, or the day after, many publications drew on a mixture of agency reports and despatches by their own correspondents; many of the smaller papers relied wholly on agency reports, probably chiefly provided by the Cricket Reporting Agency. Australian newspapers drew on cables sent by Reuters, who sent score updates which were sometimes different from those that appeared domestically. British evening, daily and weekly newspapers and periodicals provided a rich variety of material on Jessop's match and specifically his innings. As the game took place between Monday and Wednesday, this was not a story best suited to weeklies, but a number of titles provided original and insightful articles on the Saturday and Sunday after the match.

The digital British Newspaper Archive, which is an ongoing project to place online the British Library's vast collection of newspapers, was a central and invaluable resource. It renders hundreds of national and regional papers not only readily available but also searchable at speed, greatly increasing the chances of tracking down relevant material. The newspapers.com site was also useful for titles not in the British Newspaper Archive, as was http://trove.nla.gov.au for publications in Australia.

The following proved the most useful:

EVENING NEWSPAPERS, WEDNESDAY 13 AUGUST

London/South: *Westminster Gazette, Evening News, Echo, Pall Mall Gazette, St James's Gazette, Southern Daily Echo*
Midlands: *Nottingham Evening Post, Birmingham Evening Despatch, Birmingham Post, Coventry Evening Telegraph, Leicester Daily Mercury*
Yorkshire/North East: *Sheffield Evening Telegraph, Yorkshire Evening Post, Halifax Evening Courier, North East Daily Gazette*
Lancashire: *Manchester Evening News*
South-West: *Gloucestershire Echo*

MORNING NEWSPAPERS, THURSDAY 14 AUGUST

London: *Daily Express, Morning Leader, Daily Mail, Sportsman, Sporting Life, Daily News, Daily Telegraph, The Times, Standard, Morning Post. Cricket: A Weekly Record of the Game*, published in London, also appeared on Thursday morning.
Yorkshire/North East: *Sheffield Daily Telegraph, Yorkshire Post and Leeds Intelligencer, Leeds Mercury, Shields Daily Gazette*
Midlands: *Birmingham Daily Mail, Birmingham Daily Gazette, Derby Daily Telegraph*
South-West: *Western Daily Press*

EVENING NEWSPAPERS, THURSDAY 14 AUGUST

London: *Westminster Gazette, Evening News, St James's Gazette, Pall Mall Gazette*
Yorkshire/North East: *Yorkshire Evening Post, Sheffield Evening Telegraph*
Lancashire: *Manchester Evening News*
Scotland: *Edinburgh Evening News, Dundee Evening Post*

SUBSEQUENT DAYS

Friday 15 August: *Daily Mail, Hull Daily Mail*
Saturday 16 August: *Field, Illustrated Sporting and Dramatic News, Globe, Nottingham Evening Post, Cheltenham Chronicle, Runcorn Guardian, Horfield and Bishopston Record*
Sunday 17 August: *Lloyd's Weekly, Weekly Despatch*
Monday 18 August: *Athletic News and Cyclists' Journal, Leeds Mercury, Scottish Referee*
Tuesday 19 August: *Daily Express*
Friday 22 August: *Dover Express*
Saturday 23 August: *Country Life Illustrated, Burnley Gazette*

OTHER NEWSPAPERS AND PERIODICALS

Strand Magazine, South London Press, Uttoxeter New Era, Sketch, Black & White, Truth, St Andrews Citizen

BOOKS AND ACADEMIC PAPERS

Alcock, C. W. and Lord Alverstone, *Surrey Cricket: Its History and Associations* (Longmans and Co., 1902)

Batchelder, Alf, *Hugh Trumble: A Cricketer's Life* (Melbourne Cricket Club and Australian Scholarly Publishing, 2009)

Beanland, V. A. S., *Great Games and Great Players* (W. H. Allen, 1945)

Beldam, George, and Fry, Charles B., *Great Batsmen: Their Methods at a Glance* (Macmillan, 1905)

Britton, C. J., *G.L. Jessop: a Complete Record of His Performances in First-Class Cricket* (Cornish Brothers, 1935)

Brodribb, Gerald, *The Croucher: A Biography of Gilbert Jessop* (London Magazine Editions, 1974)

Brown, Lionel H., *Victor Trumper and the 1902 Australians* (Martin Secker & Warburg Ltd, 1981)

Catton, J. A. H., *Wickets and Goals* (Chapman & Hall, 1926)

Haigh, Gideon, *The Big Ship: Warwick Armstrong and the Making of Modern Cricket* (Text Publishing, 2001)

Haigh, Gideon, *Stroke of Genius: Victor Trumper and the Shot that Changed Cricket* (Simon & Schuster, 2016)

Hodgson, R. L., *Cricket Memories by a Country Vicar* (Methuen, 1930)

Jessop, Gilbert, *A Cricketer's Log* (Hodder & Stoughton, 1922)

Lee, Alan J., *The Origins of the Popular Press in England, 1855–1914* (Croom Helm, 1976)

Roberts, Andrew, *The Chief: The Life of Lord Northcliffe Britain's Greatest Press Baron* (Simon & Schuster, 2022)

Rogerson, Sidney, *Wilfred Rhodes* (Hollis & Carter, 1960)

Tate, Stephen, *The Professionalisation of Sports Journalism c 1850–1939 with particular reference to the career of James Catton* (University of Central Lancashire, 2007)

Thomson, A. A., *Cricket My Happiness* (Museum Press, 1956)

Travers, Ben, *94 Declared* (Elm Tree Books, 1981)

Uttley, Paul, *Gilbert L. Jessop* (Gloucestershire County Cricket Club Heritage Trust, 2024)

White, Jerry, *London in the Twentieth Century: A City and Its People* (Viking Adult, 2001)

Wodehouse, P. G., *Over Seventy: An Autobiography – With Digressions* (Herbert Jenkins Limited, 1957)

Images

Gilbert Jessop: Bob Thomas / Popperfoto / Getty Images
Jessop's bat (commemorative plaque): courtesy of the author
Jessop's bat (in full): courtesy of the author
"The Croucher": © Illustrated London News Ltd. / Mary Evans
England XI at Sheffield: © Illustrated London News Ltd. / Mary Evans
Frank Stanley Jackson: George Beldam / Popperfoto / Getty Images
Charles Fry: Popperfoto / Getty Images
1902 Australian Team: Paul Popper / Popperfoto / Getty Images
Oval Scoreboard: Hudson & Kearns in *Country Life* (August 23, 1902)
Hirst and Braund: Hudson & Kearns in *Country Life* (August 23, 1902)
Jessop batting: George Beldam, found in *England Versus Australia: Pictorial History of Every Test Match Since 1877* by David Frith (London: BBC Books, 1977/1993)
Crowd rushing the field: George Beldam, found in England Versus Australia: Pictorial History of Every Test Match Since 1877 by David Frith (London: BBC Books, 1977/1993)
Panorama of the Oval: *The Archives Photographs Series: Surrey County Cricket Club* compiled by William A Powell (NPI Media Group, 1996)
Jonny Bairstow: Philip Brown / Popperfoto / Getty Images
Harry Brook: Philip Brown / Popperfoto / Getty Images
Brendan McCullum and Ben Stokes: Philip Brown / Popperfoto / Getty Images

Acknowledgements

Charles Davis was, as far as I know, the first person in modern times to attempt to construct a ball-by-ball timeline for Jessop's innings. He was very helpful in responding to my early inquiries about how he had done this, and the problems he encountered, as well as alerting me to the difficulties of tracing early Test match scorebooks, and that these books were not in any case always free from errors. His website http://www.sportstats.com.au contains interesting material on these topics, as well as many linear scores.

David Studham of the Melbourne Cricket Club library also gave me useful information on those early scorebooks from England–Australia tours which survive. The late Roger Gibbons of the Gloucestershire CCC Heritage Trust could not have been more obliging when I visited the museum at the County Ground in Bristol in November 2024 and allowed me to handle the bat used by Jessop, which was on loan from the Lord's museum at the time, and go through Gerald Brodribb's papers, which included some material which did not make it into his biography of Jessop. Thanks also to the ever-helpful England media officer Danny Reuben for arranging to measure Harry Brook's bat by way of comparison with Jessop's. To Ian Marshall at Bloomsbury, thank you for believing in the idea, for your guidance, and for directing me towards some of the particulars of Lord Northcliffe's part in the newspaper revolution circa 1900. Thanks also to Richard Collins for his sensitive copy-edit.

I must also acknowledge Dr Lucy Jessop, Gilbert's granddaughter, for her early assistance; Pat Jessop, his daughter-in-law; and Rodney Ulyate. My wife, Gayle, has supported me through many books but perhaps not one written in such a short, intense period as this, in which I disappeared into an Edwardian-era haze in my study. I could not have done it without you.

When I first suggested a book on Jessop to David Luxton in the spring of 2024, I confidently informed him that The Croucher's England record would not survive another summer's assault from the Bazballers, and that any book had to be about both Jessop and the man who would topple him from his perch. David rightly told me to focus on Jessop and his story, for it was as intriguing as it was astonishing, and worth further exploration, as well as offering a slice of a vanished world. In fact, Jessop's record survived not only the summer but the winter as well. It may have fallen by the time this book is read but whenever it yields, it will never surrender its magic.

Index

A Note on Author

SIMON WILDE has been cricket correspondent of the *Sunday Times* since 1998 and has reported on around 330 England Test matches and numerous World Cups. He has written twelve books, three of which were shortlisted for the William Hill Sports Book of the Year. His most recent works have been the acclaimed *England: The Biography*, a history of the men's national team, and *The Tour*, which chronicles the England team's travels overseas since 1877 and which won the MCC/Cricket Society Book of the Year prize.

A Note on the Type

The text of this book is set in Linotype Stempel Garamond, a version of Garamond adapted and first used by the Stempel foundry in 1924. It is one of several versions of Garamond based on the designs of Claude Garamond. It is thought that Garamond based his font on Bembo, cut in 1495 by Francesco Griffo in collaboration with the Italian printer Aldus Manutius. Garamond types were first used in books printed in Paris around 1532. Many of the present-day versions of this type are based on the *Typi Academiae* of Jean Jannon cut in Sedan in 1615.

Claude Garamond was born in Paris in 1480. He learned how to cut type from his father and by the age of fifteen he was able to fashion steel punches the size of a pica with great precision. At the age of sixty he was commissioned by King Francis I to design a Greek alphabet, and for this he was given the honourable title of royal type founder. He died in 1561.